Donated by...

The

Jost-Ore

E. J. Jost
Buffalo
6/4/80

To the memory
of Brett

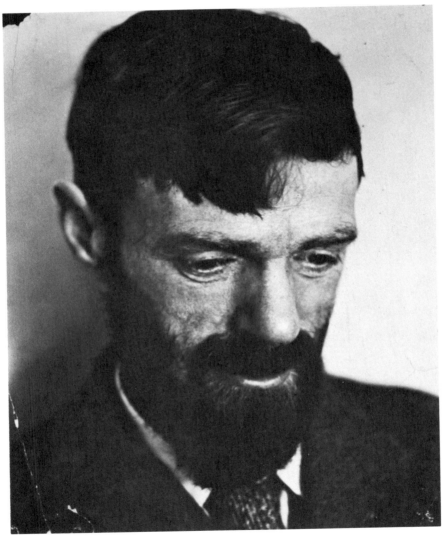

photo: Edward Weston

D. H. LAWRENCE
LETTERS TO THOMAS AND ADELE SELTZER
Edited by Gerald M. Lacy

Santa Barbara
BLACK SPARROW PRESS
1976

Frontispiece portrait of D. H. Lawrence is from a previously unpublished photograph by Edward Weston taken in Mexico City on 4 November 1924.

LIBRARY OF CONGRESS CATALOGING IN PUBLICATION DATA

Lawrence, David Herbert, 1885-1930.
    Letters to Thomas & Adele Seltzer.

    Bibliography: p. 288
    1. Lawrence, David Herbert, 1885-1930—Correspondence. 2. Seltzer, Thomas. 3. Seltzer, Adele Szold, 1876-   I. Seltzer, Thomas. II. Seltzer, Adele Szold, 1876-   III.Lacy, Gerald M. IV. Title.
PR6023.A93Z5354 1976   823'.9'12 [B]   76-10782
ISBN 0-87685-224-X
ISBN 0-87685-225-8 pbk.

TABLE OF CONTENTS

INTRODUCTION

by

Gerald M. Lacy

When it is completed in 1983, the Cambridge University Press edition of *The Letters of D. H. Lawrence* will contain over 5,000 letters and postcards, over half of them published for the first time. But since the publication of the letters to S. S. Koteliansky, Louie Burrows, and Martin Secker, few extensive collections of letters to one recipient remain substantially unpublished.[1] The present collection is one of the exceptions. Of the 135 letters from D. H. Lawrence and Frieda Lawrence to Thomas and Adele Seltzer in this volume, only five have previously appeared in print. Almost all of the letters written by the Seltzers are presented for the first time; of these, the effusive and revealing letters written by Adele Seltzer to her friend Dorothy Hoskins are of special interest,[2] as are the informative letters from Thomas Seltzer to Lawrence's American agent Robert Mountsier. Many of the photographs of the Lawrences and the Seltzers are also new. And finally the engaging "Biographical Narrative" of the Seltzers by Alexandra Lee Levin and Lawrence L. Levin presents in a well-documented manner the Seltzer side of the relationship. With the appearance of this volume, we thus not only learn more about the specific details concerning the twenty Lawrence titles published by Seltzer (their composition, their design, their texts, and their reception by the public),[3] particulars of numerous periodical contributions by Lawrence, and the working alliance between the English author and the American publisher, but also we see the literary and pecuniary struggles of both men during what are very likely the most crucial moments of their careers.

Notes to the Introduction will be found on p. xiv.

We have in the volume nearly all of the letters (at least two are missing and apparently lost) which Lawrence wrote to Seltzer. The correspondence begins with Lawrence's first cautiously optimistic letter written in 1919 to the soon-to-be dissolved publishing firm of Scott and Seltzer, progresses through the six years of Seltzer's operation as an independent publisher, and ends with his final letter in 1928, asking Seltzer, whose publishing firm had collapsed and been taken over by his nephews the Boni brothers, to release all rights to his Lawrence titles. The regularity of the exchange, however, starts to lapse earlier, and the tone of partnership and familiarity alters in 1925 when Seltzer, obviously in serious financial trouble, was informed that Lawrence had decided to offer his next novel *St. Mawr* to the more propitious management of Alfred Knopf.

> The new publishers, the Knopfs, are set up in great style, in their offices on Fifth Avenue—deep carpets, and sylphs in a shred of black satin and a shred of brilliant undergarment darting by. But the Knopfs seem really sound and reliable; I am afraid the Seltzers had too many 'feelings.' (D. H. Lawrence to Mr. and Mrs. William Hawk, 27 September 1925)

For one of the correspondents, this breach in the five-year association was a grave one: Thomas Seltzer Inc. published only thirteen books after 1925, and 1926 was its last year in full operation. The popularity of Lawrence titles had played a significant role in Seltzer's affairs; during the six years of publishing under his own imprint, he had published more books by Lawrence than by any other author. The association recorded here thus spans the entire publishing career of Thomas Seltzer. The primary interest of this volume, however, concerns the letters written by Lawrence to the Seltzers and the record they give of Lawrence's rise as a successful and established author.

We learn more about Adele Seltzer from this volume than we do about Thomas. The "Biographical Narrative" is the fullest account and it tells us a great deal about the origins and history of Thomas and Adele Seltzer. While Thomas's letters reveal very little direct information about his nature, they do suggest the image of a man harassed and often nearly overcome by the demands of his profession. Adele's letters, on the other hand, reveal a great deal about her character. And this is especially relevant when we note that, in Lawrence's opinion, it was Adele's "poison streak," her "bad influence" that contributed to Seltzer's downfall. These remarks are somewhat like other spleenful comments which Lawrence would make when a relationship for some reason turned sour. Adele said in her letters that she wanted "bestsellers," but she wanted these in order to be able to publish "the classical stuff." I cannot help thinking that she, and perhaps Thomas, never saw that even approaching Lawrence in such terms as "bestsellers" was a fundamental misconception, a tactic which brought about a somewhat spiteful response.

> But you won't be like Adele Seltzer and ask me to come back with a best seller under my arm. It's very nice for those whose line it is, and very nasty for those whose line it isn't, to be called upon for best sellers. Anyhow, it's on the knees of the gods. (Lawrence to Martin Secker, 8 January 1927)

Adele's request, probably innocent and well-meant, very likely caused Lawrence to evaluate her as he did after the association was over. Lawrence's sense of mission ("it's on the knees of the gods") and Adele's equally understandable pragmatism, strongly tinged with a sense of the quixotic, may have simply collided. For Adele, the result was doubly painful, for her request for a best seller came at a moment when her husband's firm desperately needed some literary miracle to save them.

When we consider what Lawrence wrote to him and what he said about him to others, Thomas Seltzer appears to have been a man who courageously faced some large battles, but at the same time, a man somehow small in more than a physical sense (he was barely five feet tall), somehow lacking in decisiveness and enduring forthright action: perhaps he was too selfless to be cunning, perhaps he was without real financial acumen, perhaps he did not really know the quality or lack of it in some of the works he published toward the end, perhaps he could not forecast sales. At any rate, the small firm of Thomas Seltzer, Inc., failed, after an initial period of success, and we last see Seltzer in a letter written during the depression, cutting a rather pathetic if well-meaning figure. In 1933 he wrote to his old friend William C. Bullitt in the U.S. State Department inquiring about a possible diplomatic position in Russia. One may admire Seltzer for this evidence of his tenacity, and Mrs. Levin informs me that Seltzer's characteristic tongue-in-cheek humor is evident in the letter, but reading it from the perspective of this volume, we are made uncomfortably aware of the alteration from an important publisher to an applicant for a government position. Seltzer brings up the possible recognition of Russia, and then adds:

> I should be a splendid person in Moscow or some other place in Russia, doing some sort of work for the United States and leaving to others for the nonce to attend to the publications of D. H. Lawrence, Marcel Proust, etc.
>
> Seriously, I am looking for a job and perhaps the government can find some use for me in connection with Russia, if recognition comes. I know Russian well enough to have translated works by Gorky, Andreyev, and other authors. I can brush it up, so that within a month or so I could speak it with a fair amount of fluency. I have not been connected with any political party for years, hence am without taint.

Bullitt replied that it seemed "unlikely that additional men from the outside" would be needed. The last years of both Seltzers were spent, as the Levins suggest, exploring various "avenues to hoped-for solvency."

But literary history has judged that Thomas fought the right battles, whether always successfully or not: Morris Ernst, the attorney who defended Joyce's *Ulysses* against the censors in 1933, notes the importance of Seltzer's *Casanova's Homecoming* case.

> The *Ulysses* case is the culmination of a protracted and stubborn struggle against the censors dating back to the victory over the New York Vice Society in the *Mademoiselle de Maupin* case in 1922. Coming in logical sequence after the *Well of Loneliness* case, the Dennett case, the cases involving Dr. Stopes' books, the *Casanova's Homecoming* case, the *Frankie and Johnnie* case, and the *God's*

Little Acre case, all of which have served to liberalize the law of obscenity, the victory of *Ulysses* is a climax to the salutary forward march of our courts. (Foreword to *Ulysses*, Random House, 1946)

Seltzer had one victory over the New York Society for the Suppression of Vice and lost another—no small matter, for the Vice Society was an active and effective organization. Under its founder, Anthony Comstock, who authored the Comstock Law to exclude obscene literature from the mail, the Vice Society was responsible for the "arrest of more than 3,000 persons, destroyed 50 tons of books, 28,400 pounds of stereotyped plates for printing of objectionable books, and nearly 400,000 pictures." (James D. Hart, *The Oxford Companion to American Literature*, p. 150) Such a society was obviously a power for publisher and author to carefully reckon with.

For reasons not clearly known, Seltzer gave up on the second prosecution case, even though it involved two of the same three books which had been declared inoffensive in an earlier trial. The book business had generally been bad in America in the mid 1920's, and further legal expenses would have drained precious funds from the struggling firm. But in agreeing to withdraw from circulation *Casanova's Homecoming* and *A Young Girl's Diary*, Seltzer lost two profitable items from his list and also the right to continue his damage suit for $30,000 against his accusers in the earlier trial. Perhaps he had no choice; perhaps, as G. Thomas Tanselle says, withdrawing the books from circulation was "the more expedient thing" to do. Tanselle's summation seems to be the proper evaluation of Seltzer's publishing career.

The Thomas Seltzer firm cannot lay claim to some of the distinctions achieved by certain other "little" publishers among its contemporaries. It did not (except in a few instances, like Lawrence's *Sea and Sardinia*) devote much attention to the physical product, the beauty of paper and type, as Kennerley and Knopf did; it did not attract the dazzling array of names that Knopf and Huebsch did, nor, like those two, manage to maintain surprisingly high standards over a long period of time.

But it should not, on the other hand, be thought of simply as the American publisher of D. H. Lawrence, Douglas Goldring, Gilbert Cannan, and Ramsay MacDonald. Its attention to popular novels and the sensational has its counterpart in each of these other firms, and it shares with them an interest in socialism, Russia, and psychology. Though it may be distinguished from some of them in the number of titles it gives to Jewish subjects, the Labor movement, and British popular fiction, it has enough characteristics in common with them to be recognizable as one of the group.

There can be no question that Seltzer performed an important service in making available to Americans many of the works that he did. And who is to say how much his choices were determined by the prevailing intellectual currents and to what extent they contributed to the formation of those currents? When D. H. Lawrence wrote that God had created Seltzer a little publisher, he was being critical of Seltzer's pretensions but he was also suggesting, by implication, the values of littleness—which is to say, the values of personal taste and judgement. He meant something of the same thing when he declared that "the Seltzers had too many 'feelings.' " Thomas Seltzer's career stands as an instructive illustration of the individual element in the publishing of the 1920's, of the strengths and weaknesses of being little. When one ponders Seltzer's failure or tries to account for the differences between his story and those of other small publishers, one comes back always to the man and remembers what Lawrence said. (G. Thomas Tanselle, "The Thomas Seltzer Imprint," pp. 415-416.)

The Manuscripts and Editorial Principles

Judging from the location of most of the manuscripts of Lawrence's correspondence with the Seltzers in one collection at the University of Texas, Thomas Seltzer carefully kept all of his letters from Lawrence; they passed from publisher to collector to the University where they are today. Research has not explained how the ten letters from Lawrence to the Seltzers not at Austin got separated from the main collection, nor has it been discovered what happened to the two unlocated letters known to have been written by Lawrence to the Seltzers. One is known to have been inserted in a copy of Lawrence's *Sea and Sardinia*—both the book and the letter were a gift from Adele to a friend. A second letter appeared momentarily in a recent House of Books catalogue and then disappeared when it was sold. Lawrence kept very few letters written to him, and the papers of the Seltzer firm which might have preserved copies of Seltzer's correspondence to Lawrence have not apparently survived its dissolution. (The two letters from Thomas and Adele Seltzer to Lawrence survive only because they were found in the papers of Robert Mountsier, Lawrence's American literary agent during a brief period.) With these few exceptions, therefore, the present volume makes use of *all* the significant Lawrence-Seltzer material known to exist.

The letters are given complete. Misspellings—there are very few—have been allowed to stand; I have added, however, the troublesome "sic" in those instances where there might be some confusion, e.g., where Lawrence spells "Birkindele" in two different ways within the same letter. Other editorial policies are as follows:

Punctuation:

A period is added to an abbreviation and to those squiggles in Lawrence's hand which form his closing—"Yrs." I also add an apostrophe to the possessive or contraction in those instances where the rush of handwritten composition may have allowed no time for correct grammatical rules. In a few instances a closing period has been added to a sentence. Frieda's highly idiosyncratic letters have been left largely as she wrote them, although I have added a period in those instances in which she leaves it out of her signature, "F."

Underscoring:

In three instances, I have departed from the usual substitution of italics for underscoring: in Lawrence's signature, although his usual style was to underline his name; in those instances where Lawrence has underscored more than once for particular emphasis (underscored once here), and in dates, where Lawrence usually underscores part of the day of the month, e.g. 13*th.*

Deletions:

Only the preferred word is given.

Inside Address:

All of the inside addresses (except that of Thomas Seltzer, Inc.) have been presented in a standard format: to the left and in block form.

Fortunately, Lawrence never lost sight of what is most important: his reply to this editor, as it was to the bibliographical sleuth Louis Feipel, would have likely have been that "charts," like the above listing, left him "quite cold," for "hyphen or no hyphen is one to me."

Letters to Thomas
& Adele Seltzer
from
D. H. Lawrence

*Lawrence in 1919 when he began his
association with Thomas Seltzer.*
(George Lazarus)

*Chapel Farm Cottage where the
Lawrences lived 1917-1919. Photo:
Peter Male.* (HRC)

*Douglas Goldring (1887-1960), novelist,
essayist, and the man who introduced
Lawrence to Thomas Seltzer.* (HRC)

1

Chapel Farm Cottage
Hermitage nr. Newbury, Berks
England
7 Sept. 1919

Dear Mr Seltzer

I had your cablegram—at least as enclosed. I was away, so there is some delay. I wanted moreover to go through the MS. of the novel once more.—I consider this the best of my books.—Please be careful with the MS., as it is the most complete one:—I am forwarding it to you by the next mail.

Meanwhile Martin Secker writes that he would like to publish the book next spring, under its old title "The Sisters." He has another copy.—I would like the book to come first in America. I shall never forgive England "The Rainbow."—If you wished to publish this novel, would you like me to write a short Fore-word?—And which title do you prefer, "Women in Love," or "The Sisters."

Yours Sincerely, D. H. Lawrence

Hermitage, Newbury, England is sufficient address for me. [1]

2

Hermitage—Newbury
2nd Novem. 1919

Dear Mr Seltzer

I have no news from you of "Women in Love"—presume you have MS.—Unless you are already printing, will you return the MS. *at once*, as Secker urgently wants it to print from. He is including the novel in his Spring list—title The Sisters. If you are printing, send sheets, proofs, as soon as you get them from the printer, to *Martin Secker, 17 Buckingham St., Adelphi, London W.C.* Please do this. And if you are not printing, do please send the MS to <u>Secker</u>, not to me, as soon as you get this.

Notes to the letters begin on p. 157.

If you have to write to me, will you address me at *5. Acacia Rd., St. Johns Wood, London N. W. 8.* I am going to Italy next week.

Yours Sincerely, D. H. Lawrence

3

Palazzo Ferraro
Capri
(Naples)
Italy
16 January 1920

Dear Mr Seltzer,

I hear from Huebsch that he is anxious to secure the publishing of *Women in Love.* I understood that my agent Pinker had sent him the MS. long ago. Apparently it was not so. Since Huebsch has done *The Rainbow* it is most fair that he should have the offer of *Women in Love.*[2] If you can see your way to do so, I wish you would relinquish to me again the MS of the novel, and I will at once return the £50 advance. If you have gone to the expense of the type-written copies, I will pay that bill also. Please let me know *by return.*

If you cannot see your way to relinquishing the MS., then first and foremost will you let Martin Secker have the copy you promised. He writes insistently about it, and I am concerned that he has not received it.

Then will you please draw up a short agreement according to the terms of my last letter:[3] stating definitely the royalty per-centage, the sale-price of the book, and the date before the expiration of which the book shall be published; also will you agree to send me an account of sales every six months, and to settle the account within three months of the date of rendering.

My agreement with my agent Pinker lapses now, and I wish to act as my own agent henceforth.[4] If this is to be in any way satisfactory, I must have every point of agreement between myself and my publisher precise and explicit. I don't want tedious formality. But a short, concise, explicit agreement, signed by both of us, I must have.

Yours Sincerely, D. H. Lawrence

Thomas Seltzer (1873-1943), Lawrence's
American publisher 1920-1925.
(Alexandra Levin)

4

Palazzo Ferraro
Capri
(Naples)
29 Jan. 1920

Dear Mr Seltzer

   Huebsch writes that I have put him in the cart with *Women in Love*. It is my agent's fault. I thought Huebsch had turned the book down a year ago: it seems he never saw it. Now since he did *The Rainbow* when no-one would touch it in America: and since he has stuck to my work, I *very much* want you to give me back the MS. Any expense incurred, over & above the £50 advance I had & of course including the £50, I will refund at once, but I do wish that you would cable to me that you are willing to return the MS. Anyhow, if you are going strong on Goldring's work, I'm sure you will never bring mine in with any success: not that I depreciate Goldring, far from it: but he appeals to a public that would reject me.—Moreover I don't want a semi-private publication.—I don't believe it is good for a new publisher to handle *Women in Love*. Do please cable me—"Will release Manuscript"—and send (unless that is disagreeable to you) a line to B. W. Huebsch to that effect.
   I am so sorry to be tiresome—but I honestly think it would be best all round if you left such a book alone. Huebsch has lost his reputation, in that line, already. [5]

Yours Sincerely, D. H. Lawrence

5

Fontana Vecchia
Taormina
(Messina)
Sicily
9 March 1920

Dear Seltzer

   I have your letters of Feb. 9th & Feb. 11th and contracts. Duckworth must have Canadian rights: and I thought we could agree about terms for the next novel, when it is ready. Otherwise well & good.

I am sorry about Huebsch. But Pinker let me in for this: and Huebsch was always *so* vague and friendly: now it is as it is. Let us see how *we* get on together. Huebsch should have been more to the point with me, and not have acted behind the publisher's veil. Then I should have known how much Pinker & he had to do with one another. As it was, I was a third & mystified party. Let us go ahead. Huebsch will feel I've let him down—I hate that. But I would never have done so intentionally. There, people shouldn't have veils—except in season.

Twenty five dollars seems much for a price.[6] But I suppose I must depend on a succés [sic] d'estime at the best, & at the worst, a succés de scandale. If so, let them pay for their scandal. Pah!—and for their esteem. How it wearies me.

I'm glad you like Touch & Go—and your wife likes the Rainbow—son' contento. Women in Love is best, next to The Rainbow. I am doing Mixed Marriage—it should be more popular—one withdraws awhile from battle.[7]

Yes, put at the back of Touch & Go that the dramatic agent is Walter Peacock, 20 Green St., Leicester Square. London. He is a nice man.

Now is the beginning of my day.

We've taken this house for a year—guess you know Taormina. Italy feels shaky—but Sicily won't change much till Etna erupts again—and Etna is snowy silent.

When you have anything to pay me, please pay in American dollars, it is easiest, & the exchange so favorable for me.

Send a copy of *Touch & Go* to Amy Lowell, Heath St., Brookline, Mass, will you—and a copy to Robert Mountsier, 417 West 118 Street, New York.

I really ought to find somebody to place small work— short stories & articles—in America.

I shall <u>love</u> to have a copy of Women in Love, nicely printed. Send me a proof as it comes, will you.

D. H. Lawrence

Seltzer's first publication of a Lawrence work, the play Touch and Go (New York, 1920). With a letter from Seltzer to Robert Mountsier.

Seltzer's "subscriber only" edition of Women in Love (New York, 1920). With the publisher's prospectus containing Lawrence's "short Fore-word."

6

Fontana Vecchia
Taormina
(Messina)
7 May 1920

Dear Seltzer

I had your cable saying you were sending a hundred dollars—so am awaiting a letter to know why: presumably for *Women in Love,* I don't know anything else. Meanwhile I heard from Huebsch saying you were turning over the MS. to him—I must wait for letters to enlighten me.

Secker says *you haven't sent him the typescript.* But you promised so plainly.

I have done my new novel *The Lost Girl.* It is quite proper, to my idea, & might easily be popular. It is being typed in Rome. I hope to let you have a copy, by a friend who is sailing from Naples on June 10th, going to Boston. Trust I shan't be frustrated in this despatch.

Meanwhile see if you can get a definite answer from Huebsch, as to whether he is doing the *Studies in Classic American Literature.* If not, ask him for the MS.

Meanwhile I wait for news from you in your letter with the dollars.

D. H. Lawrence

7

Fontana Vecchia
Taormina
(Messina)
14 May / 20

Dear Seltzer

I enclose letter from Pinker about my play The Widowing of Mrs Holroyd which was bought by Little Brown & Co, of Boston, some time back.[8] I said to Pinker that if you want the plates etc you will write direct to Little Brown.—The play is just going to be produced in Hammersmith.

No letters at all from America.—Hope to get the MS. of the Lost Girl off to you, by hand, by boat leaving Naples June 10th. It is being typed in Rome.

Yrs., D. H. Lawrence

8

Fontana Vecchia
Taormina
Sicily
1st June 1920

Dear Seltzer

I received your letter yesterday, with the two drafts in Lire on the Credito Italiano, Messina, representing twice $50. For the same, many thanks, they come very nicely.

I wrote to Secker about the sheets of the limited edition of *Women in Love* for Alec Waugh. If he objects, then we can't go forward with it. I will send a cable when I hear from him.—I hope by now he has really got the typed MS. from you.—I should very much like to have *proofs* of Women in Love, to correct them: but realise the horrible delays of the post. If you could post them on a ship coming direct here, I would get them back as soon as it is possible.—But if you think the delay would be too great, send me the proofs all the same, so that I can see them.

Secker said he thought he could get the new novel serialised in *The Century* in America. That would be a great protection for the other books. Secker prefers the title *The Bitter Cherry*, but I think my original *The Lost Girl* is better. The Century would have the option of the two.

I am sending this letter by hand, by the young Sicilian who owns this villa, which I rent. He is a cook, and is coming to be *chef* to some Americans in Boston. He sails with his young wife from Naples on June 11th. I shall try to send a copy of the MS. of *The Lost Girl* by him; if only the typist has finished it.

We have just come back from Malta, where I went to see a friend. [9] It is glaring hot. My health is quite all right. People like to exaggerate my delicacy. I am perfectly well, only too sensitive to shocks and influences.

I hear from Robert Mountsier in Paris, that he is returning

soon to New York. [10] He may get down to Taormina: hope he will. You will see him in New York.

Am looking forward to *Women in Love*.

D. H. Lawrence

Cicio's address in America (my landlord's, that is) is:

> Francesco Cacopardo
> c/o Mr William B. Rogers
> Potter & Rogers
> 3 Doane Street
> *Boston*
> Mass.

I have just heard from Secker that he has not yet received the typescript of Women in Love. This is really annoying. You have said so often that you were sending it.

Does nobody speak the truth?—I shan't send any MS. of *The Lost Girl* to America till that is settled about Women in Love.

D. H. L.

9

Fontana Vecchia
Taormina
Sicily
5 June 1920

Dear Seltzer

I have just been going through the Complete MS. of my *Studies in Classic American Literature*. Huebsch has had the duplicate MS. for six months, and I have no definite word even now of his intentions. No doubt he is a little scared.

Therefore I shall offer the book to you, if I don't hear from him within the course of a month from now. Let me know if you want it. I should like these essays to follow *Women in Love*. Secker will buy sheets.

You can speak to Huebsch, and tell him what I say. I will write him also. You might cable to me. *Lawrence, Taormina, Sicily* is enough address.

Yours, D. H. Lawrence

10

Fontana Vecchia
Taormina
Sicily
10 July 1920

Dear Seltzer

Your letter of June 21st today, with cheque for Lit. 240. on account of the article in the Evening News: and many thanks.[11]

I heard from Secker he has received the first half of *Women in Love:* for which thank goodness. Hope by now he has got the second half.

I just had a cable from him also—"Lost Girl excellent, greatly pleased," it says. He has just got the MS. & read it.—I am trying to get it serialised in England, perhaps in The Queen.

Secker said he thought he could get *The Century* to serialise *The Lost Girl* in America. If that were possible, it would be a shield against all possible prosecutions, I should think. I am waiting to hear from Secker. English post here is now *abominable.* Italy is the devil of a country for business.—I expect the MS. of The Lost Girl will be in Boston by now: Ciccio [sic] took it some three weeks ago. I gave him your address with The Century's also, & said I'd cable him. You would like The Century to serialise, wouldn't you? Anyhow Ciccio's address is:

> Sig. Francesco Cacopardo
> c / o Mr. William B. Rogers
> Potter & Rogers
> 3 Doane St. *Boston.* Mass.

When I hear from Secker—curse the post—I will wire Ciccio: either to send to you or The Century: with request to the latter (if they enter) to communicate with you.—I had a letter from Schofield Thayer asking me to let him see The Lost Girl for *The Dial*, for a serial. I had a *very* nice & friendly letter from Carl Hovey, of *The Metropolitan*, accepting a story of mine which had been sent to him from London, through a friend—and asking me for more.[12] —He might just possibly serialise. We ought to be able to do something.

I had funny letters from Huebsch about Women in Love: couldn't understand quite what you & he had been agreeing. I think he must be angry.

About *Studies in Classic American Literature:* I've just had a letter from Cecil Palmer asking me to let him publish them in England. I can't quite make up my mind. Secker wants to wait for American Sheets—I don't *think,* myself, that Huebsch will do them. I wrote to him saying that unless I heard definitely from him *this month,* I should offer them to you. They have none of them been printed in America: The first eight essays were printed in The English Review, November 1918—June 1919—long enough ago for them to be fresh for America.— The essays on Dana, Melville & Whitman have never been published. But *Whitman* would not do for a periodical. The earlier essays are the best for magazines. If you print the book, wait for a *revised* "Whitman." 13

I am glad you bought "The Widowing—"

Hope this letter reaches you in decent time.

Compton Mackenzie was bargaining for a yacht to go to the South Seas: and was going to ask me. 14 I very much doubt if it will come off. But if it should, I suppose we should call at New York, I think he would cross the Atlantic direct. Then I should see you.—Meanwhile it's very hot here.

I shan't do anything about publishing in America—save periodical stuff—without writing to you first and having your answer. I shall trust to you to tell me what you are doing with my work, exactly. Then we can get on. But I don't want you to feel at all hampered by me. If there is anything of mine you don't care for, say so without bothering.

Stanley Unwin asked me to finish a little book 30-40,000 words—*Education of the People*—of which I showed him a sketch 2 years ago. I will let you see this also.

I got the six copies of Touch & Go this morning: many thanks. Amusing it looks.

Have you sent me proofs of Women in Love?

Yrs., D. H. Lawrence

I have begun another novel—amusing it is.—But oh, the days are so hot just now—one lounges them away. 15

A friend of mine, Robert Mountsier, is returning to New York just now from Paris, and I am asking him to look after my business a bit. He is not a literary agent—no agent of any sort—journalist. Perhaps you know him—Curtis Brown bothers me to join him. I see he acts for you. But I don't want professional agents any more.

11

Fontana Vecchia
Taormina
Sicily
18 July [1920]

Dear Seltzer

I hear from Secker he has written to Boston to have MS. of *The Lost Girl* sent to *The Century*. I have written to the *Century* asking them to communicate with you. If they don't accept for serialising, I wish you would let Hovey, of *The Metropolitan*, see the MS.—& then Schofield Thayer, of *The Dial*, if the Metropolitan turns it down. I'm sure the best thing is to be serialised in an important periodical.

I have begun another novel: such a queer mad affair.— Secker says he is *enthusiastic* about The Lost Girl.

Yrs., D. H. Lawrence

12

Academia
Ponte delle Meravegie
1061
Venice
30 Aug. 1920

Dear Seltzer

I send you corrected proofs of Lost Girl— will let you have the rest as soon as I get them from Secker. Have been moving round this last month—think I shall leave Venice end of this week, & go to Florence. Best write to me at Taormina, where I expect I shall be by end of October.

D. H. Lawrence

13

Villa Fontana Vecchia
Taormina
Sicily
7 November 1920

Dear Seltzer

Thank you for all the proofs of *Women in Love.* I went through them. There are only very slight incorrections. I am looking forward to your volume: it comes out immediately, Mountsier says.

You will have received from Secker final corrected proofs of *The Lost Girl.* Please print from these. Secker was due to publish on 1st Novem., but Smith's & Mudies objected to page 256, so I re-wrote it for him, and I hope it will delay so that he can publish simultaneously with you. [16] I asked him to send you *at once* the revised page, so that you can please yourself. Of course the original is best.—Via England is quicker post than direct to America.

Secker intends *Women in Love* for February. I still think it the best of my books. Will you please send a copy to:
Miss Amy Lowell, Heath Street, *Brookline*, Mass.
And will you please send me *two* copies for myself. Of course you will give one copy to Mountsier.

I have various bits of work to do: haven't settled to anything serious yet.

Do hope all goes well & happily.

D. H. Lawrence

14

Fontana Vecchia
Taormina
Sicilia
22 Novem. 1920

Dear Seltzer

Thank you for the cuttings—I send them back at once— don't bother to send me any more.

15

I had your letter—look forward very much to my copies of Women in Love.

As for Italy—she'll get through the winter all right, I suppose. The South is a dead letter. Things are so shaky that nobody will give the last push.

Saluti, D. H. Lawrence

15

Villa Fontana Vecchia
Taormina
Sicily
11 Decem. 1920

Dear Seltzer

Today have come ten copies of *Women in Love.* I am very pleased indeed with it: feel it has made us friends for life: and sincerely hope so. It's a real book. Now I pray it will bring you your money quickly, and be a success in that way. It is my best book. I was glad you said you began to like it. It needs a bit of getting used to.

I was furious with Secker for letting his Lost Girl appear in New York—had Mountsier's cable—and wrote & cabled him, Secker, such a smack in the eye that he'll probably never forgive me. So much the better for me.

Be sure and tell me how this book goes: I am most anxious about it: the others I don't fret myself about so much.

I hope we can go on all the way together, you as publisher and me as writer. I haven't Mountsier's respect for big publishers like Doran & Co:—they are excellent sellers of old hat, but fatal for new: witness Methuen & The Rainbow.

Many Christmas Greetings, and New Year. This was my best Christmas present.

Yrs., D. H. Lawrence

16

[*Postcard to Thomas Seltzer*]

5 Jan. 1921

Had your cable about *Lost Girl's* start today. Hope she will really go well. Am busy with Mr. Noon. [17] Will you send a leaflet of W. in Love to Mrs. Lucile Levy

5747 Westminster

St. Louis

Mo.

U.S.A.

Apparently she would like a copy. Thank you so much for Launcelot & "Woman." Former a bit vieux jeu. [18]

D. H. L.

17

Fontana Vecchia
Taormina
Sicily
28 Feb. 1921

Dear Seltzer,

Your letter, & 6 copies of the Lost Girl, came yesterday. I like the look of the book immensely—much better than Secker's. Am glad it started well! If only it will keep on.

I believe that *Women in Love* will sell all right. Secker definitely is not publishing before 1st May. He will hardly send copies to New York before he issues the book in London, will he?

We went to Sardinia—but decided Sicily is better. It is just possible I may come to America—but there, I have said it so often. There isn't any news from here till I make up my mind to something. It is full spring in Sicily—lovely really—and Etna deep, deep in snow.

I do hope things will go well.

Yrs., D. H. Lawrence

Martin Secker's edition of The Lost Girl *(London, 1920).*

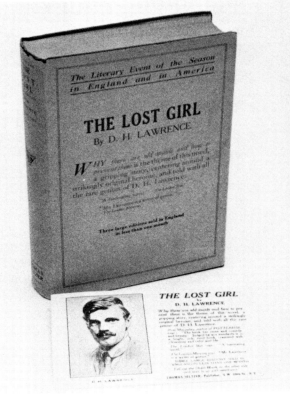

Seltzer's edition of The Lost Girl *(New York, 1921).*

P. S. I do wish you could give Mountsier some dollars for me.

D. H. L.

P.P.S.—Just come "Precipitations" & "Blind Mice" forwarded by you.[19] Many thanks. If books come for me—or letters—hand them to Mountsier will you please.

D. H. L.

18

Capri
16 April 1921

Dear Seltzer

I have left Taormina for the summer. Write me a line:

> per Adr. Frau Baronin von Richthofen
> Ludwig-Wilhelmstift
> Baden-Baden
> *Germania*

That is quite safe. Tell me how all things are. Send the copies of Psychoanalysis & the Unconscious to me there: also one copy to

> Miss Elizabeth Humes
> American Embassy
> Piazza S. Bernardo
> Rome

Don't forget.[20]

Best of wishes, D. H. Lawrence

19

per Adr. Frau Baronin von Richthofen
LudwigWilhelmstift
Baden-Baden
Germany
3 June 1921

Dear Seltzer

Today ten copies of *Psychoanalysis and the Unconscious*: beastly long title. I am always so pleased when the books come from you, they *look* so nice. Whereas Secker's are so scrubby! I got a copy of his *Women in Love* the other day, & fairly spat. He brings it out on June 10th, so he says.—Many thanks for these ten copies.

I want you to tell me fairly soon if this sells enough to make it worth while my going on with the next little volume, which continues the development of the theory of the Unconscious. I have begun it, and it should be as interesting, if not more, than this first book.

I have finished *Aaron's Rod*, writing away in the Black Forest here: so still, so strange, such a different Germany. Feels so empty—as if uninhabited: yet of course every house is crowded to the coal cellar. Yet it feels empty—life-empty: no young men. I like the big wideness of the landscape—we are living out in a village—the big magnificence. It seems all to have gone still and remote & far off, and I feel a bit as the Romans must have felt on the edge of the great Hercynian wood. They were so terrified of it. Everybody is very nice—inwardly tired and very sad. Never a uniform left, and no real authority. Yet the people by themselves obey the laws, and everything works perfectly. It is strange after the impudence & disorder of Italy.

But one feels, the old order has gone—Hohenzollern & Nietzsche & all. And the era of love & peace & democracy with it. There will be an era of war ahead: some sort of warfare, one knows not what. But Mars is the god before us: the real Mars, not Jesus in arms.

I expect Mountsier here next week. We shall wander about: perhaps stay the summer in the Austrian Tyrol, where my sister in law still has a little estate among the mountains.

Perhaps back to Florence. Mountsier wants me to go to London—but no, not England! It depresses me and makes everything feel barren.

I read Evelyn Scott's *Narrow House.* Really it is a sort of last word. After that we drop to bits, piecemeal, like lepers.— I read Magdeleine Marx's *Woman,* & didn't like it. Ugh, I detest such "Women," and long to box their ears and jump on their straw turbans—and use absolutely *low* language to the bitches.—I read Cecil Scott's *Blind Mice*—and if only he'd grinned, even up his sleeve, what a marvellous satire it would have made. But he never grinned.—Mountsier will write you everything. 21

D. H. Lawrence

Orchestra concert in Kurhaus last night—Siegfried Wagner conducted. Great men should never have sons.—Lichtenthaler Allee full of Schrieber: ach, so ugly: & they pay 800 Mark a day in the Stephanie.

I suppose you know Germany quite well.—This place will never really revive. It belongs to Turgenev & Dostoevsky & Edward VII.

This is my Schwiegermutter's address: always a safe one.

I wish you would send Evelyn Scott a copy of P. & the Unconscious—c / o Boni & Liveright.

D.H.L.

20

[*Postcard to Thomas Seltzer*]

[per Adr. Frau von Richthofen
Ludwig Wilhelmstift
Baden-Baden
Germany]
8 Juli. [1921]

Mountsier here—we leave in two days—address

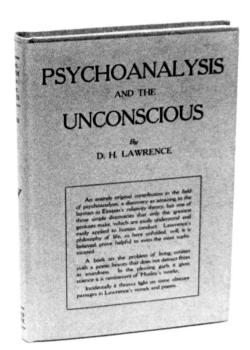

Seltzer's Psychoanalysis and the
Unconscious (*New York, 1921*).

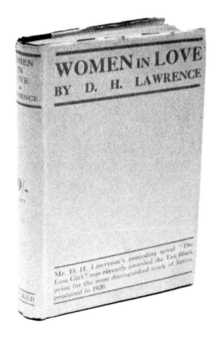

Martin Secker's "scrubby" edition of
Women in Love (*London, 1921*).

c/o Frau von Schreibershofen
Tumersback
Zell-am-See
bei Salzburg
Austria

Hope to send Aaron's Rod soon—we'll type it out at Zell—as soon as possible.

D. H. Lawrence

21

Villa Alpense
Thumersbach
Zell-am-See
bei Salzburg
Austria
30 July 1921

Dear Seltzer

Your letter of 15 July today: I had your cable in Baden.—I had to send 2nd half of *Aaron's Rod* to England to be typed after all. Expect it back next week. Then shall post it to you. I shall post your copy two weeks sooner than Secker's. He hasn't seen the book yet. Mountsier read the first half & didn't like it: takes upon himself to lecture me about it. Says it will be unpopular—Can't help it: It is what I mean, for the moment. It isn't "improper" at all: only it never turns the other cheek, and spits on ecstasy. I like it, because it kicks against the pricks. I'll send it the first possible moment.

Mountsier loathes me because I will develop my *Unconscious* ideas. But I have written the second book, & know it good. In about three years time I'll write the third book, and then—fertig. If you send me the criticisms, I'll answer them in a nice peppery introduction.

Somehow my compass will not point to America. We'll probably go to Italy in September.

Austria is Kaput & doesn't seem to care a bit.

Curtis Brown will have sent you the Juta pictures. I do hope you'll like them & have them reproduced. And I do hope Thayer will print one or two articles from *Sea & Sardinia* in

SORGONO   Jan Juta

TONARA   Jan Juta

TERRANOVA   Jan Juta

GAVOI   Jan Juta

*Four of the Jan Juta illustrations for
Lawrence's* Sea and Sardinia (*New
York, 1921*).

the Dial, & so help to pay for the pictures. Let me know. 22

Perhaps when I am cajoled into a good mood, I will write you a Tyrol story—short novel—like Wintry Peacock. Life is long.

Pleasant here—my sister in law's summer villa—with lake, boats, carriage, & snowy mountains. You can buy anything you like, with enough Krone.

Don't know anything about Hearsts. Gruesome sounding sort of name. But then it's all one boat.

Yrs., D. H. Lawrence

Very many thanks for sending the Wintry Peacock proofs.

22

[Postcard to Thomas Seltzer]

[Villa Alpense
Thumersbach
Zell-am-See
bei Salzburg
Austria]
12 August 1921

Have your cable "Cable authorisation to sell second serial rights Lost Girl." Mountsier is in Vienna at the moment, so I reply "Authorise sale serial rights—Lawrence."—Don't quite know what second serial rights are—hope you'll tell me.

D. H. Lawrence

Anyhow I hope it's something nice, & authorise sale in hopes.

D. H. L.

23

[*Postcard to Thomas Seltzer*]

[32 Via dei Bardi]
Florence
15 Sept. [1921]

I had the press cuttings of Psychoanalysis today—will answer them—they are quite amusing. [23] The book—the second part—is being typed here. I leave for Siena & Rome next week. Write to Taormina.

D. H. Lawrence

24

Fontana Vecchia
Taormina
Sicilia
8 Ottobre 1921

Dear Seltzer

I hope Mountsier has sent you the MS of Aaron's Rod. He emphatically dislikes the book, but then he is not responsible for it. I want you to write and tell me simply what you feel about it. It is the last of my serious English novels—the end of The Rainbow, Women in Love line. It had to be written—and had to come to such an end. If you wish, I will write a proper little explanatory foreword to it—not the one I sent from Zell-am-See. I want you to tell me if you consider it "dangerous"—and what bit of it you think so—and if you'd like any small alteration made. If you would, please name the specific lines.

I have begun a proper *story* novel—in the Venetian lagoons: not pretty pretty—but no sex & no problems: no love, particularly. It won't go to England at all. [24]

But I am held up at the moment going over the MS of "The Child and the Unconscious"—which follows Psychoanalysis & the Unconscious. I like it much better than *Psy. & the Uncon.* It has about 52,000 words. I have written a foreword answering the critics: rather funny. As soon as I have this ready—in a few days—I will send it you direct, introduction & all. The introduction you might perhaps offer to some periodical: it is really comical.

Friends very much want me to go to Ceylon—about February. I don't know. I may. I will collect my short stories, for a volume, to have my MSS in order—if such a thing be possible. I am tired of Europe—it is somehow finished for me—finished with Aaron's Rod. Done. I wish I could find a ship that would carry me round the world & land me somewhere in the West—New Mexico or California—and I could have a little house and two goats, somewhere away by myself in the Rocky Mountains. I may manage that.

With all this the Venice story doesn't look like getting ahead very fast.

Send me some news.

D. H. Lawrence

Do you like the title The Child and the Unconscious? or Child Consciousness?

25

Fontana Vecchia
Taormina
Sicily
22 October 1921

Dear Seltzer

I am sending you today the MS. of *Fantasia of the Unconscious:* also an introduction, a reply to some critics of Psychoanalysis & the Unconscious;—and a small introduction to Aaron's Rod.—As for a title, I don't mind if you alter it to something else.—The introduction you might like to publish in some magazine—do as you think well.—I think, if any book of mine is going to make your fortune, this Fantasia will be the one.—You may think differently.[25]

I hear from Mountsier that he is posting you Aaron's Rod. I hope you won't dislike it as much as he does.—But I want you to publish it about as it stands. I will make any small modification you wish. So write at once. You won't think of publishing it before spring. I don't want you to.—I promise you, it is the last of my "serious" novels.

I haven't heard from you for a long time—about two months. Mountsier writes that book business is very bad in America, & that we're all going to the devil. Vogue la galère.

Let me hear from you.

D. H. Lawrence

26

Fontana Vecchia
Taormina
Sicilia
26 November 1921

Dear Seltzer

The postman gave me your letter in the Corso this evening: your letter of Nov. 11th. That is a marvellous quickness.

About Aaron: I haven't got any type-written corrected MS., so don't quite know how it stands. I have only my hand-written MS—which luckily I haven't yet burned. If you really must modify Argyle—I think he is so funny, though Mountsier calls him a foul-mouthed Englishman—you can do so at your discretion, by just lifting a word or two. [26] I'll go through the Marchesa MS. tonight.

<u>Do</u> print the introduction to the Fantasia. The motto today is fight, fight, and always fight. Let them have it: they well deserve it, and they can't really do one much harm.

Of course I am dying to see *Sea and Sardinia.* Yes, I want you one day to publish the European History. [27] I feel here too near to Greece and Rome to want to write a history about them.—Curse the Austrians for not sending that cable.—If *Tortoises* is not much go as a chap-book, no more chap-books.

I have got two long stories: *The Captain's Doll,* 34,000 word[s] and *The Fox,* about the same. I will send them to Mountsier the minute I get the typescript from Florence. I think they are very interesting.

I am persisting in my idea of coming to America, as I told you. January or February I hope to sail. *Ought* I to come to New York? I see red when I think of Kennerley & *Sons &*

Lovers. [28] Would it be better if I personally were on the scene to have a shot at him?—Or can I continue to chase my ship to take me to Los Angeles or San Francisco. May be a wild-goose chase, but I'll just try. People in London urge me to go there— they say I could do things in England now. But no, England has made me too angry. I will come to the States to try it: but to fight, to fight. All the better to put their rabbity backs up.

The Fox and The Captain's Doll are so modern, so new: a new manner. Then I will send seven or so other stories, shorter.—I don't want to start anything serious now before I leave.

I have been angry at not having any definite news from New York since August. Perhaps there has not been much to say. But I always want to know exactly what is happening, so please tell me always, direct. And always send me proofs of whatever is appearing, even if you don't wait to have them returned.

To me Fantasia is important. But they'll try to push it aside as if it didn't matter. That's why it's better to go out against them tooth and nail and make them uneasy about what *they're* going to say. Print the introduction, and to hell with them. For this book one must put up a fight.

Yours, D. H. Lawrence

I have looked through the original MS. It is no good, I can't alter it. But if you like to follow the type-script, which I have often written over, in the scenes you mention, and if you like to leave out what is written over, I don't think you need fear the public much. And if you like to leave out a sentence or two, or alter a phrase or two, do so. But I can't write anything different. Follow the original typescript.

27

Fontana Vecchia
Taormina
Sicilia
9 Jan. 1922

Dear Seltzer

Today has come *Sea and Sardinia*, and a few days ago

Tortoises. [29] They are handsome books, and must have cost a good deal. But you can't call Tortoises a chap-book. Did you intend it for one? I think the pictures have come out well—only the reds a bit weary. I do hope Juta will be pleased. Poor Jannie, he has hurt his leg so badly out there on that beastly Table Mountain, and is struggling on crutches. I do hope he'll soon be on his proper feet. He is just the man for the American public—so handsome and pictorial.

Today I sent off the last of the story MSS to Mountsier. I do hope by now he has all. The three stories, The Fox, The Ladybird, and The Captain's Doll, will, I think, make a really interesting book—perhaps even a real seller. Then there is the book of short stories proper. When the MS. section of Aaron arrives from you, and I have done that, then I have finished with writing for a bit, thank god. I am sick of the the sight & thought of manuscripts. But to amuse myself on shipboard & so on I shall probably go on with a translation of the Sicilian novel "Mastro-don Gesualdo," by Giovanni Verga. It is some thirty years old already, and perhaps is already translated in America. Will you find out?—It interests me very much, as being one of the genuine emotional extremes of European literature: just as Selma Lagerlöf or Knut Hamsun may be the other extreme, northwards. But Verga seems to me more real than these. [30]

I've got this flu which keeps coming—so feel unhappy for the moment. But for this we'd probably have sailed from Bordeaux to New Orleans by the La Salles—Transatlantique SS—on January 15th. Now maybe we shall take the *Providence*, Fabre Line, from Palermo to New York, leaving Palermo February 5th. I shall cable you when it is decided, and you will please tell Mountsier.

They are in a stew here over the failure of the Banca di Sconto. Let us hope it will end all right. But Italy is rocky. I am tired of Europe—really tired in my bones. There seems to be no getting any forrarder. What I want in America is a sense of the future, and be damned to the exploited past. I believe in America one can catch up some kind of emotional impetus from the aboriginal Indian & from the aboriginal air and land, that will carry one over this crisis of the world's soul depression, into a new epoch.

Did they tell you that they gave me £100 sterling for the James Tait Black Memorial prize for the best English novel of

The last of four Lawrence titles that Seltzer published in 1921, Sea and Sardinia (New York, 1921).

Seltzer's edition of Tortoises (New York, 1921).

1920. It was judged by the Professor of English literature in Edinburgh University. [31]

It is cold here, the snow almost coming down to us, on the hills—Etna all white & black—many many little birds fluttering everywhere. Thank goodness powder has become so dear.

I look forward to seeing you. What fun it will be to be in Taos. I look forward to it immensely, & wish I could start tomorrow. Juta & Insole press me to go to Nyasaland, and trek across to Lake Tanganyika. But no, I have said I will come to America.

Be greeted, D. H. Lawrence

28

Fontana Vecchia
Taormina
Sicilia
14 Jan. 1922

Dear Seltzer

The typed MS. of *Aaron's Rod* came today. I again tried altering it. I can modify the bits of Argyle's speech. But the essential scenes of Aaron and the Marchesa it is impossible to me to alter. With all the good-will towards you and the general public that I am capable of, I can no more alter those chapters than if they were cast-iron. You can lift out whole chunks if you like. You can smash them if you like. But you can no more alter them than you can alter cast iron.

There you are. It's your dilemma. You can now do what you like with the book. Print only a limited edition—leave out anything you like for a popular edition—even if you like substitute something of your own for the offensive passages. But it is useless asking me to do any more. I shall return you the MS. on Monday. Then say no more to me. I am tired of this miserable, paltry, haffling and caffling world—dead sick of it.

D. H. Lawrence

29

Fontana Vecchia
Taormina
Sicily
20 Jan. 1922

Dear Seltzer

   This is a note simply about J. W. Nylander, who is a Finn
who is here, was once a sailor, has written sea-stories, in
Swedish, is translated into German, but not into English: and
who is poor. I am sending you by this post *Seevolk*, a volume
of stories: he says not the best. They are a bit *soft:* yet I think
"Jim Lawson"—& "Die Frau auf dem Southern Cross" good;
& even "Idyll." Would the magazines do them if they were
translated; do you think? And if so do you think you could
find a translator who would share royalties—*Swedish*, remember? And would you speak to Mountsier about it, if you think
it any good? Nylander will send you three other volumes in
German translation. The man is poor, and so modest &
shrinking: please do find time to give the matter a bit of
attention. I shall trust you to do this. 32

Yrs., D. H. Lawrence

   address J. W. Nylander
   Sleependen pr. Kristiania
   Norway

   No matter *what* your decision, be so kind as to write him a
word and tell him.

30

Fontana Vecchia
Taormina
Sicily
17 Feb. 1922

Dear Seltzer

   We are sailing from Naples on the 26th inst by the *Osterley*, for Colombo. The address: "Ardnaree", Lake View Estate, Kandy, Ceylon.

Will you be so kind as to send a copy of *The Lost Girl* and of *Sea and Sardinia* to Mrs. Leader-Williams, Palazzo Atenasio, *Taormina*—Sicily.

Hope I'll do a Ceylon novel.—Am so glad to be moving out of Europe.

D. H. Lawrence

31

Grande Albergo Santa Lucia
Quai Partenope
Napoli
I. Ordine

24 Feb. 1922

Dear Seltzer

So we have left Sicily and on Sunday—two days hence—the boat sails for Ceylon. Feel upset at going—but glad to leave Europe—will come west eastwards.

The book business is not good, Mountsier says, & everybody seems depressed. Never mind—pazienza chi va piano va lontano.

Greetings to you, D. H. Lawrence

32

Thirroul
New South Wales [Australia]
9 June 1922

Dear Seltzer

Well we've got so far— about fifty miles south of Sydney, in a little house to ourselves quite on the sea: very nice; a weird country, though. I have begun a novel, & it seems to be going well—pitched in Australia. Heaven knows if anybody will like it—no love interest at all so far—don't intend any—no sex either. [33] Amy Lowell says you are getting a reputation as an erotic publisher: she warns me. I should have thought my reputation as an "erotic" writer (poor dears) was secure. So now I'll go back on it. [34]

Will you please hand back to Mountsier the MSS. of *Mr. Noon*—till I see what I'll do further with it—and of *Birds Beasts and Flowers*. Please let him have them at once.—Did you like the Three Stories?

I do hope you didn't post copies of *Aaron's Rod* to me here or to Ceylon. Hear it is going well. Please send a copy to Amy, and to Mabel Dodge Sterne, *Taos*, and to Mrs A. L. Jenkins, Strawberry Hill, *Perth*. West Australia: also to Juta if you have his address, also to Frau Dr. Else Jaffe-Richthofen— Konradstrasse 16. *München* also to E H Brewster, c/o Thomas Cook 90 rue du Rhône, *Geneva*, Switzerland.

We think of staying here till August, then crossing to San Francisco & so to Taos. But I'll let you know definitely.

When we get to America we'll see you. Hope the Consul won't want to refuse us visas.—I should like very much to write an American novel, after this Australian one: on something the same lines. But we'll see. One has to do what one can do. Only Germany helped me to the finish of Aaron.

I want so much to know how Fantasia goes—and to see it in print. Send it to Mabel Dodge also—and to Brewster—and to my sister in law Else Jaffe.

I should expect to land in San Francisco either on Sept 4th—by the boat *Tahiti* (via Wellington, Rarotonga, Papeete) —or else on the same day by the Ventura—via Pago Pago & Honolulu. But *don't* tell anybody we are coming. We shall go to Taos. And I don't want anybody to know we are there.

Feel we shall be seeing you soon. Till then, prosper.

Yrs., D. H. Lawrence

33

"Wyewurk"
Thirroul
South Coast
N. S. W.
11 June 1922

Dear Seltzer

Wrote you yesterday—today come the copies of Aaron—
Many thanks—book looks so nice—haven't plucked up
courage to look out the cut parts yet.

Don't bother therefore to send the copies I asked you to
post. But don't post me *Fantasia* here, if you haven't done so.
Send out for me instead the five or six copies I asked you to
send—and keep the rest till I come.

I think I'm calling my new novel *Kangaroo.* It goes so
far—queer show—pray the gods to be with me, that I finish by
August.

Yrs., D. H. Lawrence

34

"Wyewurk"
Thirroul
New South Wales
21 June 1922

Dear Seltzer

We are planning to sail from Sydney on August 10th by S.S.
Tahiti, Union Line, arrive in San Francisco on the morning of
Sept 4th, all being well. You said you would come & see me as
soon as I landed in America. It would be great fun if you could
come to San Francisco & meet us: especially if both Mrs
Seltzer & you were there. We'd go to some quiet and inex-
pensive hotel—I see one can easily have a room for $1.25 or
$1.50 a day—and we wouldn't tell anybody we were there.
Except Mabel Dodge Sterne, & she might possibly come too.
Which we *might* all like: or hate. Anyhow we are pledged to
go from San Francisco to Taos. But I don't want *any* strangers

*Lawrence and Frieda in 1922 on a
pleasure trip with friends in Australia.
Photo: A. D. Forrester. (HRC)*

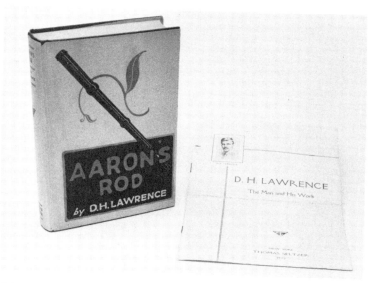

*Seltzer's edition of Aaron's Rod (New
York, 1922). With a publicity pamphlet
about Lawrence written by Adele
Seltzer.*

The cottage in New South Wales,
"Wyewurk," where the Lawrences
stayed from May to August 1922.
Photo: F. W. L. Esch. (HRC)

Mollie Skinner's "Holiday House" in
Darlington, Australia, where the
Lawrences stayed in early May 1922.
Photo: R. G. Howorth. (HRC)

to know, or any foolish reporters. Here in N.S.W. not a soul knows about me, I don't present any letters of introduction: and I like that much the best. Before we leave I shall cable you the name of the boat—*Tahiti*, via Wellington & Tahiti, arrives Sept 4th, & *Sonoma*, Oceanic Line, sails Aug 16 & arrives Sept 4th, the same—but not such a nice route. I hope Mountsier will have sent me the dollars to come with. Do ask him if he has.

I have done more than half of the novel: the Lord alone knows what anybody will think of it: no love at all, & attempt at revolution. I do hope I shall be able to finish it: not like Aaron, who stuck for two years, and Mr Noon, who has been now nearly two years at a full stop. But I think I see my way. Seven weeks today till we sail.

No, I wouldn't like to live always in Australia—unless I'd had enough of the world altogether, & wanted to lose myself. It would be a good place for that. Weird country. Has its fascination.

What fun if we saw you in Frisco.

D. H. Lawrence

I want this to catch the Niagara: then you should have it by July 20th.

If I cable the boat to you, be sure & tell Mountsier. Did you ever get the cable from Kandy, "Sailing Fremantle"? I don't believe you did.

D. H. L.

35

"Wyewurk"
Thirroul
New South Wales
18 July 1922

Dear Seltzer

Just a line to say that the advertised date of the sailing of the *Tahiti* is suddenly changed from August 10th to August 16th. So that if you *were* coming to San Francisco—I don't suppose you are—then I should think our boat would arrive September

10th instead of September 4th. Of course you can always make sure by enquiring at a shipping office—S.S. Tahiti, Union Line, New Zealand.

But I am not sure it will be the Tahiti, because I haven't got any cable of money yet from Mountsier. I hope it will come soon. They are holding me a cabin on the boat.

I finished Kangaroo on Saturday—I don't suppose you'll like it a bit. I heard from Mountsier & he said Sea & Sardinia had only sold 685. Aaron about 3000. That's few of S & S.—I hope Aaron will go on selling. Depressing to have such petty sales always.—I must come to America & try & do a novel there, that's all.

tanti saluti, D. H. Lawrence

This will catch the Makura—via Vancouver—last mail before the Tahiti.

36

Palace Hotel, San Francisco

8 Sept. 1922

Dear Seltzer

Here we are in the land of the free: sunny & warm out here, & less strenuous than I imagined, though very iron-noisy.

I thought I should have had a word from you—but there is nothing. Mountsier said he telegraphed to you. The mail is late, so we are going on without it: we leave tonight for Santa Fe, meet Mabel Dodge there. She sent me a cutting about suppression of Women in Love. Pfui!—But I haven't had any real news for ages.—I shall be glad to hear from you & to know what is happening. Apparently I have arrived in the land of the free at a crucial moment.

Yrs., D. H. Lawrence

37

12 Sept. [1922]

Dear Seltzer

I found here your letters to Australia, sent after me, but no other sign of you. I do hope you weren't intending to go to San Francisco.

Mabel Dodge met us at Lamy & brought us here—75 miles across a really wonderful desert. She has built us this summer this lovely adobe house, & made it so beautiful. Really we are quite overwhelmed. But you must come here. You can get a stage automobile from Santa Fe.

It is high up, 7000 feet, so I am just feeling a bit dizzy & sleepy, and feel as if my own self were trailing after me like a trail of smoke, some of it still in Australia. How much of me is here I don't know—just the clockwork.

Well I shall be glad to know at least where you are, & how.

D. H. Lawrence

38

Taos
New Mexico
19 Sept. 1922

Dear Seltzer

At last I have your letter. I am glad you won that case: now you ought to be able to go freely ahead.

Amy is just a cupboard that loves itself. I'm glad that by sheer intuition I gave her a few slaps last time I wrote her. She goes off my list now. [35]

I am very anxious to see *Fantasia.*

I am sorry Mountsier & you have come to daggers drawn. Or perhaps it is just as well to fight a bit. Anyhow I'll leave it to you to fight it out, because truly I know nothing about it. Mountsier doesn't tell me. And you see I've got to be friends with both of you. For my part, I think you have stuck up for me well, as a publisher, and I want us to be on good terms. We must meet & have a talk & pour a little oil of laughter on the troubled waters. Won't you run over here? Mabel Sterne will lend you a studio. She is very nice & has a good opinion of you.

I have a letter from Secker very angry, apparently, about not getting sheets of *Sea & Sardinia*. What about that? Also informing me he is doing the three novelettes under title "Ladybird" *first*, soon, before he does the book of short stories. That must be seen to. I have written him & Curtis Brown. I wonder if I'll get a novel out of here? It would be interesting if I could.

I wait a letter with more news of the "case" from you.

Yrs., D. H. Lawrence

I was away five days motoring into the Apache country to see a dance—Indian: so I am still strange here, not orienté. The place is 6000 ft. high, & takes a bit of getting used to: makes me feel dazed. I expect Mountsier will be coming over to see me—you won't have to be here both at the same time, or blood might flow.—You take the stage motor-car from Santa Fe.

39

Taos
New Mexico
22 Sept. 1922

Dear Seltzer

Will you please do a little thing for me. Send me a Spanish-English dictionary, and a book to begin to learn Spanish from. Those shilling paper folders published by Kühl or Kunze—yes, Kunze—are quite good. One needs Spanish here. I must find a teacher too.

Can you send me also a copy of James Joyce's *Ulysses*. I read it is the last thing in novels: I'd best look at it. [36]

Mabel Sterne says when you come to Taos she will be glad to put you up in her house. She has plenty of room, & servants. We shall be glad to see you any time. You take the motor stage which leaves Santa Fe at midday, 75 miles over the desert, or you take the other stage from Taos Junction, only about 30 miles.

I hope you will get your $25000 damages from the Vice man.

Yrs., D. H. Lawrence

Could you send me too that Herman Melville book— "Herman Melville, Poet & Mystic."—I will go over the "Studies in C. A. Literature" again. 37

Any news of Fantasia yet?

Have you got the MS. copy of Studies in Classic American Literature? I should like to go through them again.

D. H. L.

40

Taos, New Mexico
Friday, 7 October [1922]

Dear Seltzer

I received the Spanish Dictionary & Grammar & Melville book, for which many thanks. Couldn't you find *Ulysses*? If you could just *lend* it to me, to read. I suppose I ought to read it.

<u>Why</u> have you not written me one line to here? Are you so very busy, or just holding off?

Mountsier says he's posted me the typescript of the Australian novel *Kangaroo.* I'll revise it when it comes. He wants it published this fall. I am neutral. He wants me to cut out my own long "war" experience, condense it to a couple of pages for Kangaroo, & publish the "experience" apart, perhaps with "Democracy." 38 What do you say to this? I am doubtful. I asked Mountsier to send you the other typed MS of Kangaroo *at once.* I want you also, quickly, to send me on all you have to say. I am willing to make revisions of all sorts. Do you think the Australian Govt. or the Diggers might resent anything? Let me know this as soon as possible.

Send me please the MS. of Birds Beasts & Flowers, so I can go through it again.

<u>Where</u> is Fantasia?

I *wish* you had got Sons & Lovers. <u>Can't</u> we do anything? [39]
Be sure & write about Kangaroo immediately.

Yrs., D. H. Lawrence

41

Taos, New Mexico
16 October 1922

Dear Seltzer

Thank you for your letter.—All right then, January. [40]
I think we shall stay the winter here—but it will be cold—sunny too.

Have gone through Kangaroo—many changes—it is now as I wish it. I want to *keep in* the war-experience piece: and I have made a new last chapter. Now it is as I want it, and it is good. I'm glad it's done. You'll like it much better.

I'm still waiting for Fantasia.

Yrs., D. H. Lawrence

42

Taos
New Mexico
6 Nov. 1922

Dear Seltzer

The books all came today—Fantasia, England my England, Women in Love & Ulysses: all very nice, but a terrible wrapper on Women in Love. [41] —I hope they will do well for us.—I take it Ulysses is just *lent*, & I will return it to the sender—who is he?—in about a week's time.

We must begin to arrange your visit. We plan to go to Santo Domingo pueblo—about two hours from Santa Fe—on the 23rd or 24th December. How would it be if you met us in Santa Fe & we all went to the dance? Mabel Sterne's car would hold us. Let me know: letters seem to take long.

We have just come back from a camping on a little

abandoned ranch Mrs. S. has about 16 miles from here—on the Rockies foothills.[42] —Lobo. I think my wife & I will go & live there: but come here for your visit: or part of it at least: part we might all spend at Lobo. Is Mrs Seltzer coming? We shall all be glad to see her. Now let us fix up this visit, or we shall be getting criss-cross.

Tell me about your proposals for spring publication. I sent Mountsier the Corrected MS of Kangaroo to New York.

Yrs., D. H. Lawrence

We should be in Santa Fe on Dec. 24th.

43

Taos
New Mexico
19 Novem. 1922

Dear Seltzer

Will you do a little thing for me. Please have your clerk send a parcel of books to my sister—including Aaron's Rod, England my England, Fantasia, Psychoanalysis & the Unconscious, & your Bee book, & perhaps Batouala, and any other you think she would like.[43] Make her a nice parcel, & charge it all to me. The address:

Mrs. L. A. Clarke
Grosvenor Rd.
Ripley near Derby
England

If you send them book post, it saves customs fuss.

Mountsier is at last in New York, so you will settle everything with him—I hope the books go well enough.

Please also send a copy of Aaron's Rod and a copy of England my England to

Mrs. S. King
480 Main St.
Carlton near Nottingham
England

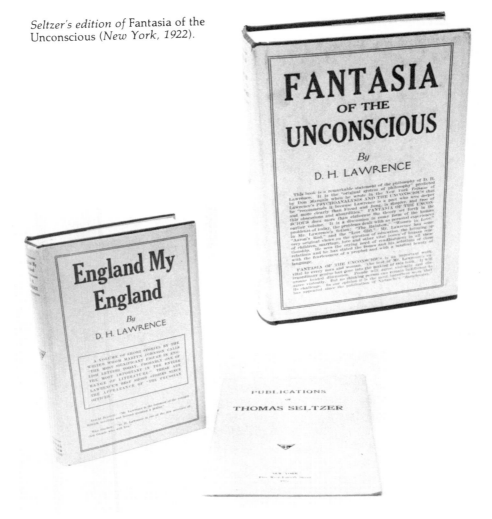

Seltzer's edition of Fantasia of the Unconscious (*New York, 1922*).

Seltzer's edition of England My England (*New York, 1922*). *With the publisher's current catalog.*

The "terrible" dust jacket of Seltzer's popular edition of Women in Love (*New York, 1922*).

Don't fail to send these, will you. I want them to have the books for Christmas. 44

Let me know about your coming here for Christmas. It has snowed deep, but thank goodness melted again in the hot sun.

I hope Mountsier has given you *Kangaroo*.

Greetings, D. H. Lawrence

I am busy with Studies in Classic A. Lit.—you'll like them much better, I think: much sharper, quicker.

D. H. L.

44

FRIEDA LAWRENCE TO ADELE SELTZER

Del Monte Ranch
Questa
New Mexico
[November-December 1922]

Dear Mrs Seltzer,

We are looking forward to your visit—You will find it a different sort of life after New York—Bring warm clothes and old clothes and riding things if you like riding—It's primitive to say the least of it—but plenty of wood and cream and chickens. I hope you can come on the 25th for the Indian's deer dance!

This is in a hurry as letters dally ages!

Yours sincerely, Frieda Lawrence

45

Taos
Tuesday, [?21 November 1922]

Dear Seltzer

Just a word to tell you our news. We are going a little way from Taos, to the Del Monte ranch, about 17 miles away. We shall have a good 5-roomed log cabin there—& a lovely wild place. This is a bit too much Mabel Dodge. You must come there. We are due to go on Friday next—day after Thanksgiving. But I'll write you the exact address when we get there. It's only 1½ hrs. in a car: three hours on horseback.

Two young Danes—artists—go with us, & they will have a 3-room cabin on the ranch, so we shall have company. In the big house are the young Hawks—Bill & his wife—& Elizabeth. [45] They are nice: the father a "gentleman"—but not rich. It's a lonely, lovely place—under the mountains, over the desert: very open.

The Danes—Knud Merrull [i.e. Merrild] & Kai Götzsche—don't have much money. Merrull is a *very* clever designer, head of the Artists Decorators Society in Copenhagen. I want you to let him design my book-jackets; and do some woodcuts for Birds Beasts—pay the ordinary price. Will you do that? I will have him send a design for *Kangaroo* jacket. And then if you can give him a bit more work, please do. Because he has a great sense of beauty, and is modern. You'll see when you come. [46]

We shall be so pleased to see Mrs Seltzer too.

Of course there is no breach with Mabel Sterne—no doubt she will want us all to come & stay here a bit, when you come.

I've nearly done Studies. It is the American Demon indeed. Lord knows what you'll think of them. But they'll make a nice little book: much shorter.

I'll write again directly.

I sent back Ulysses to Mr Wubbenhorst—thought it was only a loan. Thank you so much for getting it me. But I do not want you to pay for books for me. Please charge them to me, or I feel uneasy.

And when you come, if you can lend me Herman Melville's "Pierre" and "Mardi," I should like it. They belong only to a set, I believe.

"Ulysses" wearied me: so like a schoolmaster with dirt & stuff in his head: sometimes good, though: but too mental. I thought the Ben Hecht book silly: not a bit good. [47]

Yrs., D. H. Lawrence

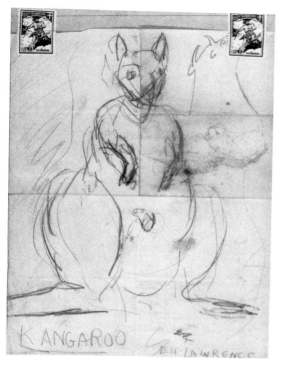

Three preliminary sketches by Knud Merrild for the dust jacket of Lawrence's Kangaroo. *(HRC)*

Five caricatures of Lawrence by Knud Merrild. (HRC)

46

Del Monte Ranch
Questa
New Mexico
Sunday, 2 Decem. [3 December] 1922

Dear Seltzer

Well we have moved—are cosy in a 5-room old log cabin among the pines above the desert. It is here you'll have to come. But come to Taos all the same, & probably we'll all stay at Mabel Sterne's for a day or two. I am glad to be on free territory once more—but we remain quite friendly. She was always nice—only somewhat blind to anything except her own way. I'll meet you at Taos.

It is rough here—really—and snow. But the house warm, even if there's no furniture. Will Mrs Seltzer mind? Will you?

We spent the morning sawing a pretty big tree into lengths—one of the Danes & I. We get our own fuel. This afternoon we rode through sleet and slush to San Cristobal—through the trees, downhill. They are littlish piñon trees, nothing tall. Me on a "pacing" horse with swivel legs. A pacer, they call it!

Don't come if you mind roughness. Otherwise it's great fun, & very beautiful wild country.

I'll try & get *Studies* finished

Yrs., D. H. Lawrence

I am not sure if we'll go to the Santo Domingo dance—but probably *not*.

47

[*Postcard*]

[Dec. 1922]

Dear Thomas

Bring me if you can the figures for the income tax—I must get that done. The Kingfisher fishing in the ink is for you—

twist the top & it's an inkwell. Il Penseroso is for Adele.

D. H. L.

Bring me that brown copy of The Rainbow if it's handy, & I'll expurgate it.

48

Del Monte Ranch
Questa
New Mexico
5 Dec. 1922

Dear Seltzer

I have your letter of Nov. 28, & clippings.

I will meet you then in *Taos* on the 25th—if you come straight through. If you don't care about going to Santa Fe, then everybody says it is best to come to Denver, Colorado, change there on to the Denver & Rio Grande railway, and come down to *Taos Junction Station* changing, I think, at Alamos again. This is only 25 miles from Taos, and the stage runs every day. Sometimes the Santa Fe stage doesn't run for two or three days. We'll probably stay a day or two in Taos, then come here. So glad Mrs Seltzer can come.—I told you, we are only 17 miles from Taos.

You know the Insel Verlag has published a translation of The Rainbow.

I know Murry too well to care what he says, one way or another. "When I open my mouth let no dog bark."

Have done all "Studies" except the last two—sent the first VIII to Mountsier. Will finish in a week (Deo volente).

Do you really want to publish my James Joyce remarks? No, I don't think it's quite fair to him.

It is fine here—but rough. Will you mind that?

Do please send books to these people, for Christmas.

D. H. L.

Thomas Seltzer. (Alexandra Levin)

49

Del Monte Ranch
Questa
New Mexico
Thursday, 4 Jan. 1923

Dear Seltzer

I imagine Mountsier is going to settle down to ranch life &
forget literary agency for the time being. Anyway I won't have
him doing anything I don't want.—Personally he is being very
nice: he'll like the life here—has gone riding today to Questa
with Rachel Hawk: to the satisfaction of both. I'm glad he
enjoys himself. Best that he should forget books. He talked
only of some contracts he had had drawn up, starting with a
15% royaltly. I don't know how that affects you. In England I
start at 15%. But I want to be quite just, and you to be the
same. I shall go through the *Studies in Classic American
Literature* MS. & let you have it as soon as the last four
typewritten chapters come from New York. If you want to
make any minor alterations, you are free to do so. Mountsier
wants *Studies* published first, before Kangaroo. What do you
think?

I enclose the last words of *Kangaroo*: the last page. Don't
lose it.

Looking at Merrild's book-jacket designs again, I think that
one for *Kangaroo* with the small figure in the middle is rather
weak & abstract-looking: might lead one to expect something
theoretic.

I am going through the Verga MS.—*Black Bread*—the short
sketches: then I'll send it you. I want to know what you think
of *Mastro-Don Gesualdo*.

Tell me how your trip west was. And what you think of the
trip to Mexico. [48]

What a rush you had for that Stage—or that train! And
Oakley's car arrived at 10:45, if you please!

It is a lovely day. If Adele Szold were here we'd go riding.
As it is I'll just stroll down to the post-box with this
letter.—Yesterday William killed a steer—and that young Pips
would not be kept away—became shamefully sick—got well
spanked—and so has gone to live with the Danes. There let

her stay. She's got no loyalty. [49] To me, loyalty is far before love. Love seems usually to be just a dirty excuse for disloyalties.

Tell Adele Szold the white bowl had a pudding made in it this morning.

Yrs., D. H. Lawrence

50

FRIEDA LAWRENCE TO ADELE SELTZER

Friday, 12th I. 23
Del Monte Ranch

To-day comes your letter and I never thanked you for the beautiful white bowl William brought back—I could not have thanked you sufficiently at once as I did not know the innumerable uses it can be put to—I am sure if there were a baby it would be bathed in it—glad you had a nice day in Santa Fe—We have had lovely weather, have ridden and walked and picknicked and cleaned and the only fly in the ointment is "Rachel's" uncertain temper—Mountsier helps on the land and forgets that he is an agent—I would rather like to see the spring here and then I would like to come East—but Lawrence may want Mexico—We had a letter from Thomas— otherwise nothing interesting happens, letters from Germany very sad—Also Katherine Mansfield is in a new kind of community [50] near Paris about 60 people, wanting to lead the simple life (at this late hour) they are mostly rich—Lawrence is just writing with Pips on his right arm—My pen is rotten I try in vain to get it into a good humour—Did the girls in the office like their "Mitgebringsel?" I am so glad you are both no longer only a name to us—Please send me my knickers as soon as possible my others are dying—It seemed a pity that your stay was so short—

All good wishes to you, Frieda Lawrence

51

Del Monte Ranch
Questa
New Mexico
Friday, 19 January 1923

Dear Seltzer

I have packed up for you *Studies in Classic American Literature.* I want you to publish them this spring. If you want anything altered or eliminated, tell me the page & line—I have a third MS.—and I will send you the revision. Don't bother to post the MS.

Also in the parcel is *Ladybird.* I had a long & friendly letter from Curtis Brown with very favorable offers for Kangaroo. But I don't trust Secker. And Curtis Brown says Secker is making a fine book of *Ladybird*, and will bring it out in March. I knew that was what they were up to. Hurry up your printers. If you have proofs of Captain's Doll & Fox, & there is time, let me see proofs. I will send them back at once. But be sure & be ready with the book *early* in March. That Secker shall not steal a march on us, and leave us stranded in April.

Also in the parcel the three book-jackets, which I like very much. Hope you will like them too.

Also the Götzsche drawing. The Dial might do it with my *Indian* article, which they are printing in instalments. [51] Or you might have some other bright idea. It would help nicely to advertise. I wrote the names on the back.

Also in the parcel thousands of contracts. [52] As I said before, I want you to agree to all you possibly can. What is impossible write plainly to Mountsier, also to me—if anything is impossible.

Mountsier suggests *Captain's Doll, Studies,* and *Birds Beasts & Flowers* for this spring, leaving *Kangaroo* till early autumn. I think this wise. Do you?—And Mountsier says you really don't want Birds Beasts decorated or illustrated. If you really dislike it, we will just make a title-page and a rather exceptionally beautiful jacket, with animals on it. Would you like that?—I never want you to agree to anything that really goes badly against your grain. Don't hesitate to tell me.

We still think of Old Mexico in March. I read Stephen Graham's letter in the Santa Fe newspaper about the death of

Wilfred Ewart in Mexico City. Is Stephen Graham back in New York? If so do ask him what the travelling is like—and the journey down from El Paso to Mexico City: and any advice he has to give. [53]

Oh, Curtis Brown has a publisher wants to do *Mastro don Gesualdo* in August in England. [54] Tell me quickly what you want to do about it. That lawyer Stern told Mountsier that in 1888 the copyright laws weren't fixed between Italy and U.S.A. Had you better make sure.—So warm here. Many greetings

Yrs., D. H. Lawrence

Mrs Seltzer will recognize me on Laddie, Merrild on Brownie, the buggy-horse, & Götzsche on Pinto. Götzsche is doing a real forcible portrait of me in my leather shirt & blue overalls—if he doesn't spoil it.

D. H. L.

52

FRIEDA LAWRENCE TO ADELE SELTZER

Del Monte
21. I. 23

Dear Adele Seltzer,

That letter was to you—Did it not say Mrs. Thom. *S—? Anyhow it was* meant *for you—We have had* lovely *weather so far; Mountsier sits in his room all day and writes another of his beastly European articles—I detest him for it—We can both see now what you said about him and yet is there really nothing else in him? He keeps the old mess going, when we all live and fight for something* new *in this ugly world—And as you said his spirit is just opposed to L's! If he is* hopeless, *we wont have any more of him—Anyhow it would amuse you how L keeps him under! I wonder what we shall do—New York or Mexico—Someday we shall see you in Europe, and I regret that things were'nt nicer for you here—Mostly we have had nicer* places *anyhow—It's a bit sordid here, I thought I could conquer it, but you cant—Is'nt the drawing of the riders*

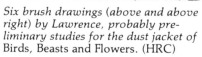

Six brush drawings (above and above right) by Lawrence, probably preliminary studies for the dust jacket of Birds, Beasts and Flowers. *(HRC)*

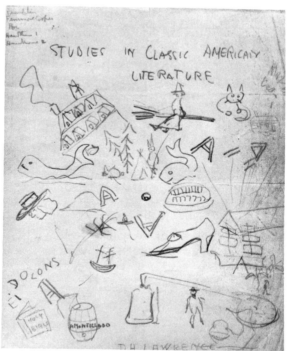

Sketch by Lawrence titled "Studies
in Classic American Literature."
(HRC)

amusing—*I was* so *pleased you liked Mastro Don, it belongs to the past as you said but in a* living *way—and I find the great phases of the past a relief from this dull present—You will like the "Liaisons dangereuses" good too—Take that letter, I ask you for knickers in it!! Also send it* insured—

Best wishes from us both, Frieda L.

It is a treat to get Vanity Fair and Punch! Thank you so much!

53

Del Monte Ranch
Questa
New Mexico
23 January 1923

Dear Seltzer

I have suddenly realised—or Mountsier has—that Hearsts have not yet used *The Captain's Doll.* Is that so? If so, will you find out when they *can* use it, quickly, & let Curtis Brown know. Because as I told you Secker is due to bring the thing out in March. I should like you to have it out that month too.

I enclose a letter to Curtis Brown—you read it and add a word when you have found out from Hearst. [55]

Tell Adele Szold the underwear came for Frieda today, and I will send a cheque for the five dollars when I write to her.

Hurt my hand a bit with a log of wood.

Hope you have my letters, & MSS, & all: am waiting to hear from you.

Find I have $2,200 in the bank. Suppose that will take me to Mexico.

Am busy doing the Birds Beasts. They will soon be done. Will you tell me as soon as you can what format you want the book to have, exactly: the size & all: and exactly what decoration you want it to have.

It is very cold again. I don't like winter. I shall be rather glad to go south to Mexico. Tell me about it, if there is anything to tell.

Yrs., D. H. Lawrence

A letter from Curtis Brown just arrived saying Secker is publishing *Ladybird* "almost immediately." Do please find out the earliest date at which it may be published, and send enclosed cable to Curtis Brown.

D. H. L.

P. S. I will send Curtis Brown's letter direct—not enclose it. But do please write him as soon as you can:

Curtis Brown
6 Henrietta St.
Covent Garden
London W. C. 2

54

Del Monte Ranch
Questa
New Mexico
28 Jan. 1923

Dear Adele Szold

Der Mountsier ist heute weg—fort—gegangen—etc. Gott sei dank. I suppose he'll be in New York in 15 days time: staying a few days in Taos—& Denver.

But I'll write Seltzer.

Thank you for sending Frieda's parcel. I wish you would send something else. Merrild has a flute & Götzsche a fiddle & we sing songs: but they want music. Could you send us a book of English songs, & one of German: just the *simple* ordinary good songs, with simple music. I would like, if you can get it, *The Oxford Song Book*, in English. If there is a simple Italian book too, we'll have that as well. It doesn't matter if there is only mandoline accompaniment music.

I am waiting to hear from Seltzer about things.

I enclose cheque for ten dollars, five of which I owe you for that Frieda parcel.

Leb wohl, D. H. Lawrence

55

Del Monte Ranch
Questa
New Mexico
1st Feby. 1923

Dear Seltzer

I got your telegram about an article this morning. Have just finished enclosed. [56] If they don't want it, burn it.

The pen came: looks very grand. Of course I'm a bit scared of it. But when I get some proper ink from Taos I'll sit down and write to you with it, and thank you.

Mountsier left on Sunday. I wished it. Whatever friendship I felt for him before, I don't feel now. I have told him I want single control of all my money. But I haven't yet broken with him as my agent, because I feel he tried. But I think the break has got to come. Voyons!

I am finishing the Birds Beasts MS. I shall send it straight to you. It makes a very interesting book.

I wait to hear from you. We still think of Mexico. I don't want Adele Szold to give a party for me, like Gilbert. [57] No. Tell her I had her letter.

Would you order for me *Terry's Guide to Mexico*—I believe that is the best.—Do I bother you a great deal?

Stormy weather here.

There is a poem to Bibbles, tell Adele Szold.

Götzsche finished his portrait of me. Quite interesting, in my blue overall-trousers & leather shirt. They say it has got my get-rid-of-Mountsier face. Cela peut être.

Frieda sewing glad-rags as if for a departure into the world somewhere.

Saluti, D. H. Lawrence

56

Del Monte Ranch
Questa
New Mexico
3 Feby. 1923

Dear Seltzer

I had your letter yesterday.

On the main point, of Mountsier, I do agree with you. I have this minute written to him—Mountsier—that I wish to break my agreement with him, and that in future I wish to handle all my business personally.

What about future payments to him? Is he still to have the 10% on all contracts drawn up by him? I don't want to be mean with him. Advise me at once.

You know too that he was starting a lawsuit against Kennerley, for recovery of *Sons & Lovers* royalties, through that lawyer Stern: the suit to cost me from $300 to $500 dollars. What shall we do about this? Let it go on?

Also he is serving, through Stern, the notices on Huebsch, for the taking back of the books Huebsch has in his control. The notices must be served one by one, as the books fall due.

We must be very careful about these things.

If you telegraph, send a night message to Del Monte Ranch, *Valdez*, New Mexico. The telegraph is a bit quicker that way.

Yrs., D. H. Lawrence

If it is really necessary I will come to New York, but would prefer not to come till the end of March.

D. H. L.

I just heard from Murry that Katherine Mansfield, his wife, died suddenly. I'm sorry.—Would you post him a copy of *Fantasia* and of *England my England* and *Psychoanalysis* to care

S. Koteliansky
5 Acacia Rd.
St. Johns Wood
London N. W. 5

And please send a copy of *Psychoanalysis* & *Fantasia* to Koteliansky himself.

D. H. L.

57

FRIEDA LAWRENCE TO ADELE SELTZER

Del Monte
3. II. 23

Dear Adele S—

So Mountsier is off the map—When Thomas's letter came about Kanguoroo [sic] it was so different from the things Mountsier said—He told me if I had any influence on Lawr I ought to make him sit still and write novels like Sons & Lovers. Can you see an endless row of Sons & Loverses? Well M is a thing of the past—Lawr is just riding to Valdez to post the grand finale of a letter—Lawr thinks he must go to New York then about affairs—but we may first go to Mexico—Also you have got a girl in your office whom Mountsier used to take out to the theatre and question about Seltzer affairs, how I hate those ways—My news from Germany are very sad—still I am so glad they are putting up a fight—We shall help my Jaffe sister, it'[s] hard for her, she has been so well off—We had a desperate letter from Murry Katherine Mansfield is dead—It grieved us both deeply—She was such an exquisite creature and we had real fun with them—This paper is vile—The letters take such a time—So you are entertaining Gilbert, I wonder if he knows that Mary is very ill with appendicitis; in spite of his lofty airs Gilbert is really a pathetic figure—We have jolly evenings with the Danes— Please send me my dyed rags as soon as you can, that I can fix them—I always like to make glad rags for the spring—It has snowed very hard, two pigs have drowned in the pond—Rachel is down in spirits, I think it is an infant—The Pips is chased by all the big dogs on the ranch, she is a real female now—I hope Thomas liked the article on the novel—I did—Dont work too hard—The house in Stamford sounds attractive—

Good luck, Frieda Lawrence

58

WESTERN UNION TELEGRAM

[To]

Thomas Seltzer
5 West Fiftieth Street
New York, N. Y.

[?9 February 1923; published
New York Times, 11 February 1923.]

Let Judge John Ford confine his judgement to court of law, and not try to perch in seats that are too high for him. Also let him take away the circulating library tickets from Miss Ford, lest worse befall her. She evidently needs an account at a candy shop, because of course "Women in Love" wasn't written for the Ford family any more than apples are apples for their sake. Father and mother and daughter should all leave the tree of knowledge alone. The Judge won't succeed in chopping it down, with his horrified hatchet. Many better men have tried and failed.58

D. H. Lawrence

59

Del Monte Ranch
Questa
New Mexico
10 Feb. 1923

Dear Seltzer

I write this with your new pen, which is a great success.
We were in Taos two days; came back yesterday. I sent you a night letter for Judge Ford et famille. Bet you didn't print it.
I met Mountsier twice: told him simply I wished to discontinue with him: firstly, because he did not believe in me & what I was doing, but was antagonistic in spirit: secondly, because he had so annoyed you, you didn't want to deal with

him. In answer to the first he said if that was my opinion, there was no use arguing about it. To which I replied, it was my opinion. In answer to the latter he said various things. — But altogether he gave me the impression he has a *bad conscience* about something: I don't know what. He hates losing the *job*, but, *au fond*, is really relieved, I think, to be released. He gave me back some MS. & Huebsch contracts, and is to send me a letter saying what he thinks he ought to get, in the way of continuing of commissions to him. He may not stay long in Taos. Then I shall ask him back for all papers & MSS of mine. I asked him to write everybody concerned & say he had ceased to be my agent.

The two points of importance seem the Huebsch notices and the Kennerley business: both in the hands of the lawyer Stern. The Huebsch notices must be served in presence of *witness* seven years after date of <u>publication</u> *of book*. Notice for Rainbow is already served—no reply from Huebsch. And then the Kennerley case, the lawyer says, cannot come to *court for two years*—and Stern is "pessimistic." Mountsier advises that I continue this business *with Stern personally*. What do you say?

I have your letter of Feb. 1st. I had your telegram about Mountsier yesterday, saying you will wire again. I think it is very annoying, the *Hearst* delay. I wanted those three stories out this spring. And it will be a blow to Secker. Pity nothing can be done. Magazines should have a date limit.

I was annoyed to learn from Mountsier that Seldes had the English copy of *Kangaroo*, had carted it off to Berlin; Curtis Brown hasn't got it yet. I have asked Curtis Brown to communicate direct with me & you about it. Whatever Seldes decides, I don't really want The Dial to print a *bit* of the book. [59]

We won't worry about Mountsier any more. He has a bad will, I have done with him, save for winding-up trifles. Enough.

I am anxious to hear from you about the order in which the new books are to appear. Am really sorry The Captain's Doll is held up. I *don't want you* to get a book ready for publication without letting Curtis Brown know. He sent me a very favorable contract for *Kangaroo*, from Secker. But I said I wouldn't sign it till Secker satisfied me about *Fantasia, Psychoanalysis, Studies,* and *England my England.* Secker agrees to pay 15% up to 2000, then 20% on the next 3000, and after that, 25%. But I won't sign till I am satisfied about those other books. [60]

I think to go to Mexico City about middle of next month. Don't bother about the Melville books or the Bernal Diaz. The former I can get in England, the latter in Mexico. But I should be glad if you could send me Terry's "Guide to Mexico", as I asked. We'd probably be in New York by end of May again, stay till July. Tell Adele Szold the house sounds attractive. It would be fun.

I think when you get used to it you'll like Merrild's *Kangaroo* jacket. I didn't like it at first; now think perhaps it's the best. I do want them to have a few dollars to be able to go on their way with. Otherwise I must give them, and it's so much better for their pride if they can earn them. Götzsche was so pleased when he heard Adele Szold liked the drawing. [61] We wonder what she'd think of the portrait.—Did you see this month's *Dial*?

Tell me soon about *Birds Beasts*: format & everything.

I've got to fill up income-tax papers—have asked Mountsier to let me know what I've earned exactly. Hope he will do so.

Let's settle as much business as possible before I go to Mexico. And if possible, do let me see an exact MS. of Birds Beasts. I have that book at heart.

Yrs., D. H. Lawrence

I am thinking perhaps it would be better to close my account with the Charleroi Savings & Trust Co, & you open another account for me in a New York bank. What do you think?

D. H. L.

P. P. S. I found the *Almond Blossom* poem. Enclose it here. So the MS. of Birds Beasts can be complete.

D. H. L.

60

[Del Monte]
Saturday 10. II 23

Dear Adele S,

We found each a long letter yesterday from each of you! You would have laughed over the last Mountsier days! Lawrence made him feel so small even Pips, you will admire his judgment, detested Mountsier—On the very last day after Lawr. had told him, he wanted him to go—I was left alone with him for lunch—Lawr took some sandwiches and went off—Mountsier very sad, he had no home, no father, no mother—in Colombo some little native beggar boys run by the side of your rickshaw and say; Lady, give penny, no daddy no mummy, no breakfast—Lady, give penny!! He used to talk to me and with that fatal inevitability I knew he was'nt our sort and we not his—I did not even feel cross I just knew—He is a poor hollow nut, like so many people he clings to the social shell, no wonder it's all they have got if they are hollow inside! I fear Gilbert is another one—He hates Lawrence now, he cant patronise him anymore! We were both so pleased that Thomas S. is somebody in the world. I feel L's and his success very bound up—I thought it mean of M. to say anything about the Women in Love contract of course we none of us thought it would sell as it has done neither did Mr Mountsier beforehand. [62] *He wanted to turn Lawr & Thomas into enemies—Lawrence knows well enough what he owes to you both it's more than dollars, the dollars came after as a result of your belief in his genius. I think you are right to take your stand definitely and finally, it's no good messing with people that are'nt worth it, or giving into them—"Entweder oder"—Lawr wants to go to Mexico, he thinks he might write his American novel there—You know he would like to write a novel of each continent—if possible—It's awfully nice that we have so many dollars, Lawrence will feel free and I can help my people—Then we shall come to New York, it would certainly be nice for a change to live more comfortably, then in the autumn we would go to Taormina and keep our Fontana Vecchia as headquarters—We love it both and you*

68

would have to come and see us—I also want to see my children in England! I am looking forward now to move on—Taos is rather awful with its spite, they all detest each other—The Danes have been a tower of strength. They are really nice and you ought to hear our "concerts" in the evening—They also heartily detested Montsiger [sic]—Wytter [sic] Bynner came with an enormous motor full of Americans, I liked the thin little Johnson, but he looked so cold and frail—What fun it will be, when you show us New York. Our poor Catherine Mansfield is buried near Paris, it was so sad and again so inevitable that she had to die—She chose a death road and dare not face reality! It's been a wonderful day, you never saw this place at its best—

Now I must go to the post!

Auf Wiedersehen, Frieda

I think it's a disgrace for the Allies this Ruhr business— Where is their love of justice, fair play, freedom now? They need never talk again! 63

Dear Adele Szold

Did you get my letter asking you for song books and enclosing ten dollars? Mail is a bit shaky out here.—I want you to have Birds Beasts under your wing, to see they are nice & shapely.—It's been so cold—now a bit warmer. And the Montsiger [sic] business made me so sick. We are keen on Mexico for a trip: & the Danes pining to scrape a bit of money together to go too. They are having an exhibition in Santa Fe. Witter Bynner came here one day & wants to go too: but no, no Americans if possible. I feel sore with all Americans for the moment. Where are those sweets?—Baking day, & I've made buns. Pity you aren't here to tea.

A riverderci [sic], D. H. L.

Did Thomas print my wire to Judge Ford intact? Tell me.

61

Del Monte Ranch
Questa
New Mexico
Sunday, 17 Feb. 1923

Dear Seltzer

I return proofs of *Ladybird* today.

I got the assignments for the *White Peacock* from Mountsier.

There are two parcels for me, I get notices, at Jaroso [Jerosa, Colorado]. These will be from Adele Szold: & many thanks to her. But don't send things by *express* to here, please: send parcel post. Jaroso is 52 miles away, in Colorado: the nearest station on the Questa side. And I have a struggle to get the things forwarded.

And do please answer all my questions soon, & write to Merrild. I think to leave for Old Mexico about the 15th March via El Paso: have written about tickets: they don't cost much. So let us get everything settled as far as possible before we go: about the books.

Grüsse, D. H. Lawrence

62

Del Monte Ranch
Questa
New Mexico
20 Feby. 1923

Dear Seltzer

I have your telegram this morning—Tuesday. Enclose it. Am so glad Hearsts' have freed *The Capt's Doll.* Now you can publish it next month. I sent proofs yesterday of *Ladybird.* Did you tell Curtis Brown? I am writing to Secker today so shall let him know the book is free. You write Curtis Brown.

Yes, you attend to everything for me, that Stern has on hand: the Kennerley business and the Huebsch contracts. I wrote to Huebsch telling him to act with you, & with me, not with Mountsier. I enclose a letter for Stern, the lawyer, which you can hand on.—I enclose also Mountsier's letter about further royalties. Let me know what you think about this. And particularly let me know about a new banking account. I think I shall get a letter of credit from the Charleroi people, and pretty well close the old account.

And in future, keep my twelve presentation copies, please, & have them sent off from your office as I ask you. I enclose a list of addresses for *The Captain's Doll.* Send to me just two copies.

I hope everything will go well.

Tanti belli saluti, D. H. Lawrence

Copies of *The Captain's Doll.* to be sent out
1. Knud Merrild
1. Kai Götzsche
1. Mrs Elizabeth Freeman, The Desert Inn, *Palm Springs,* California.
1. Mr. & Mrs Joseph Brewis, 640 Riverside Drive, *New York City.*
1. Mrs. Lee Witt, *Taos.* New Mexico.
1. Mrs. Mable Sterne. *Taos.* New Mexico.
1. Frau Baronin von Richthofen, Ludwig-Wilhelmstift, Baden-Baden Germany.
1. Frau Professor Else Jaffé, Konradstr. 16, Munich, *Germany.*
1. Frau Johanna von Schriebershofen, Dahlmannstr. 5, Charlottenburg bei *Berlin.,* Germany.
1. Dr. E. Tuchmann, 34 Würtembergischerstr, *Berlin.,* Germany.
1. W. Siebenhaar, Registrar Generals Office, *Perth,* West Australia.
1. Miss Ruth Wheelock, American Consulate, *Palermo.* Sicily.
1. Mrs. Humes, c/o J. C. Humes, 315 Shawmut Bank Bldg., *Boston.* Mass.

D. H. Lawrence

63

Del Monte Ranch
Questa
New Mexico
Feb. 22, 1923

Dear Seltzer

Your letter this evening also the Guide to Mexico & other books, & sweets. For all of which very many thanks, & *please charge them to me:* I mean all the books and expenses.

Sorry about *Sons and Lovers* cheap edition. That's a waste. You can only serve notices on Huebsch six months after date of <u>publication</u> of each book: not expiration of contracts. You must find out these dates from Huebsch; or I must. How is he going to act? I wrote him about Mountsier & told him to act with you on any necessary point. If you want the Huebsch contracts, I will send them, & you can keep them for me, or deposit them for me.

Yes, you do things with Stern. (What about this Stern?) But *always* tell me. If you must act quickly, on your own responsibility sometimes, do so. But always tell me plainly everything. That was how Huebsch annoyed me: he just left me out. So in the end I left him out. And glad I did. Always tell me openly what you are doing and intend doing with my things, else I get angry, and then I don't care any more.—I wrote Stern to act with you.

I wrote to Secker *Captain's Doll* was released, and he was to fix date of simultaneous publication with you.—I told you I wrote Curtis Brown I would sign no contract with Secker for *Kangaroo* till Secker satisfied me about *Fantasia* & *Studies* & *England my England.*

I am glad you sent Merrild the money. I think, truly, the Kangaroo jacket will have more effect than you imagine. Merrild will do the jacket for *Birds Beasts,* in bright, tangled colour. Size 6⅝ by 8½ inches. I take it you want *no* interior decoration. But you should tell me, since I asked you.

Mountsier made out the total of my year's income, and the total of the deductions, so I shall pay in this state, where there is no *State* tax: only the 4%. But do please as far as possible keep track of my income for the current year: & expenses you pay to Stern for me, and things like that.[64]

Did you read *Mastro-Don Gesualdo*? Do when you have time, and let me know. Because Curtis Brown wants an answer for England. Blackwell wants to publish it in August or September. [65]

Secker pledged to do advertising for £100 sterling, on Kangaroo. I don't know, I'm sure, what he is really about. But the figures are as I tell you. I don't trust him very far. Yes, if you go to England, do speak for me. But I'll stick to Secker if he will print all of me.

I will send you *The White Peacock* papers. Stern has served the notice for The Rainbow.

Let me have proofs of everything as soon as they come off the press, no matter where I am.

If you can get me an interesting letter of introduction to anybody in Mexico, do. I liked that book *The Mexican People*. Do you know anything about Pinchon or Gutierrez de Lara, the authors? [66]

We are due to leave here in 3 weeks today.

I shall look for the contracts. Yes, put in the seven year clause, and give me the copyrights. Then I shall feel freer. But I had better have a place in New York to keep my papers in. Would you suggest a part of a safe in a bank?—or Stern? I must also get Mountsier to transfer all papers when he returns to New York. He is still in Taos.

Don't forget to answer me, too, about a banking account.

I seem to give you a great deal of trouble. But everything is coming straight. And we will make a success of things.

Thank you so much for all the books and music and the trouble you have taken.

Yrs., D. H. Lawrence

64

Del Monte Ranch
Questa
New Mexico
2 March 1923

Dear Seltzer

Your letter of Feb. 24.

My account in the Charleroi bank will expire this month. Please open me an account in the Chase National Bank: and do as you say, keep me a constant 2000 dollars to my credit. If I leave the rest in the Seltzer corporation, *can I get it out any time I may want it?* If so, I will leave the balance in your business.

I had a letter from Curtis Brown. Secker will publish *Studies, Fantasia & Psychoanalysis* as one book, *England my England,* all before the end of this year. So I let him go ahead. I don't know if Cape is any better. I have got the *Kangaroo* contract still unsigned: it binds me to offer my next novel to Secker. I want to see what he does with these pending books, first.

Curtis Brown said Blackwell wanted to do *Mastro-don Gesualdo* in August. September would be all right. I must have proofs of this.

We leave here not later than 18th inst.—Remember to send me proofs of everything. I wish I could have proofs of *Studies* before I go: & that MS. of *Birds Beasts.* But if you print early you can send proofs early.—*White Peacock* is quite free. I'll send you the papers for it.

Grüsse, D. H. Lawrence

Curtis Brown urges me to stay with Secker.
Hope to receive *your* contracts before I leave.

D. H. L.

65

Del Monte Ranch
Questa
New Mexico
3 March 1923

Dear Seltzer

I sent you B. W. Huebsch's letter about *The Rainbow* last night. [67] Enclosed I send you the contracts for:

> *Three Novels* (Doran, covers The Rainbow)—including a letter about copyrights.
> *Italian Days. Amores* (Doran)
> *Prussian Officer.* (Doran)
> *Look! We Have Come Through* (Huebsch)
> *The White Peacock* (Duffield—transfer papers complete).

Please keep these for me very carefully till I come to New York and can arrange a safe-deposit for all my papers.

On the back is a copy of my letter to Huebsch. I think we ought to let him get through this edition, anyhow. Best let Stern deal with him in this matter. Try and be amicable and fair.

You see Doran started at 15% on this contract.

I am writing to Stern and tell him you will show him the Huebsch letter.

Telegraph to me—I must know how this is to be settled before I leave.

Yrs. ever, D. H. Lawrence

P. S. Would you send a copy of *England my England* to

Mrs Elizabeth Freeman
The Desert Inn
Palm Springs
California

66

Del Monte Ranch
Questa
New Mexico
9 March 1923

Dear Seltzer

Your letter of March 3rd.—Thank you for the card from Lincoln Steffens.[68]

All right, we'll drop Stern after he has arranged this bit of Huebsch matter with you. I thought he'd better do that: you and Huebsch might bite one another's heads off. But please yourself. I'll write no more to Stern.

I sent the Huebsch contracts.

I have at last finally settled with Mountsier that he is to have 10% of this year's receipts from you—your March & September payments: & then *finito!* He has already got $170 on acc. from Dial.

By the way, would it bother you to keep the two *Dials* with my *Indians & an Englishman* article in them.

I think, really, you are right not to make interior decorations for *Birds Beasts.* But poor Merrild was so set on it. He has done a design for each section-cover. I told him that you would *not* use them for the ordinary edition, but that if you liked them, & if ever you wanted to print a decorated edition, you might use them for that. I think the book-jacket has a nice free feeling: hope you'll like it. Götzsche has done a jacket for *Mastro-don Gesualdo,* which I like. But I don't want you to feel pestered about these. If you don't really want them, pay for them out of my money.

Damn Ford & the suppressionists. But other events will take place, that will overwhelm this small fry.[69]

I've still got a bit of my cold. Want very much to go south. So does Frieda. I think Witter Bynner & Willard Johnson are coming along to Mexico City. Have learnt quite a lot of Spanish. Feel the U.S.A. so terribly sterile, even *negative.* I tell you what, there is no life of the blood here. The blood can't flow properly. Only nerves, nerve-vibration, nerve-irritation. It wearies the inside of my bones. I want to go. Voglio andarmene.

I enclose a letter from Paris. Give 'em *England my England*

& *Capt's Doll* if you feel like it, & let 'em read & digest. Canaille!

Enclose also a letter from a periodical *Tempo.* I wrote the Oliver Jenkins & told him to ask you for a poem from *Birds Beasts.* Give 'em *Elephant,* or one of the Taos or Lobo poems. And fix a *mild* price for the poor dears. [70]

Am looking for MS. of *Birds Beasts.* I hope you'll print the books *early,* & send me proofs. Have you not got proofs of *Studies* yet? I wanted to see them. Guess Secker will print Studies before *Fantasia.*

Be sure you send a complete *Birds Beasts* to Curtis Brown.

I shall depart to Mexico leaving myself in your hands. We go next week.

Vale! D. H. L.

OLIVER JENKINS TO D. H. LAWRENCE

Tempo, A Magazine of Poetry and Prose

D. H. Lawrence, Esq.
Taos, New Mexico
March 3, 1923

Dear Mr. Lawrence:

TEMPO *which has been appearing regularly for two years as a verse magazine is about to enter the field as a potential journal of prose and poetry. The next number which we are to issue in May will be a classic if we can make it so. All of which comes to this: I have the audacity to ask you for a poem or story for* TEMPO.

The following authors have been enthusiastic enough to contribute something for the May number: Waldo Frank, Amy Lowell, Ben Hecht (?), Henry Bellamann, etc. I have reasons to expect to add Carl Sandburg, James Oppenheim, Joseph Hergesheimer, Charles Finger and Eliot to this list. Won't you help me to fulfil my desire? I want to put out a magazine that will back all the others of its kind off the boards. I think that I can do it—what do you think?

If you will just give me the satisfaction of a reply, whether you like the idea or not, I'll certainly appreciate it. And in closing I take this opportunity to thank you for the pleasure of WOMEN in LOVE, THE LOST GIRL, *many of your poems and articles, have brought to me.*

Cordially yours, Oliver Jenkins

Please understand that TEMPO *is just starting and is not wealthy, but we will use all authors fairly. If you send anything, just state your own price and we'll do our best.*

67

WESTERN UNION TELEGRAM

MAR 12 1923

THOS SELTZER
5 WEST 50 ST NEWYORK NY

PROCEED WITH HUEBSCH BUT BE FRIENDLY

LAWRENCE

68

Del Monte Ranch
Questa
New Mexico
14 March 1923

Dear Seltzer

I telegraphed you: "Proceed with Huebsch, but be friendly." If he's *really* got an edition in the press, you *can't* squash it. Don't do that.—I'll put a copy of my letter to Huebsch on the back.

I've got *Birds Beasts* MS. Will send it you before I leave. I've got my Letter of Credit.

Will you please pay in a thousand dollars to my account in the *Charleroi Savings and Trust Co. Charleroi. Penna.* This can be the last we will pay in to that account. But I want some money there, so I can draw a cheque or so from the cheque-book I've got. Please pay it in as soon as you get this letter.

I send you the last poem I shall write in the US this time: *The American Eagle*. Some one might like to print it. I think I would like it put *last* in the *Birds Beasts* MS, among the *ghosts*.

When will *The Captain's Doll* be out?

Please send a complete MS. of <u>Birds Beasts</u> *to Curtis Brown at once.*

We expect to be in Santa Fe on Monday—leave Wednesday. If you have a last word, you could telegraph *care Witter Bynner. Santa Fe.*

I can't bear to leave the Bimsey. Either Götzsche or Mrs Freeman, who is coming to Mexico in May, shall bring him to us: or I will come back here for him.

Mountsier says he will probably leave Taos about 1st April.

I do hope everything will go well with you. I feel the Ford fuss won't come to much. But don't overwork and make yourself ill.

I'll write a note & thank Steffens. Am sorry about Gutierrez de Lara: feel I should have liked him.

We are in the midst of packing. The sky is trying to snow. Mabel Sterne has gone to California: got herself into too great a mess with Indians etc. Nina Witt & Lee came yesterday: been in Boston since Christmas: are a bit dreary. Expect Witter Bynner goes with us to Mexico.

I put my trust in you.

D. H. Lawrence

I shall call at the post-office Mexico City for post restante letters.

Taos Junction   Monday 18 march 1923

Dear Seltzer

I just had your telegram about Huebsch as we left Taos. I haven't any Huebsch *Women-in-Love* correspondence. But very little passed. Pinker had the MS. two years. I thought of course he had tried everybody. Came your letter asking for the book – I sent you my MS.. Then I had a letter & cable from Huebsch saying he hadn't seen the MS (who knows if he had!) I cabled you, please release *Women-in-Love*. You had sent me £50. sterling – & you replied you couldn't release. That was all. Ask Huebsch to show you my letter. He once said to Mountsier that I was a liar, & that he could prove it from letters. He went to look for said letters & couldn't find them. — I remember that against him, you may be sure. And I will write

and remind him of it. Anyhow I acted in absolute good faith in the *Women in Love* matter. You have the correspondence.

Huebsch never answered my letters from Taos.

I do hope it will straighten out without ugliness. Go softly.

Yrs   D H Lawrence

Letter of 18 [19] March 1923. (HRC)

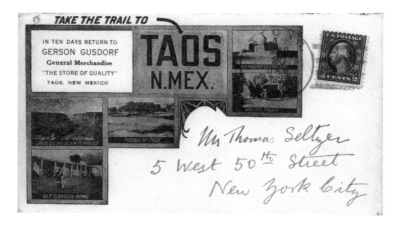

TAKE THE TRAIL TO

IN TEN DAYS RETURN TO
GERSON GUSDORF
General Merchandise
"THE STORE OF QUALITY"
TAOS, NEW MEXICO

TAOS N.MEX.

Mr Thomas Seltzer
5 West 50th Street
New York City

Mr Thomas Seltzer
5 West 50th Street
New York City

TAOS: Capital of Taos County,

mistress of the beautiful Taos Valley, famous for three centuries for its fertile soil, its flocks, herds, grain and fruit; its lofty mountains with valuable deposits of gold, silver and copper; its crystal lakes, mountain streams and medicinal hot springs.

Its delightful climate; its unique Indian village with most remarkable communal buildings in known world, built nearly four centuries ago. Taos County contains 200,000 acres government and 60,000 acres state land waiting for settlers.

Taos may also be reached from Trinidad, Raton and the east via beautiful Cimarron Canon and over either Taos or Red River Pass; from Las Vegas via Mora and Los Alamitos Pass and from Santa Fe via scenic Rio Grande Canon.

Taos may be reached by automobile from Denver, Colorado Springs and Pueblo, via La Veta Pass.

Come to Taos. Its the land of opportunity for artisans and homeseekers, a mecca for artists, archeologists and tourists.

69

Gerson Gusdorf
General Merchandise
Taos, New Mexico

Taos Junction
Monday, 18 [19] March 1923

Dear Seltzer

I just had your telegram about Huebsch as we left Taos. I haven't any Huebsch *Women-in-Love* correspondence. But very little passed. Pinker had the MS. two years. I thought of course he had tried everybody. Came your letter asking for the book—I sent you my MS. Then I had a letter & cable from Huebsch saying he *hadn't* seen the MS (who knows if he had?). I cabled you, *please release Women-in-Love.* You had sent me £50 sterling—& you replied you couldn't release. That was all. Ask Huebsch to show you my letters. He once said to Mountsier that I was a liar, & that he could prove it from letters. He went to look for said letters & couldn't find them.—I remember that against him, you may be sure. And I will write and remind him of it. Anyhow I acted in absolute good faith in the Women in Love matter. You have the correspondence.

Huebsch never answered my letters from Taos.

I do hope it will straighten out without ugliness. Go softly.

Yrs., D. H. Lawrence

70

Witter Bynner
P. O. Box 1061
Santa Fe, N. M.

Tuesday, [?20 March 1923]

Dear Adele Szold

This is the key to the little trunk with arctics & sheepskins. You can use anything any time you may want.

We leave today at 4.0 *without* the Bynners. They follow Friday.—I wrote Thomas from Taos Junction.

Adios, D. H. L.

71

Hotel Monte Carlo
Mexico City
30 March 1923

Dear Seltzer

The enclosed came today.[71] I don't know which parcel it refers to. If it is Frieda's dyed stuff, we got the parcels all right, but didn't pay any C.O.D. charges—only the excess charge for bringing the things from Jaroso [sic] station. There was no request for any payment C.O.D. I received two parcels from Jaroso, Express: the dyed stuffs,—and sweets & books (Young Girls Diary etc). Nothing else.

I hate to bother you about this. But would you just see to it. If you did send a C.O.D. parcel, please pay for it from my account.

D. H. Lawrence

Bynner has turned up: hating this city! I like it better than at first.

72

Hotel Monte Carlo
Avenue Uruguay 69
Mexico
4 April 1923

Dear Seltzer

Your letter about *Sons & Lovers:* also Stern's, just now. Witter Bynner is here. He says he has seen an advertisement of Mitchell Kennerley, announcing a new edition of *Sons & Lovers* (not the Boni & Liveright popular edition). Bynner says Kennerley probably has a stock of *Sons & Lovers* in hand, &

*Willard Johnson, Witter Bynner and
Lawrence at rear of Bynner's home in
Santa Fe before starting for Mexico in
March 1923.* (HRC)

will go on selling—& underselling—you. Do you know about this? If he transfers *plates* & *copyright*, what about his already printed stock?

Do I lose the $1100 dollars from Kennerley altogether?

It seems to me there is a mistake in this Release paper: that it should say *Mitchell Kennerley* where it says *David H. Lawrence*, there in the middle. However, I send the thing signed, to you, & you can do what is necessary. I think this address is quite safe.

Grüsse, D. H. Lawrence

P. S. To save time I have the form typed out, take both to the American Consul, & send you both.

D. H. L.

Consul says it's all right now.

D. H. L.

73

Hotel Monte Carlo
Aven. Uruguay 69
Mexico
8 April 1923

Dear Seltzer

Your letter about Kennerley's further swindle come.

I don't like kow-towing to Kennerley & letting him off everything. I would rather you took proceedings against him on my behalf. I *hate* letting him blankly swindle me. It would be better to bring a claim against him for breach of contract in not paying royalties, demand payments, & restitution of all rights to me. If the case cannot come on for a long time, bring an injunction to stop further sale of *Sons & Lovers*—stop Boni & Liveright as well as Kennerley.

It is time now to fight, not to be aimiable [sic] & yielding. But sorry you have all the trouble.—But *black their eyes*.

D. H. Lawrence

You will only succeed by *fighting:* and fighting again. That brings success.

D. H. L.

74

Hotel Monte Carlo
Av. Uruguay 69
Mexico City
Monday, 8 [9] April 1923

Dear Thomas

I wrote you yesterday, best fight Kennerley. Best fight all round. You'll see they'll all try now to put a spoke in your wheel. Think you're going too fast. So fight 'em. Run risks if one must. But don't conciliate any further.

As for me, when it comes near time to book tickets to England, I don't want to go. England makes me feel sick to think of: it would try to drag me down to the old thing. So I shall look for a house here in Mexico. I really like the country, feel I might like to live here. We shall go to Guadalajara & look round.—Meanwhile this address is good.

And you are caught in the toils of family & sickness and nurses & impending funerals. I am sorry for you. Don't let it drag you down too. *Let the dead bury their dead.* We've got to live forward.

I feel I would like to settle down & do a novel here.

We were in Cuernavaca—where Zapato held out so long. Dead, dead, beautiful cathedrals—dead Spain—dead!—but underneath, live peons.—Soldiers everywhere—riding on roof of trains to guard them—soldiers, soldiers—And ruins! Nearly all the big haciendas and big houses are ruins, shells. A great deal of waste country.

Yet I feel I should like a little hacienda—house, and a few acres of land for fruit—perhaps get Götzsche to come & help me work it. He is very helpful where there is work—& one would need to be a tiny bit reinforced in this country.

Met one or two liberals—but am weary of this liberation. It is almost as fatal as capital: perhaps worse. Criminal to want to educate these peons with our education.

Tell me one or two things:

1. Is "The Captain's Doll" out yet.

2. What about *Studies in C. A. Literature?*—

3. I presume you got the completed MS. of *Birds Beasts*, with the additional *American Eagle* poem. Also the two cover designs from Götzsche & Merrild. Hope you liked them & sent the money for them.

4. When will you be printing these things? Can I have proofs?

5. Are you sending me the *Contracts*—& statement for this half year's payment?—I had word from Charleroi Savings & Trust Co. that you deposited $500 to my credit there. That will do for the time being. But if I find a house of course I shall want money. I'd really like to settle down.

6. Curtis Brown wrote urging me to let his American Office handle my stuff. Would it be simpler if I did this?

Hope things are straightening up.—With Kennerley I think it would really be best to start an action & bring an injunction to stop the sale of Sons & Lovers at once. Put a spoke in <u>his</u> wheel.—

Saluti, D. H. Lawrence

75

FRIEDA LAWRENCE TO ADELE SELTZER

Hotel Monte Carlo
8. IV. 23

Dear Adele,

(Excuse pencil, it's all I have)

Your letter came, your sister's illness and cancer of all things, but it can be cured you know in many instances [72] *— Lawr's mother died of it, he has a horror of it—We begin to like Mexico—the peons are jolly and alive, we shall try and find a hacienda, a little land and a house with a patio and a fountain in it—We saw a big bullfight—A wild and low excited crowd 4 bands, then a nice young bull and the men with their mantles dodging it so quickly, the bull jumped the barrier and the attendants jumping so cleverly was fun—but*

87

then oh horrors, blindfolded horses led up to it by picadores who prick the bull with lances, the bull of course thinks it's the horse that hurts him, and with his horns he goes for the horse—I know no more, I fled and Lawr white with rage followed me—My last impression—a smell of flesh and blood and a heap of bowels on the ground—vile and degraded the whole thing—Very interesting an old pre-Aztec place with temples and pyramids and terrible carvings—Xexalcoatl the God of sacrifice human hearts his specialty—We have a nice little Italian hotel, friendly and pleasant—it is'nt dead here like Europe—but I must see my mother and children—We went to see a learned Mrs Nutall—she liked us but was frightened of us—belongs to the old sort, When I mentioned Steffens an old American judge (dont know his name) nearly jumped out of his skin—Judges dont seem our line in America! 73 I am afraid Thomas will have a worse time than ever, they will hate his success—I hope and trust he can stand them or withstand them—I would be glad if Kennerley got it, he is such a scoundrel! The impudence, selling something that is'nt his to sell and then wanting more! I am sorry for all the nasty fighting Thomas has to do! And no end to it—Let us know how your sister is—Glad you liked the tray—Bynner and Johnson with us, Bynner does'nt affect us much one way or another—the boy is nice but such a "jeune fille", rather stupid that—We enjoy a town after Del Monte—Dont reckon on our coming at any time—You know what Lawr is—but I hope we shall see you before long, dont overdo it, either of you—This illness will be a strain on you—All this Spanishness here is disappearing all ruin—and something native pushed through the old dead leaves—Countries who have no unconscious peasant life to draw strength from are doomed—

All good to you, F.

76

[*Postcard*]

Orizaba, [Mexico]
21 April [1923]

Dear Adele Szold

I do wonder how is your house of troubles. We go back to Mexico City tomorrow and I shall find mail.—I've had enough of Mexico—it's quite nice, but I've had enough. And I want to go back to England. No reason why—but I just want to. So I think we'll sail for New York in about a week's time. I'd like to see Thomas & you again before I leave this continent. We ought to be in New York by the 7th May, easily. I'll send a telegram—and if you are still in the bigger apartment—the Lord be with you—can we go in the little one, and not have a servant, except perhaps a char-woman twice a week? Frieda is crazy to wash dishes again. I should never be able to write on this continent—something in the spirit opposes one's going forth.—Do hope your troubles aren't thickening.

D. H. L.

Spud Johnson & me descending the pyramid.

77

[*Postcard*]

Hotel Monte Carlo
Mexico D. F.
27 April [1923]

Dear Thomas

I am going this evening to Lake Chapala in Guadalajara, to see if we might like to live there a while. If that is no good, we shall come to New York—shan't bother any more with here. Isn't this a nice photograph—in the cloisters of Cuernavaca cathedral. Nothing further from you

D. H. L.

89

Verso of postcard (see letter 76).
Willard Johnson and Lawrence
descending the Pyramid at Teotihuacan
near Mexico City in April 1923. (HRC)

Lawrence in the cloisters of the
Cuernavaca cathedral in 1923. (Yale)

78

Zaragoza No. 4
Chapala (Jalisco)
Mexico
2 May 1923

Dear Thomas

Here we are in a little house of our own on Lake Chapala, a big lake not far from Guadalajara (2 hours). Frieda joined me from Mexico this morning, & we moved in. It is hot and sunny and nice: lots of room.

F. brought your letter. I suppose all the papers will come on, contracts etc. So far nothing. I <u>do</u> hope you haven't posted me presentation copies here: I do hope you got my list, & sent them out from New York.

About the book-jackets for *Mastro-don* and for *Birds Beasts*, they were enclosed in the final corrected MS. of *Birds Beasts* sent just before I left Taos—by registered mail. Surely you got that packet. If you look it up you will find the things. I'm afraid that, what with Judge Ford and the rest you have hardly time to keep track of everything.

You will see the Judge Ford business won't hurt in the long run, but meanwhile what a curse. I can tell you are almost snowed under.

Murry cabled that he is starting a new monthly & wanted to use a chapter from Fantasia, wanted also a story: haven't got latter.

I shall begin a novel now, as soon as I can take breath.

I won't let Curtis Brown handle my American side. But don't you get too overwhelmed with work. It is what I am afraid of.

Don't I change from day to day about staying here? However, I am fixed now for a time at least. I believe you'd like it immensely. Splendid to have you both come.

Be sure & look up that corrected MS. of *Birds Beasts* & those two book-jackets, and let me know.

Hope you got my letter enclosing the one to Huebsch, with cheque to Huebsch, paying him back. Mind you send this.

I wonder if any of the letters get lost.

How is Adele Szold?

Saluti, D. H. L.

Frieda and Lawrence at the window of
their house at Zaragoza No. 4,
Chapala, Jalisco, in 1923. Photo:
Witter Bynner. (HRC)

79

Zaragoza #4
Chapala
Jal.
Mexico
9 May 1923

Dear Thomas

I just sent you the first lot of *Studies* proofs: as far as end of
Poe. I do hope you get them in time. I'd like the revisions
made. There are one or two serious alterations in the first
essay, that are important to me.

I repeat again, I <u>do</u> wish you would print *Kangaroo* and
Birds Beasts & *Mastro-don* <u>early</u>, <u>soon</u>, so that I can have
proofs in plenty of time. And I would like *two sets* of proofs,
please. I'll write Miss Leener too, and tell her this.

You are doing *Mastro-don* for September, aren't you? I am
settling this with Curtis Brown. Tell me for sure.

I send the massive list of corrections of errors from Mr
Feipel, who is evidently in the Brooklyn Library. Pity he can't
have revised proofs, if he's such a bird. His charts leave me
quite cold.[74]

Nothing has come from you except that first batch of
Studies proofs: and the *transfers* of copyright.

It is hot here in Chapala. I like it. I have made two false
starts at a novel here. Shall make a third start tomorrow.

Mexico is queer: very savage underneath. It still is unsafe to
live in the country: & not very safe anywhere. Somebody
tried to get in here last night. It seems to me Mexico will never
be safe. I have my ups & downs of feeling about the place. It
will end, I suppose, in my staying as long as it takes me to
write a novel—if I *can* write a novel here—then coming to
New York for a time, then going to England. But I never know
what I shall finally do.

Did you hear Mabel Sterne has married Tony & is going to
take a ranch to live a "freer life," and invite *paying* guests.
You might see what she charges. She is now Mrs Antonio
Lujan.—It gives me a sort of end-of-the-world feeling. Mexico
does that too. It feels like the end of the world. *Ruat caelum!*

I keep wondering how your domestic affairs are: how is
Adele Szold's sister, how is New York altogether?—Also

how are they taking Captain's Doll? They won't care for it, if England likes it.

Poor Gilbert has a dreadful face, in your Announcements List.

We went to Guadalajara yesterday. It's a burnt dry town. I didn't care for it much. Pearl of the west! Mostly old shell! Mexico altogether is terribly heavy, as if it had hardly the energy to get up and live. Though it's not really a case of energy. The soul of the country sulks, and won't look up. Sulks emptily through the ages.

I can read Spanish fairly well now.

Fight on! D. H. L.

80

Zaragoza #4
Chapala
Jalisco
22 May [1923]

Dear Adele Szold

Your letter about Thomas & his nose—bad luck. The enemy almost gets us down, sometimes. Am having a hard fight myself. The enemy of all the world. Doesn't want me to write my novel either. Pazienza! Curse Kennerley, curse Huebsch, curse Boni & curse Liveright. May their bones rot inside their bodies. Curse the enormous enemy. May it burst swollen.

A hacienda!—You don't know Mexico. We have to have a young man with a pistol sleep on the terrace outside the door. I am not allowed to walk alone outside the narrow precincts of the village: for fear of being stopped, robbed, & what not. It gets awfully boring. It's really just petty crime. But the government has no control outside the towns & villages. The country is a sort of no-man's-land as far as security goes. If I thought of a little hacienda I'd have to buy a revolver for the first furnishing—& get the Danes to come down & arm them too as a military guard.—It's safe enough inside the town or here in Chapala—unless you're supposed to have money in the house.—All rather boring. I like the lake—and though the day from 12 to 4.0 is pretty hot, the rest is quite pleasant. And it won't get any hotter. The rains are coming.—All the Mexicans with property seem to want the United States to take over the country—Mexico enter the U.S. federation.—But I hate the *cramped* feeling of not being allowed to go freely in the country, having to watch every man to see if he's a rascal. The people here are quite nice. And at first everything *seems* so normal. Then one begins gradually to realise the uncertainty, & the limitations.

We've never had definite news of Sons & Lovers. I don't get *any* parcels—though some are in Mexico—nor do I get the balance of the *Studies* proofs. Don't trust the post.—Tell us if Thomas is better, & how Kennerley settled at last.

D. H. L.

81

Zaragoza #4
Chapala
Jal.
Sat., [? 26 May 1923]

Dear Seltzer

This is to ask you if you have yet got any proofs of *Kangaroo*—also of *Birds Beasts* & of *Mastro-don Gesualdo*— and to beg you please to send me *duplicate* galleys of all, by *Printed Matter* post—not by parcel.

Hope you're well.

D. H. L.

82

[*Postcard*]

Zaragoza # 4
Chapala
Jal.
8 June [1923]

Dear Thomas—

This is to tell you that we are definitely leaving here at the end of this month: so don't post any mail here after the 19th. We ought to be in New York by July 15th. I'd like to stay there long enough to do all those *proofs,* and perhaps go through my novel: but we'd have to be in the country for that. We'll see.—Haven't heard from you for some time. Hot here. Novel more than half done.

D. H. L.

83

FRIEDA LAWRENCE TO ADELE SELTZER

Chapala
10. VI. 23

Dear Adele,

Thank you very much for your offer of tinned things! No, we get good food, all this tropical fruit and we have bought chickens that lay eggs and then we eat the chickens—It's been so hot for a day or two but then the terrific rain came—and it's still attractive—We do things with Bynner & Spud like going across the lake or into Guadalajara! Lawr—is at page 350 of a most surprising novel—Lawr—says it will take Thomas all his time to publish it—I think it is the most splendid thing he ever did—I look forward to seeing you in less *than three weeks—As New York is so hot we will only stay 2 or 3 days; if you had thought of having us in your house* dont *do it; it will mean so much bother for so short a time, put us in a hotel near—We will go into the country—*

is'nt there a nice little old new England inn any where? And you would have to come—Bynner says New Hampshire is pretty, is that too far [for] you? I wish you could have see this, there is something uncowed *in these natives that fascinates us all—It's given us a lot, the country so hard and wild and unsentimental! How is Thomas, is he really quite well? Are you suffering from the heat already? How is your sister, not well I fear—Europe lies in front of me like an unknown country, because we are changed—Dont work too hard in the heat, because it pulls the strength out of you—Have'nt we triumphed over our enemies, Revenge is the joy of the gods—We shall have a lot to tell you when we come—*

So auf Wiedersehen, Frieda

I like my new novel best of all—much. But it['s] perhaps too different for most folks: two-thirds done. Pray the gods for the rest.

D. H. L.

Long while since I heard from Thomas. I'll bring him a serape. Do you want anything? Say quick.

D. H. L.

We leave this house about 26th—see that no mail comes after 17th or 18th.

We might have a tiny cottage somewhere for a month—not far from New York.

I think I might like to stay long enough to go all through the novel & all the rest of proofs.

D. H. L.

84

Chapala, Jal.
15 June 1923

Dear Thomas

Your letter & statement today.—I should still be poor *sans* Women in Love, shouldn't I?

All right, I'll go over the Whitman essay again. Wait for it.

The Esmeralda becalmed on Lake Chapala, July 1923. Dr. Purnell, Witter Bynner, Willard Johnson, Idella Purnell Stone, Frieda and Lawrence. (HRC)

Lawrence at the mast of the Esmeralda during the trip up the lake. Photo: Witter Bynner. (HRC)

The novel has gone well. Shall I call it *Quetzalcoatl?* Or will people be afraid to ask for a book with that name.—I've done 415 MS. pages—expect about another 100. It interests me, means more to me than any other novel of mine. This is my real novel of America. But you may just hold up your hands with horror. No sex.[75]

Now it comes near time to leave here, I don't much want to go. I give up this house on the 30th—if novel isn't finished, shall stay in Hotel Arzapalo long enough to get it done. Bynner & Spud still there. By the way, if ever you want a man clerk, do you think you might have Spud Johnson? He's very reliable & does good work. I think he ought to have a proper job, not be just Bynner's amanuensis.

Murry's *Adelphi* came. How feeble it is! Oh God, am I going back to Europe to that?[76]

I don't really want to go back to Europe. But Frieda wants to see her mother. Perhaps I shall have to go, this once. But feel sure I shan't stay.—Perhaps round the world again, & try to do a novel in India or China: the East. Then to America, & perhaps back to Mexico. So far, I think I like Mexico best of all the places, to live in. As Adele Sz. said, the life of the blood. I'm sad to go. But I suppose it's best, for the moment.

Don't give anybody that bit of the bull-fight unless you think well. I don't feel like supporting the knock-kneed *Adelphi.* Katherine Mansfield's ugly bits etc.

So sorry you've been seedy. But you'll be better now.

Rainy season here—cool again.

Ships sail from Vera Cruz every Sunday. We *might* sail on July 8th—arrive N.Y. 15th or 16th

Have you really sent the books to the printer?

D. H. L.

Fantasia will sell later—like *Women in Love.* Pazienza!

85

29 June [1923]

Dear Thomas

Now comes word we must be vaccinated—which may possibly delay us a week. I'll let you know at once.

*Idella Purnell Stone, Lawrence,
Frieda, Willard Johnson and Dr.
Purnell, taken on Johnson's 26th
birthday, in Chapala. Photo: Witter
Bynner.* (HRC)

*Witter Bynner and Willard Johnson in
Chapala, 1923.* (HRC)

I've sent some books by post—trunks so full.

Saluti, D. H. L.

86

Chapala
30 June [1923]

Dear Thomas

They have altered the sailings of the Ward Line ships from Sunday to Thursday—so expect to sail Thursday 12th July and arrive Thursday 19th.

D. H. L.

passport photographs

87

FRANCIS LOUIS TO D. H. LAWRENCE

County Hospital,
Durham
England
June 1st 1923

It seems rather incongruous introducing the jargon of pseudo-scientific technique into your otherwise striking piece of imaginative writing in the "Adelphi": but will you consider it an impertinence if I venture to congratulate you on your truly wonderful physiological & psychological systems? What a powerful light you shed upon the aetiology of phthisis and "neurasthenia of the heart"!

Yours etc., Francis Louis

[? July 1923]

This is about the Chapter from Fantasia in the Adelphi— which that brat Murry never acknowledged as from Fantasia. This man might be useful—I suppose he is a doctor. I wrote a note to him & asked him to reply care of you. Would you mind sending him a copy of Psychoanalysis & of Fantasia?

D. H. L.

88

Hotel Arzapalo
Chapala
Jal.
9 July 1923

Dear Thomas

We leave Chapala today—it is doubtful if we can get out of Vera Cruz—very Bolshevist there, and strike imminent if not already on—won't let ships leave—so we think to leave by rail, via *Laredo*, probably stop of [sic] a day or two in New Orleans—arrive in New York somewhere about the 20th. I'll let you know.

D. H. L.

89

219 West 100th Street
New York

Tuesday night, [?21 August 1923]

Dear Adele

Well then, goodbye for the moment. [77] We'll meet again before very long: & some time we'll make a bit of a life in unison. I'm not going to allow this world to have its own way entirely with us all.—"So he said: Fight on! Fight on!" Since we know we *can* make a life together, we won't break the thread of it. We'll keep an invisible thread holding us together. "See if I am not Lord of the dark & moving hosts
  Before I die."
There's the world—and there's me & the ones who are with me. And we'll possess ourselves of the future, see if we don't.

"Peace I leave you; my peace I give unto you—"
Greet Schnitz also Fritz

D. H. L.

90

Palace Hotel
San Francisco
Wed. morning
[?22 August 1923, ?New York]

Dear Adele

Raining. Am just leaving.

Enclosed the ticket for that dyed dress. You won't mind paying for it with Amy's cheque? [78] And if F. writes she wants the dress, we can send it. Otherwise let it lie here—or let the Brewis' take it to England in October. They leave about mid October—the landlord said he would renew their lease for 3 years at same terms as present $1,450 a year. It's quite a nice flat in a modern building, with a sitting-room overlooking the river: gives a sense of space, which is good.

> Mrs Joseph Brewis
> 640 Riverside Drive
> end of 141st St.

If you think you might like it ring up Brewis at the Butterick building. But I don't suppose you want to change.

> au revoir
> je m'en vais
> me ne vo
> salgo.
> jetzt geh'ich
> Adios!

D. H. L.

Thomas Seltzer. (Alexandra Levin)

91

10 Saybrook St.
Buffalo
Saturday [?25 August 1923]

Dear Thomas

I am still here. Thank you for sending on cablegram & letter—you did right to open cablegram.

The queerest thing in the world, being in Buffalo & going round their "blue blood." It's almost like Cranford: more old-fashioned than anything still surviving in Europe: and really a genuine nice feeling among them—and a pathos. A mixture of Virgins of the Rocks & Cranford and The Wide Wide World.

I've not been to Niagara yet—am due to go today. Lunching out there with Mabel Sterne's mother. You would hardly know me, I am so well-behaved. A perfect chameleon. But the same old sphinx of a me looking at the different grimaces of the sphinx of life. I think I learn more about the old *genuine* America here, than anywhere.

Well, now we know one another, so we can go on with our mutual burden separately. I am glad to have stayed that month with you & Adele. I find a real reassurance in it.

Damnation to have missed two trains.

It has been cold as hell here—bit warmer. This dree, dree lake! The town is like Manchester sixty years ago—or Nottingham—very easy and sort of nice middle-class, BOURgeois.

Vamos! Vamonos! D. H. L.

92

R. M. S. P. "ORBITA"

Sunday, [*?26 August 1923*]

Dear Adele,

Here I write proudly with my new fountainpen—Has Schnitz grown into a young lady—yet? I am having a good trip—fresh and sunny and I have'nt done much except knit your shawl and on Tuesday I get to London—I feel so cross with Lawrence, when I hear him *talk about loyalty—Pah, he only thinks of himself—I am glad to be alone and I will* not *go back to him and his eternal hounding me, it's too ignominious! I will* not *stand his bad temper any more if I never see him again—I wrote him so—He can go to blazes, I have had enough—The worm that turns—I think I shall like England, but am not sure—I like their gentle ways on the boat—have a waiter like the Prince of Wales and a jolly scotch stewardess —made friends with a violinist, woman, and a spinster who of course wants to write—I think England is different since the war—I post this directly on my arrival and also the shawl, it's been much admired—Thank you and Thomas awfully for the jolly time you gave us—Hope you are not working too hard—Do send me all the news, did Lawr go to Los Angeles?* [79] *My love to you both.*

Frieda

93

46 Lancaster Avenue
Buffalo, N. Y.
27 Aug. 1923

Dear Seltzer

I wish you would send to Miss Mary Wilkeson, at the above address, a copy of *The Lost Girl* and of *The Captain's Doll* and to Mrs Effingham Burnett

Columbia Avenue
Wanakah
Erie County. Hamburg N. Y.
a copy of *Aaron's Rod.* To the same address, to Mrs John
Knox Freeman, a copy of *Women in Love.*
I am leaving tonight for Chicago.—Pax tecum.

D. H. L.

94

care Knud Merrild
628 W. 27th St.
Los Angeles
Friday, 30th [August 1923]

Dear Thomas

I got here safely last night. Thank you for sending on F's
cablegram. I do so wonder how she likes it.—The Danes met
me at the station with that ancient Lizzie of Del Monte fame.
They are working on a room at Santa Monica—20 miles out.
Perhaps I shall go & stay in the hotel there for a week. But this
address is good.—I want do to the article for Canby, & if I
can, put together Miss Skinner's Australian novel—which is
good, if only threaded.—The letters sent on, one I enclose—the
other from Prince Bibesco wanting to see him. Don't care for
him much, but like her.—Merrild rather down in the mouth
because he hasn't much success: Götzsche working at a job &
not complaining.—I think of Birkindele, & wonder how you
are getting on.[80] Tell Adele I don't forget her.—Now I am
here I feel like going back to Mexico—it seems realer to me
than the U.S.—Let me know when the MS of Quetzalcoatl is
typed, & let me have a copy if you can before I start moving
again. And tell me how you are & what is happening. I feel I
have to keep an eye on everything, like the eye of God, for
fear the devil pounces in.

Salud. D. H. L.

95

FRIEDA LAWRENCE TO THOMAS AND ADELE SELTZER

5 Accacia [sic] *Rd.*
St. John's Wood
London N. W. 8
Sunday, [September 1923]

Dear friends,

Here I am, that is to say not at the above address but at Cath. Carswell's. England is so gentle and quiet—I saw Murry yesterday, we did talk and he said how he realised that Lawrence was a greater man than he was and how bitter it was for him to come to that conclusion, and how he has hated L— but now he had for ever accepted him, no matter what Lawr did—After all it almost takes greatness to see that another man is greater than you—Saw Secker also, he is a steady kind of a man, quite genuine I should say, I rather liked him, though he has'nt Thomas's spark—Captain's Doll sold nearly 6000—I have a banking account of my own and feel an important female—Everybody is very nice but I miss the something that I found in both of you—Except Murry—Nobody has suffered or fought over here—Lawr always said it—Adele, I have not quite finished your shawl yet—the minute it is, I send it—I will get rooms in Hampstead for a month, I cannot face another journey this minute, and I cant go to Lawr' sister for a fortnight, she has a little son—I do wonder what L. is doing—Whether he will come, but oh the climate, I shiver in my very soul—It would never do for a winter—Had 2 nice letters from L. saying how he hated parting with you both—How you, Adele, would love this place! So perfect— How is Birkindale? I wait for news from you—Dear Adele, would it be a great nuisance for you to send me a corduroy coat, that's in the household trunk—I shall need it, have nothing warm enough and it will do—The dyed dress you need'nt send it's too cold—

[manuscript ends here]

96

FRIEDA LAWRENCE TO ADELE SELTZER

5 Acacia Rd
St John's Wood
Hampstead N W
[September 1923]

Dear Adele,

You dont know how in spirit you sit with me on Parliament Hill and look across London with the Dome of St Paul's and Westminster Abbey and the houses of parliament showing.— How you would love it! It is a great relief to find no air-guns and no war any more—Lawr does not know how all khaki is gone and the ugly spirit—I am discovering London for myself! There is a great relief everywhere! England is a great country still! Only I still dont like the women! Narrow gutted is Lawr' word! David Garnett showed me his wife, she is like his mother, all sufragettes [sic] at heart! No wonder Englishmen marry Americans! Could'nt you and Thomas both come—I could take a biggish flat where you could stay when I come back from Germany! Lawrence writes: dont come to U.S.A. And I wont—So Thomas need not hurry! I go to Germany on the 28, Murry goes to Switzerland, we travel together via Paris, he will show me Fontainebleau where Katherine stayed—I see a lot of Cath. Carswell, she is so nice, but has a nasty child and a failure of a husband! To-day I see my children—to-morrow spend a night at Secker's place in the country—next week I go to L's sisters—Good-bye for to-day— Much love to you both.

Frieda

97

Los Angeles
Sat., 22 Sept. [1923]

Dear Thomas

Götzsche and I leave on Monday for Mexico: for Guaymas

& Navajoa first. We are going down the West Coast, not as before. The railway only runs as far as Tepic.

F. doesn't seem to like England much. Here in California people live so much from the outside, it's almost fascinating. But a great bore. Drunk with trivial externalities: that is California.

I am getting a letter of credit from the Bank of California, so be <u>sure</u> & have money for me in the New York bank. Don't ever let me overdraw there, on your honour.

I wish I had more *respect* for the world & its people. One turns to the Lord Almighty and shuts one's eyes, people are such shells of emptiness.

I shall be glad to have news from you: how is your prosecution case? [81] I have been thinking of that. How is *Studies* doing, & *Kangaroo*, & when are *Birds Beasts* and *Mastro-don* ready? Send me all news as soon as you can.—Say if you are buying or leasing Birkendale [sic], if the well is still dry, if the lunatics got hydrophobia in the draught, if Schnitz is large, if still coy with Fritz. Adele's letter about the Crambseys was so lugubrious! And the Hammerslaugh, how did he wind up? Like a twisted rat?

I wish very much I were at Birkindele with you and that dish-washing demon of an Adele this week-end, to see the sun go down and the moon over the Lassieless pasture, and say a few wise things and hear a few, after all this *senselessness* out here.

And yet there seems a *wee* bit of gruesomeness among those New Jersey hills.—I wonder what Adele is doing with her Robot. [82]

Sei mir gegrüsst, D. H. L.

98

[*Postcard*]

[Los Angeles]
Monday, 24. Sept. [1923]

Dear Adele—

I am setting off tomorrow with Götzsche down the west

coast, by train, to Mexico again. I am glad to go. America drys up the natural springs of one's soul. But I've had quite a nice time here—people are very nice to me.—It's a very selfish place, Southern California, in a rather simple way. People care about *nothing* but just the moment. But also that can be pleasant.—I wonder very much if you have bought Birkindele, & if the well is dry. I knew it was getting low when I left. You must simply have had to *starve* the dishes, at washing-up time.—Götzsche is just posting the portrait of me. I like it.—And I posted Kath. Mansfield's last book. I think it's a downright cheek to ask the public to buy that waste-paper basket. 83 Also I posted in the parcel the first part of the *Boy in the Bush*, the Western Australia novel. 84 I think it's very amusing. Ask Thomas to have it typed out when there's time.—I can understand better & better how *bored* you are by New York—even by a publishing business & books—even mine. I feel like that. Oh to get away from the world! Only to get away and be by oneself with the things that live.—I shall write at once from Mexico. I seem to hear little from anybody. Write in readiness.

D. H. L.

99

Los Angeles
25 Sept. [1923]

Dear Thomas

These are the two keys of the two trunks in your cellar. If Frieda comes she will want them: especially at a frontier. Perhaps best tie them on to one of the trunks.

Sorry to bother you.

D. H. L.

111

Tepic is 3000 ft up. — Poor Götzsche sweats like
Niobe. I am visibly thinner.
There is no railway on from Tepic, so we
shall have to go by stage & a day on mules,
across the barranca, if we are to get to
Guadalajara.

There is a certain fascination also
about this place. It is very like the
South Sea Isles in quality: as remote &
soft and sensuous also, with an awful
naked sea-front with rocks with flying
staircases & half-built houses & delapidation.
— No money here. — And cocoa-nut palms
like snakes on end. But good cocoa to drink.
And a green bay with tropical huts &
natives very like islanders, soft, dark, some
almost black, & handsome. That Pacific
blue-black in the eyes & hair, fathomless
timeless. They don't know the meaning of time:
And they can't care. All the walls and
nooks of our time-enclosure are down for them.
Their eternity is so vast, they can't care at all.
Their blue-black eyes.
     I have learnt something from them:
the vastness of Pacific time, unhistoried, undivided.
Archronities running on the floor full speed.
I think Frieda would like her countryman
Götzsche here. Adios D.H.L.

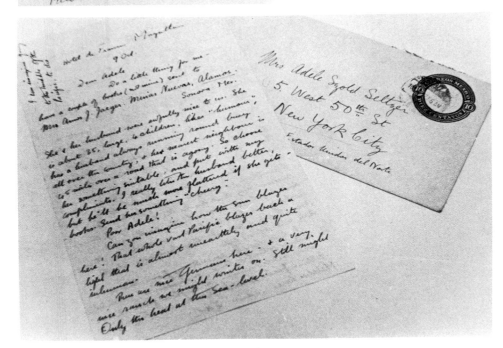

Letter of 9 October 1923. (William Pieper)

100

Hotel de France
Mazatlan, [Mexico]
9 Oct. [1923]

Dear Adele

Do a little thing for me—have a couple of books (not mine) sent to Mrs Amos J. Jaeger, Minas Nuevas, *Alamos*, Sonora, Mex. She & her husband were awfully nice to us. She is about 35, large, 4 children, likes "humour," has a husband always running round busy all over the country, & her nearest neighbor is 45 miles over a road that is agony. So choose her something suitable: and put with my compliments. I really like the husband better, but he'll be much more flattered if she gets books. Send her something "cheery."

Poor Adele!

Can you imagine how the sun blazes here! That whole vast Pacific blazes back a light that is almost unearthly and quite inhuman.

There are nice Germans here—& a very nice ranch we might winter on. Still might. Only the heat at the sea-level.

Tepic is 3000 feet up.—Poor Götzsche sweats like Niobe—I am visibly thinner.

There is no railway on from Tepic, so we shall have to go by stage & a day on mules, across the barranca, if we are to get to Guadalajara.

There is a certain fascination also about the place. It's very like the South Sea Isles in quality: as remote & soft and sensuous also, with an awful naked sea-front with rocks with flying staircases & half-built houses & delapidation.—No money here.—And Cocoa-nut palms like snakes on end. But good cocos to drink. And a queer bay with tropical huts & natives very like islanders, soft, dark, some almost black, & handsome. That Pacific blue-black in the eyes & hair, fathomless, timeless. They don't know the meaning of time. And they *can't* care. All the walls and nooks of our time-enclosure are down for them. Their eternity is so vast, they can't care at all. Their blue-black eyes.

I have learnt something from them. The vastness of Pacific time, unhistoried, undivided.

Cockroaches running on the floor full speed.

I think Frieda would like her countryman Melcher here.

Adios, D. H. L.

I can imagine going to the middle of the Pacific, to die.

101

Hotel Garcia
Guadalajara
Jal.
18 Oct. 1923

Dear Thomas.

We got here yesterday—very lovely the towers of Guadalajara under the October sky. It was quite a trip from Tepic. We rode mule back from Ixtlan over the mountains & down the barranca to La Quemada: a beautiful ride over a very rocky road. Nine hours in the saddle. Got to La Quemada, the other end of the S. Pacific Ry, to find no train, a land-slide, the line slipped away. La Quemada a sort of railway-camp, for the new construction. A lot of ill-bred hounds who think they are engineers: louts & canaille. The S. Pacific is American, and a hateful concern. I was glad to get off it. It trails a sort of blight all down the west coast. Really, Americanism is a disease or a vice or both.—We slept in a shed & rose at dawn, got more mules, and rode for six hours across to Etzatlan, the town on the Mex. National Railway. This upland country in Mexico has a certain splendid beauty. I like it very much. And I like so much the real Mexico again, where the Americans haven't canned all the life. At the depths of me, Thomas Tomasito, I hate the Americans. There is still some strange raw splendour in Mexico. And it is green and full of flowers now, yellow and pink.

I found various mail from you forwarded from Los Angeles. Macy is a dead fish, bientôt il sera pourri. [85] Pour les autres, ils sont des poissons demi-morts. It's no good, that world has got to perish. But we have got to put something through before it perishes. And we are doing it. It's a fight all the way. Tant Mieux. Miserable Midianites, one has to bite slowly through their heart-strings.

You say you put $500 to my account in the Metropolitan

bank: I suppose you mean the National Chase. I must settle with Mountsier.

I have letters from Frieda, saying England is best after all, & wanting me to come back. But now I am here I would rather stay the winter, anyhow. I must finish Quetzalcoatl. By the way, I want you to read that MS. and tell me just what you think. Because I must go all over it again, and am open to suggestion. This winter I must finish it. (Dear Adele, in parenthesis, I should like your opinion of Quetzalcoatl, if the sight of a MS. is not too nauseating to you). I expect you got the MS. also of The Boy in the Bush. I want you to tell me about that. I think it would be best to publish it *before* Quetzalcoatl, & we must decide whether it is to be under my name & Miss Skinner's, or a nom de plume, or what. I think I shall go ahead with that, the Boy, to finish it before I try Quetzalcoatl again, because this is much more important to me, my Quetzalcoatl. The Boy might be popular—unless the ending is a bit startling—I sometimes feel that, when these two books are off my hands, I shall give up writing for a time—perhaps a few years. I get so tired of the continual feeling of canaillerie one gets from the public & from people. Toujours canaille.—As Adele says, let people cease to exist for one. They easily can—especially here. Meanwhile, adelante! Quasi consummatum est, Domine!

Adios   D. H. L.

102

Guadalajara
Jal.
Mexico
[?20-21 October 1923]

Dear Thomas

Your letter with Macy's review of Studies & with the review of Mastro-don came last night. These people have *no* guts.—I wrote Macy a little letter. Wish you saw it. It tickled me.

I send you the Cooper letter. These people are nothing but sieves for gnats. I shan't answer Cooper.[86]

I'll see if I can write a few little sketches for Vanity Fair. Don't worry about the price.—Do you know, I'd much rather be printed in Vanity Fair than in these old high-brow weak-gutted Nations.

I am dying to see Mastro-don & the Poems. But at the moment I don't mind if America doesn't like me, because I feel a great disgust for America.—Send me just *one* copy of each by book post, care Dr. Purnell. [87] But don't send MS. yet.

Mabel Sterne (Mabel Lujan—or Luhan) wrote that when she had heard how I reviled her she was very angry: till at last it dawned on her that I was right, that her way of <u>will</u> was wrong. So she had given it up. But it left her feeling rather out of work.

Now I call that sporting. So of course I have also buried the hatchet. And am watching for the leopard to change her spots.

F. seems to want me to go back. I might be driven to make a visit, if I could fix myself up a bit of a place here before I left.—I like being in Mexico. It gives one a certain strength and a power of mockery of all the macyerie.—But I wouldn't mind going with you to England, for a visit—if I could fix up here. I'd like to travel with you over.

I wish you would send a copy of *Sea and Sardinia* to

> Señor
> Don Walther Melcher
> Casa Melcher
> *Mazatlan*, Sinaloa, Mexico.

Also a copy of *Kangaroo* & a copy of *The Captain's Doll* to

> Señor
> Don Federico Unger
> Casa Melcher—same address.

They are both Germans, & very nice to me in Mazatlan.

Adele won't really be sorry to be in New York, when winter comes: and that will be best for you both. By this time next year, she ought to be able to afford herself a house with Schnitzes & even Robots if she wants 'em: and Lassies that don't cough and are not aged in years, and rooms uncontaminated by Hammerslachts. Tout vient.

Did you get the Götzsche portrait of me? And did you like it?

116

Have you got the *Boy in the Bush* MS., with the book for Adele? Let me know.—I mean the first half sent from Los Angeles.

I feel I want to go into the country soon.

D. H. L.

Monday 22nd Oct

Dear Thomas—

I have had no mail except the one letter from you and the one forwarded from Curtis Brown—& the Adelphi.—Nothing from Frieda, so don't know where she is. I went to Chapala for the day yesterday—the lake <u>so</u> beautiful. And yet the lake I knew was gone—something gone, & it was alien to me. I think I shall go to Europe soon—don't be surprised if you get a telegram saying I am leaving. I might go direct—or might come to New York. I'll let you know. Anyhow see you in England. If I don't come to New York you could bring the trunks. Would you?

Tell F. if you have her address.

D. H. L.

103

Hotel Garcia
Guadalajara
Jal.
28 Oct. 1923

Dear Adele

I got your symposium of Fritz Schnitz Thomas & Lawrence: and neither you nor Aline able to tell t'other from which. Perhaps by now you have extricated me from the whirl of fluff etc in which Schnitz coruscated, and you can be a sensible woman once more. Anyhow I'm going to treat you as such.

Are you <u>really</u> cross about leaving Birkindele? Don't be. There was a bit of a shadow over it somewhere, and that shadow would have sunk in. I believe you have had the best out of Birkindele. Leave it now, to its owner & Coffin & the Robot, and its own *rather* evil daimon. Labour & wait. You'll

117

have a better place in the country than Birkindele, before long. Something more cheerful.

I am still here. Frieda writes she will not come back. "The lady loves her will." Muy bien, qué la tenga. Let her have it. —I suppose I shall go back to England. They all press me so hard. But I shan't hurry. There is something good about Mexico, something that opens again, at least in part, the floodgates of one's soul. The USA & the world shut the floodgates of my soul tight. And here they begin to open, and the life flows, even if it flows in oneself alone. —But there is a sort of *basic* childishness about these people, that for me is the only manliness. When I say childishness, I only mean they don't superimpose ideas & ideals, but follow the stream of the blood. A certain innocence, even if sometimes evil. And a certain childlike patience & stoicism. —I like it really, our tough, dry, papier-mâché world recedes. —It's queer that F. hates it. —Sometimes I am driven to hating the white-white world, with its whiteness like a leprosy.

I suppose I shall go back some time in December, to see Murry & work on the Adelphi a bit. I think the Adelphi improves. I think I may put some of myself into it, for 1924, and see if anything results. F. declares England is still best. Murry declares England will again lead the world. But I myself know that England alone cannot. She must be juxtaposed with something that is in the dark volcanic blood of these people. One thing alone won't work: nor one spirit alone. It needs a polarity of two.

Send me a line care Dr G. Purnell, Galeana 150. Guadalajara.

Tell me: 1. Did you get Götzsche's painting of me—did you like it? (He loves this place, wants to paint it all)
2. Did you read Quetzalcoatl? Tell me what you think.

hasta otra vez, D. H. L.

118

104

care Dr. G. Purnell
Galeana #150
Guadalajara, Jal.
28 Oct. [1923]

Dear Thomas

This is just a note. I think I shall stay on till mid-December here. Send me mail, & a copy of Birds Beasts & Mastro-don each to above. Tell me:

1. Did you get Götzsche's portrait of me—did you like it?
2. Is *Quetzalcoatl* typed? What you think of it. (But don't send it till I ask for it)
3. Have you got *The Boy in the Bush* MS. If the office is busy, have it typed by a hired typist. I will pay for it. Very soon I'll send you another booklet of it. It's really good, and I want it out in the spring before Quetzalcoatl: & I want Miss Skinner to see it before it comes out & to decide how—under what name or names, it shall appear.
4. If you go to England, will you take the two trunks from your basement? I sent you the keys. I suppose you have them. Take the trunks for Frieda. I will pay all costs. Forgive this bother.
5. I think I shall sail direct from Vera Cruz. I feel still a certain disgust for the USA & New York.
6. I *don't* think I shall get to England till about January 1st—don't want to spend Christmas with my people. But if I change I'll let you know at once.

Write to me now, & tell me everything.

D. H. L.

Don't be impatient with me for bothering you.—You might have somebody worse.

I paid Mountsier his $404.—Acabado!

105

Hotel Garcia
Guadalajara, Jal.
3 November 1923

Dear Thomas

I got the telegram yesterday: *Cable from Frieda Lawrence cone* was what it said. I suppose F. cabled for me to come to England. *A la bonne heure!*—But I intend to leave next week for Mexico City, and look for a ship. If I can I shall find a cargo boat or cheaper boat because Götzsche wants to go home to Denmark. It's the best for him too.—He is painting quite busily here.

Today I have got *Mastro-don* and *Birds-Beasts*. Both look very nice indeed, especially *Birds-Beasts*. Isn't my jacket nice too! I am pleased with that book. The *canaille* of a public isn't worthy of it.

Yesterday I sent Adele a vase from the native Tlaquepaque factory just near here. It is common earthenware, only cost three or four pesos, but very interesting I think: perhaps more suited to an office than a home. I could only send it by express in a basket: I paid the express as far as *Ciudad Juarez*—that is El Paso border—couldn't pay any more. I hope it'll come, & come unbroken, so you can see what it's like. It was to be shipped across the border by Angeles y Velarde. Agentes Aduanales, *Ciudad Juarez* (Chihuahua).

I am busy with the Australian novel. I told you I would like it to come in spring, if possible before Quetzalcoatl. I wish, if you are coming to England, you would bring the MS with you. I think I'll take all this remainder & have it typed in London.

And do please take the trunks across the water if you go.

I hope very much to be in London when you come. Meet on my native soil.

Mexico is sunny & lovely. These are the fiesta days of Todos Santos & Todos Muertos. They make All Souls day a great feast: & sell toys of skeleton men on skeleton horses, skeletons in coffins, skeletons like jack-in-the-boxes—skeletons of marzipan—skeletons on bulls, skeleton bullfighters fighting skeleton bulls.—Bones! And they seem fascinated. They all buy little toys. Galeana St is crowded—like a sort of Arabian nights, booths, awnings, water-carriers, baloons, big hats, sarapes, candles, lanterns. Quite amusing, but un peu trop enfantil. *Hoy voladeros!*

I wish you'd send two copies of *Mastro-don,* and one copy each of *Birds Beasts* & *Kangaroo* to:

> Baningenieur V. Götzsche
> *Gentofte*
> Bregnevej. 5.
> Denmark

Götzsche wants them.

I am looking for a letter from you.

D. H. L.

106

FRIEDA LAWRENCE TO THOMAS SELTZER

110 Heath St.
Hampstead N. W.
Saturday the 9. XII 23

Dear Thomas,

I was awfully glad to get your letter, I began to get anxious especially as Lawr. wrote he had'nt heard—Thank you for giving me all the news—I will send you those manuscripts—Kot & Murry will meet Lawrence & bring him here in triumph (anyhow I hope so!) We had never been away from each other so long—It's been good for both of us I think—I have had a great time with my children, they are so jolly & young & natural & you can imagine what a pleasure it is to have them in my life again, when they eat my "Leberwurst" out of the kitchen and take my "glad rags!" Monty has just got the job he wanted out of 600! Murry was so nice with them—I have seen a lot of the Adelphi people and I do like Murry—I had great discussions with Kot, who is really a very decent person, I do wonder how Lawrence will find England, it does feel two-penny in so many ways and yet has produced such big men, last not least: D. H. L—But there's been such a stupid general election! It's very sad you cant be here for Lawr'[s]

Seltzer's edition of The Captain's Doll *(New York, 1923). The dust jacket is by Knud Merrild.*

Seltzer's edition of Studies in Classic American Literature (*New York, 1923*).

Seltzer's final Lawrence title in 1923, Mastro-don Gesualdo (*New York, 1923*).

Seltzer's edition of Kangaroo (*New York, 1923*). *With the publisher's current catalog.*

Seltzer's edition of Birds, Beasts and Flowers (*New York, 1923*). *The dust jacket is almost certainly by Lawrence.*

reception feast—Murry is responsible for the "drinks"! [88] *Tell Adele she is an old slowcoach never to write! But this weather; 3 days fog like "Mord und Totschlag! Also Boni & Liveright came to Cath. Carswells! I had to come—with a rather nice Australian woman in a big car—and Curtis Brown wrote, would'nt Lawr like to go to Knopf!! So there's that for Curtis B—! No-where in the bookshops do I see L's books here! I suppose you are terribly busy! Hampstead is such a village! Adele would love it! I wish I could see your Laurentian temple! Lots of letters came for Lawr—Have you also Trokris?*
I do hope you can come!

With love, Frieda

Please send our trunks! I have no sheets & things!
I want also birds, beasts & another American Literature.

107

110 Heath St.
Hampstead
London N. W. 3.
14 Dec. [1923]

Dear Thomas

Am here—loathe London—hate England—feel like an animal in a trap. It all seems so dead & dark & buried—even *buried.* I want to get back west—Taos is heaven in comparison, even if Mexico for the time is impossible. It's good to see Frieda again, but then I can take her with me, out of this cold stew.

Shall see Curtis B. tomorrow & get MSS.—I hope he has them all safe: will write you.

I hope business is good—there were slightly alarming reports here, from America. But I trust you to keep me informed.—Till tomorrow.

D. H. L.

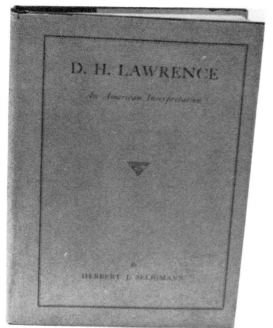

Seltzer's edition of D. H. Lawrence: An American Interpretation *by Herbert J. Seligmann (New York, 1924). The first book on Lawrence.*

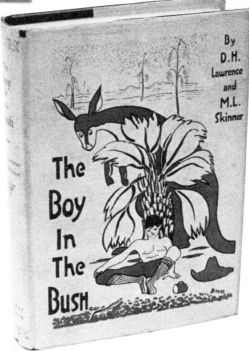

Seltzer's edition of The Boy in the Bush *by Lawrence and Mollie Skinner (New York, 1924). The dust jacket is by Dorothy Brett.*

108

110 Heath St.
Hampstead N.W.3
17 Dec. [1923]

Dear Thomas

Have you sent the MSS of *Boy in the Bush* & *Quetzalcoatl:* neither is here. I had a thrilled letter from Miss Skinner, very pleased at our collaboration. She is nice.—I had a letter from Mountsier—417 W. 118th St—thanking me for the $404.00 & saying would I deduct a $22 he owes me from the "third & last payment." How's that for cheek—when I just said the money I received in March & Sept 1923. Damn him. He'll get no third & last. He still warns me sententiously against you & myself. He's a fool. I'll have no more to do with him.

I'm in bed with a bad cold. I *loathe* every minute of it here. I expect to be in Paris before Jan. 1st—then I want to go to Spain for a time—then back to America. I think by March we shall be coming west once more. I can't stand this side. Murry wants me to link up with him—he wants to travel with me: talks of India & the Ursprung of the Aryan races. But hell can have the Aryan races, & India along with it.

God get me out of here.

You heard that Boni was here—& Knopf. I don't believe there's any point in coming here.

Why didn't you write me a letter for my arrival? What's amiss with Adele, that there's no sound from her, not even thank you for Frieda's shawl or for the vase? I feel something's the matter—what is it?—Curtis urging me to have an American agent etc—God knows. I shall have to see about my income tax in the U.S.A. I suppose if I'm back in early March I can pay it myself. Let me know. And tell me what's wrong with you.

Don't bring those boxes of ours. I don't want 'em here, & I won't cart 'em round any more. I don't care what happens to them.

D. H. L.

126

109

110 Heath St.
Hampstead N. W. 3
24 Decem. 1923

Dear Thomas

I haven't had a word from you since I am back.

I am still waiting for that MS of *Boy in the Bush*. I have all the typescript from Curtis Brown—am hung up for your part.

I saw Secker. He complained bitterly of your treatment of him over plates for *Sea & Sardinia*, also of your refusal to answer him about *Mastro-don Gesualdo*. They urge me to let Curtis Brown act for me in New York to simplify matters. Have you settled anything with Blackwell about Mastro-don?

I am doing a series of articles for the Adelphi. The February number will contain a very caustic article by me, against England: "On Coming Home." Also another article, the first of a series: "On Being Religious."—I want to write further "On Being a Man"—and: "On Writing a Book"—& "On Reading a Book." Probably I shall expand it to six essays. 89

We happened to be talking about Magnus—Murry wants very much to see that *Memoir of Maurice Magnus*—he thinks he would like it very much, as a serial, in the Adelphi. Will you please post it to me, with Magnus' own MS. of the Foreign Legion,—to care The Adelphi. 18 York Buildings. Adelphi W. C. 2. I should be glad if you would post this at once.

I still think of going to Paris in January, and on to Spain. Then come to America and go west in early spring. I want to go back to Mexico when I can, & finish *Quetzalcoatl*. Murry talks of coming with us: says he too wants to break away. The idea is, if we get the Adelphi planted in America, after about six months or a year, to publish it from that side & get more American contributors: but to keep it if possible a little "world" magazine. One can only try.—Dorothy Brett, an old friend, wants to come too. She is deaf—& paints pictures—& is a daughter of Viscount Esher.

I don't know if you still think of coming to England—as a place, it is dismal enough.

Best wishes to you & Adele for the New Year. I am a bit annoyed with you.

D. H. L.

110

110 Heath St.
Hampstead N. W. 3
22 Jan. 1924

Dear Thomas

I had your cable last week, and answered Accept—the $5000 for film rights of *Women in Love.*

They have been waiting very anxiously to hear from you about the *Adelphi.*

We leave for Paris in the morning—expect to be there about a fortnight, then to Baden-Baden for about ten days. I think we shall come to New York early in March, to pay my *income tax.* If I am not there in time, I shall trust you to pay it for me. The papers of last year are in that green *iron* trunk in your basement—and at the *end* of a green MS. book you'll find what figures I made for the early year. For the latter half of the year you have all the figures. I paid $70.00 tax—to the Inland Revenue Officer in Albuquerque, New Mexico, last year. This year it will be more.

I have had a great struggle getting *Boy in the Bush* done—you sent me only one copy. I had to have everything re-typed. And somehow everything seemed to me so confusing and difficult, I asked Curtis Brown to act for me in America through his New York branch. I have given him the MS. of Boy in the Bush, with instructions to try it for serial purpose—somewhat cut down. But of course he is to give you the MS for book publication at the earliest possible date.—He also will try to place a few articles for me. You are so frightfully busy, I can't bear to worry you any more.—Things will be just the same between us as before—only Curtis Brown will act for me. And whatever you really want, I will get him to comply with. I have told him that. We'll make an arrangement about the money when I see you. Meanwhile pay in what you can, will you, because I shall have to be spending American money to come across the Atlantic.—I shall try & be in New York by first week in March—pay my tax—and go west, to Santa Fe or Taos. Murry & Brett will either come along, or follow a little later.—I'm sure you'll get on perfectly simply & well with Curtis Brown, & it'll be better if I don't have to think about it.—I very much want to come back &

finish the Mexican novel for the autumn. Couldn't do it here. Besides I don't like it here.

Perhaps better address me care Curtis Brown, or else care S. Koteliansky. Send the Magnus Memoirs *and* the Magnus MS. to Koteliansky at the Adelphi, when it's typed out, please.

We'll be able to talk everything over peacefully when I come. Greet Adele and thank her for her letter. It pours with rain here.

Wiedersehen, D. H. Lawrence

111

[Postcard to Adele Szold Seltzer]

Hotel de Versailles
60 Bvd. Montparnasse
Paris
24 Jan. [1924]

We came here yesterday—Paris looking very lovely still, in the winter sunshine & the frost. Frieda buying clothes.—I suppose we shall stay about two weeks, before going to Baden-Baden.

D. H. L.

112

Shakespeare and Company
Sylvia Beach
12, Rue de L'Odéon
Paris, (VIe)

4 Feb. 1924

Dear Seltzer

I wish you would send a copy of my photograph to Miss Beach at this address. This is quite a famous little modern library: sells my books.

We go on Wednesday to Strasburg for Baden-Baden. Be <u>sure</u> to let me know about the income tax—I've only had one letter from you since I am in Europe.

une poignée, D. H. Lawrence

113

Hotel Versailles
60 Bvd. Montparnasse
Paris 6
21 Feb. [1924]

Dear Thomas

We are back here from Baden-Baden—still without having any word from you—which is almost mysterious. I intend to go to London on Tuesday, and sail about 5th March to New York, to be in time to pay my income tax and arrange with you & Curtis Brown in New York about the *Boy in the Bush.* [90] Then once I am fixed up with Curtis Brown I needn't bother about the business end of our relationship any more.

I have been drawing cheques on the National Chase Bank: hope you have kept my account supplied. Also I wonder if you disposed of the film rights of *Women in Love.*

But I suppose I shall know when I see you.

Yrs., D. H. Lawrence

114

Taos
New Mexico
4 April 1924

Dear Thomas

I enclose a letter from Molly Skinner. If you have time, I wish you would make the alterations she wishes: at least the smaller ones. If you want to omit the last two chapters, I don't care. What do I care any more about the pruderies or not the pruderies? I wish you'd send her just a line, to say what alterations you *are* making, at her request, so she knows she is not ignored. She is nice, anyhow. Send her a little letter of information, please.

Taos is very nice: alternates between hot sun & birds singing, and deep snow & silence. Mabel is very mild: no longer mythological. F. and I are in the two-storey house, Brett in the studio, & we eat in the big house. All goes smoothly: Mabel is wiser, has had a very bad time last year. And she was never small. Seems to me quite all right now. Touch wood!—As for Lee Witt, he is addled. Nina is divorcing him—rightly.—Tony arrived with the car, & Jaime de Angulo, last night: same as ever. He's a good soul—but, Brett says, a bit like an old nurse. Verdad!

Will you please send to Willa Cather, 5. Bank St, Washington Square, New York a copy of *Kangaroo* and a copy of *The Captain's Doll.*—And please send to Walter Ufer. Taos. New Mexico a copy of *The Lost Girl.*

I am busy doing a few short stories—I wish they'd stay shorter. But they are the result of Europe, & perhaps a bit dismal.

I do hope business will go better.

D. H. L.

Mabel has given Frieda the ranch above Lobo—legally made over.

Miss M. L. Skinner
"Leittrdale," Darlington nr Perth, West Australia.

115

Taos
New Mexico
10 April 1924

Dear Thomas

I just heard from Secker he wants to publish the *Magnus* Memoir & the Foreign Legion thing this autumn—& he wants American rights; to sell sheets to America. Will you let Barmby know your wishes in the matter, and he'll communicate with Curtis Brown, who will arrange the whole affair for me.

I don't think the new edition of *Movements in European History* will be ready yet, but I have asked Curtis Brown to let the Oxford Press people know that you would like to do the book this side with illustrations, when it is ready.

I told you F. has got her little ranch here: and I think we shall stay till late autumn—therefore I shan't get the Quetzal-coatl novel done this year. I don't feel much like working at anything just now. The winter was a bad one.

Sometime at your leisure, would you send me that translation of Max Havelaar, that the man in Australia did—W. Siebenhaar. [91] I should like to go through it to see what there really is in it. The MS. is in the safe, I think.

Brett sent you a jacket design today. I hope you like it—I do—& that it comes well in time. If you need to make any modifications in it, do just as you please. [92]

Hope all goes well.

D. H. L.

116

S. B. LILJEGREN   TO   D. H. LAWRENCE

Lund
31-3-24

Dear Sir,

I have been asked by Prof. Hans Hecht, of Göttingen, to write a students' handbook of mod. Engl. literature. The work is to be illustrated, portraits of the most important authors inserted, etc. As you seem to me to be one of the most remarkable living Engl. novelists, I should like to ask you for a portrait & what information about your life and work you will care to give. If your publisher sends your next novel to me, I might review it here, as you are totally unknown in Sweden (which is a pity).

I am, dear Sir, yours very truly

S. B. Liljegren
Prof. Engl. Lit.
University of Lund,
Sweden

Taos
Good Friday [18 April 1924]

Dear Thomas

Will you send this man a photograph & that biographical book, if you think of it. [93]

Secker talks of deferring *Boy in the Bush* till Sept. 1st. I am quite willing—I suppose you are. Settle with Curtis Brown anyhow.

We want to go next week up to Frieda's ranch, with a workman, to build up the log houses. That will have to be done. Then we'll get a bit of furniture & spend the summer there—Deo volente—Meanwhile all well here—very well, in fact. Only a bit more solitude one wants.

Deep snow yesterday.

D. H. L.

117

Taos
New Mexico
2 May 1924

Dear Thomas

I send you here the design for the book-jacket. I took Brett's design & worked it out in the two colours myself—think it is very effective, don't you?

I am sending by the same post the duplicate of Secker's proofs for *The Boy in the Bush*. There are a few alterations— not much. I think I have eliminated to fit the insertions, so it won't mean any moving of the type.

We've had cold & snow again. But now it is soft, and on Monday we are going up to the ranch with a couple of Indians & a workman, to start repairing the house. I feel like getting out there. I feel, more than I ever did, that I should like to be right away from the world.

We get on all right down here, however. Mabel is really very much changed—for the better, I think.

Hope all goes well.

Yrs., D. H. L.

133

118

Taos
New Mexico
4 May 1924

Dear Thomas

We have packed up ready to go to the ranch tomorrow. We shall have to get letters via Del Monte, so the address will be

care Del Monte Ranch
Questa New Mexico

I am thinking of my income tax: I may as well pay the second half now. I believe Miss Kameny paid $43.47. Let me know if this is right, and I'll send a check to the Collector of Inland Revenue at Albuquerque.

I shall be glad to be on the hills again, near the trees, now the warm weather has at last come. Bynner wants us to go down to Mexico, but I suppose we shall wait, now, for autumn.

Saluti, D. H. L.

119

FRIEDA LAWRENCE TO ADELE SELTZER

Del Monte Ranch
New Mexico
[May 1924]

Dear Adele,

Well, we sit on my estate with 6 Indians, Lawrence making adobe bricks and working hard, It is a lovely place—I give Mabel Lawrence's Manus kript of Sons & Lovers, which my sister told me she had! I do hope you find another "Birkindale" and a Schnitz! We saw our Pips, older wiser & sadder, Ida Rowe [sic] was here, I remember dimly that you spoke of her! I shall be glad now when we are tidier here; Mabel not as well as she used to be, she is not small and then you can get on! [94]

Just a line to send you my greetings

Frieda

We had a little 6 week old bear!

120

Del Monte Ranch
Questa
New Mexico
18 May 1924

Dear Thomas

We have come down to Taos for the week-end, to rest, after a very strenuous fortnight up at the ranch. With three Indians and a Mexican carpenter we have built up the 3-room log cabin—& very good little house—and made adobes for the chimney. Now there's a thunder-storm—& my adobes will get wet—Tomorrow we are going back—on horseback—and I hope in the coming week to get the houses all finished, roofs shingled and all. Then we shall move into the 3-room cabin, Mabel can have the 2-room when she likes, and Brett will have a tiny one-roomer. We've got four horses in the clearing, and saddles—so we are set up.—You know the ranch is about 2 miles up from Del Monte, & a good deal wilder. I think we should enjoy it for the summer, and in the autumn, about October, go down to Mexico.—By the way I had a letter from Manuel Gamio—quite a famous man down there, head of the Anthropologist Department. He sent me his book, & wants me to go & see him in Mexico. 95 I shall be glad to do so.—I wish you would send him a couple of my books—perhaps *Kangaroo* & *Captain's Doll*. Do you think he would like those? Señor Dr. Manuel Gamio

> Dirección de Antropologia
> Filomena Mata 4
> *Mexico. D. F.*

I must go down in the autumn to finish *Quetzalcoatl*. And I think Gamio will be a most useful man to discuss it with.

What are you settling about publishing the *Boy*? I hope you

135

The kitchen at Kiowa Ranch in New Mexico, 1924. (HRC)

Lawrence milking his cow Susan at his ranch in New Mexico. Friedel Jaffe, Frieda's nephew, looking on. (HRC)

Lawrence and Frieda at a meal on the porch of the ranch. (HRC)

Lawrence and Frieda baking bread at Kiowa Ranch, 1924. (HRC)

can arrange satisfactorily with Barmby.—I'm glad I've got some money in the bank, to fix up this ranch—but I'm being very economical. Of course, once the *work* is done, we shall spend very little.—And naturally I don't write when I slave building the house—my arms feel so heavy, like a navvy's, though they look as thin as ever. And after riding over 20 miles yesterday, my legs feel a bit heavy too.—I hope later to be able to find someone who might work the ranch & make a *little* living out of it—it could easily be done—so that the place needn't be abandoned in the winter.—Taos is looking very lovely, full spring, plum-blossom like wild snow up the trails, and green, green alfalfa, apple orchards in bloom, the dobe houses almost pink in the sun. It is almost arcadian. But of course, the under spirit in this country is never arcady.

I'm sorry business is still bad—but hope you're pulling through all right. Greet Adele—I hope she's well & sporting.

D. H. L.

Mabel is not at all well, in health, I think—so she is quiet and subdued, different—much nicer really.

By the way, when I get back to the ranch I'll post my second half of the *income tax* to Albuequerque, unless word from you prevents me. I'd rather pay it here.

121

Del Monte Ranch
Questa
New Mexico
Monday [?26 May 1924]

Dear Thomas

Will you please send a copy of *Psychoanalysis & the Unconscious*, & *The Captain's Doll* to Dr. W. C. H. Osborne

> Gisela-Strasse 1
> *München*
> Germany

He wants to translate Fantasia.
We've moved into our long cabin—great fun.

D. H. L.

Thank you for paying my tax.
Saw your picture with your infant "prodigy." [96]

122

Del Monte Ranch
Questa
New Mexico
19 June 1924

Dear Thomas

Will you please send a copy of *Sea & Sardinia* to Clarence Thompson, care Mrs Luhan. Taos. New Mex.

We are down in Taos for a day or two—hot weather, but windy & a big fire burning on the mountains—terrified lest it come this way. We get to be very fond of the ranch, the three of us alone, with three horses—ride every day. I was working at a couple of short stories—The *Smart Set* bought one called *The Border Line*—the New Decameron another, for anthology —and the Theatre Arts Monthly has a little article of mine, with two little drawings, of mine. Don't know when they all appear. [97] —There was a man here yesterday, George Creel— quite nice, not so very—said he'd give me a letter to Calles if I want it. Manuel Gamio writes very friendly from Mexico.— Clarence Thompson is a young New Yorker staying here—nice boy—& there is Mrs. Sprague—Always somebody at Mabel's, when one descends from the hills.

I hope all goes well with you. It is high summer with a big moon—has Adele got a nice cottage?—We've got a Pips pup, 1 month, called Jerome, & Geronimo in Spanish.

D. H. L.

The Hawks had three horses struck dead by lightning 10 days ago: Laddie, & Shadow, & Blackie—all that we used to ride.

Tell Adele my mare is called Poppy, & F. has a grey horse, the Azul—Brett has old Bessie.

Lawrence near Kiowa Ranch, 1924. (HRC)

Kiowa Ranch as it was during Lawrence's stay. (HRC)

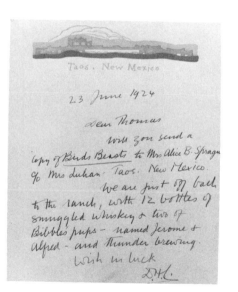

Taos . New Mexico

23 June 1924

Dear Thomas
    will you send a
copy of Birds Beasts to Mrs Alice B. Sprague
% Mrs Luhan Taos. New Mexico.
        We are just off back
to the ranch, with 12 bottles of
smuggled whiskey & two of
Bibble's pups — named Jerome &
Alfred — and thunder brewing.
        Wish us luck
                D.H.L.

Letterhead frequently used by Lawrence during his stay in New Mexico. (HRC)

Adobe oven at Kiowa Ranch as it was during Lawrence's stay. (HRC)

123

Taos, New Mexico

23 June 1924

Dear Thomas

Will you send a copy of *Birds Beasts* to Mrs Alice B. Sprague, c / o Mrs Luhan, Taos, New Mexico.

We are just off back to the ranch, with 12 bottles of smuggled whiskey & two of Bibbles' pups—named Jerome & Alfred—and thunder brewing.

Wish us luck.

D. H. L.

124

Del Monte Ranch
Questa
New Mexico
23 July 1924

Dear Thomas

I have your letter about the Magnus book, among other things. I really don't care very much what you do about that. When I did the proofs, it seemed to me interesting, but so very much passed into the past, & so very European. Maybe America wouldn't be interested.—Anyhow I <u>don't</u> think it's any good publishing my essay without the Magnus part. If you buy sheets from Secker, you can wait a bit about it, I suppose. Anyhow personally I don't care if the book is not published over here.

By the way, did you send $100.00 to Miss Skinner. She is in London with the MS. of another novel: took a 3rd class return but luckily got a 1st class passenger to nurse. If you didn't send her the hundred, I wish you would—to

140

Miss M. L. Skinner
c / o Agent Gen. for West Australia
Australia House
Strand
London W. C. 2

If you want the *Boy* to wait till Sept. 1st, insist on it with Curtis Brown. Myself I don't see what difference it makes: but since Secker held you up, there's no need for you to fit in to a day. But I don't want it to be later than Sept. 1st.

I heard that you were in a low way financially. I hope it's not true, but fear it is. Yet I believe you can weather through.—I think you have made an inward mistake, between your gods. You say you are a sacrifice to the arts. I'm afraid it's an unwilling sacrifice. No Thomas. You wanted to be a big publisher, & to beat Knopf etc. But men must serve at the altar they're dedicated to. You're not born for success in the Knopf sense, any more than I am. I don't "sacrifice" myself: but I do devote myself: and to something more than the arts. You began by so doing. You began to serve—and to serve, let us say, the arts. Then you wanted the arts to serve you, to make you a rich & prosperous publisher. So you sat down between two stools. And it is distasteful.

A man must follow his inner destiny. And it was your destiny to serve something—let us say the creative truth. That isn't the destiny of a Doran, let us say. He makes the creative truth serve him, for money. Every man has his destiny. If you truly serve "the arts," they won't let you down. They won't make you very rich, but they'll give you enough. Only a man has to devote himself. And your excursions into the popular field are only absurd.

We sit very quietly here. My adventure after all is the great adventure, which may be yours as well as mine. In early October I want to go down to Old Mexico, & finish *Quetzalcoatl*. Meanwhile we live, circumstantially, from day to day, with the hills & the trees.

F. says she will write to Adele. I hope you do really like the summer cottage.

Yrs., D. H. L.

125

Del Monte Ranch
Questa
New Mexico
8 Aug. 1924

Dear Thomas

Carlo Linati—you remember he had an article on Verga in the Dial—writes from Milan that he wants to do an article on me for the chief Italian newspaper—the *Corriere della Sera.* Of course he wants books given him. I asked Secker to send them—it is good publicity, I suppose. Only would you send *Sons & Lovers,* &, if it is ready, *The Rainbow.* You can write Linati & tell him anything you think he ought to know—that is, if you wish.

Sig. Carlo Linati, 33 Via Farini
Milan. Italy.

I had the covers of the *Boy*—very nice. Tell me the day of publication: & send me a copy for myself. I already had a Secker copy. When are the *Little Novels of Sicily* coming? I see it in your list. Send me a copy.

You knew that a Professor McDonald, at the Drexel Institute, Philadelphia, was doing a Bibliography of my books?

No Thomas, I don't think you are cut out as a Big Publisher. It's a bad race. Patience, tenacity, the long fight, the long hope, the inevitable victory—that's it.

We are going with Mabel to the Hopi Land—about 10 days—to see the Snake Dance. And in early October to Mexico. The summer is passing. But it is very lovely here now.

I like the *Boy's* jacket.

Remember us to Adele. So glad you like the cottage & the country where you are.

Yrs., D. H. L.

126

[*Postcard to Adele Seltzer*]

Laguna, [New Mexico]
Friday, [?15 August 1924]

F. & I are going with Mabel & Tony to the Hopi country in
Arizona to see the snake dance—hot down here, but I like
it—only the motorcar always wearies one.

D. H. L.

127

[*Postcard to Thomas Seltzer*]

St. Michaels
[Apache Reservation, Arizona]
16 Aug. [1924]

Stayed a night here with the Days, on the Navajo
Reservation—awfully nice.—Will you send me a copy of *The
Lost Girl* to the ranch: I suppose we shall be back there in nine
or ten days: we left Brett at home.

D. H. L.

128

Del Monte Ranch
Questa
New Mexico
26 Aug. 1924

Dear Thomas

We got back from that trip last night: rather tired. I'm not
really fond of "tripping," & I hate sitting in a motor-car.
When I said Frieda had this ranch from Mabel Lujan as a

143

gift, I ought to have said that Frieda, in return, made Mabel a gift of the MS. of *Sons & Lovers*. The ranch was worth only about a thousand dollars: Mabel had paid twelve hundred for it, & had let it go to ruin for six years. Swinburne Hale & others at Taos cry out on me for a fool: said why didn't I pay the $1000 & keep the MS.—But we like the ranch, anyhow.

Only all this expostulation about the *Sons & Lovers* MS. makes me feel I ought to be more careful of the rest of my MSS. You have them all in safe deposit in my name, haven't you?—I wish you would arrange it that Barmby has access to the safe deposit, so he can put in all the MSS as I send them to him, and keep track of everything. Let us arrange this as soon as possible, so that it's done before I go to Mexico.

And before I go to Mexico, I should like you to put some more money to my account, as I shall need a fairly large letter of credit to take with me.

I am trying hard to find someone to live at the ranch during the winter. I am afraid, if we just shut it up, the Mexicans will break in and make a smash.

I wish you would send a copy of *Pyschoanalysis & the Unconscious* and a copy of *Fantasia* to

> Clarence Thompson
> The Harvard Club
> 27 West 44th St.
> New York

And will you send to me here, please, a copy of *Birds Beasts*, for Swinburne Hale.

We shan't take very much luggage down to Mexico this time: leave everything here, & make this our centre.

Is *The Boy* out yet? I do hope he will do well, & you'll have a good autumn.

Yrs., D. H. L.

129

Del Monte Ranch
Questa
New Mexico
2 Oct. 1924

Dear Thomas

I wish you would send a copy of *Touch & Go* & *Widowing of Mrs Holroyd* to

> Carlo Linati
> *Camerlata*
> (Como), Italy

He says he would like to see if he could translate one for the theatre.

We leave here next week: stay a day or two in Taos: then on to Mexico. I will send you an address. But c/o

> The British Consulate
> 1. Aven Madero
> Mexico D. F.

will find me.

Is *The Boy in the Bush* out? Why didn't you send me just one copy? Have you sent out my six—or five—copies as I asked?—I am glad you could pay some more money into Curtis Brown: now I can travel with a more easy mind.

> Yrs., D. H. Lawrence

130

c/o The British Consulate
Av. Madero #2
Mexico D.F.
15 Feb. 1925

Dear Seltzer

Yes, I agreed at last with Barmby that he should offer the

145

Lawrence, Doña Maria Jarquin de Monors and Ramon Allenta on 18 December 1924 visiting the Church of Soledad. Doña Maria was proprietress of Hotel Francia, Oaxaca, where the Lawrences twice stayed. Photo: Dorothy Brett. (HRC)

Lawrence and Frieda before the steps leading up to the atrium and side door of the Church of Soledad. Photo: Dorothy Brett. (HRC)

Frieda, Lawrence and Padre Edward Rickards, the Lawrence's landlord, in the padre's garden. Photo: Dorothy Brett. (HRC)

Donald Miller, Frieda, Lawrence and José Garcia at the Hall of Columns at Mitla, Oaxaca. Photo: Dorothy Brett. (HRC)

short novel *St. Mawr* to Knopf. It seemed better all round: in the end even better for you.—But that does not mean I shall never offer you anything more. I am not so very sure that one exclusive publisher is wisest. Let us see how things work out: & if Knopf does one book, why should you not do another, if you wish to?

We hope to sail in about a fortnight's time to England, though I am not sure how long we shall stay.—Curtis Brown's address finds me.

Yrs., D. H. Lawrence

131

Imperial Hotel
Mexico D. F.
5 March 1925

Dear Seltzer

I've been so sick with malaria—thought I'd die. We sail for England on the 17th from Veracruz—get there 3rd April.— Will you send to

> Señor Genaro Estrada
> Secretaria de Relaciones Exteriores
> Mexico D. F.

a copy of Seligman's [sic] book on me—Estrada is under-secretary for foreign affairs, & wants to write a critique on me.

Yrs., D. H. Lawrence

132

c/o Del Monte Ranch
Questa
New Mexico
13 May 1925

Dear Seltzer

I had your book about the dinner yesterday, and your letter

DAVID H. LAWRENCE AND HIS WIFE SAIL FROM NEW
YORK FOR ENGLAND EN ROUTE TO EGYPT, AFTER FIVE
YEARS SPENT IN MEXICO AND AUSTRALIA

Lawrence and Frieda on board ship
after visiting the Seltzers in New York
for the last time, September 1925.
Note original caption. (International
Newsreel)

Lawrence and his English publisher
Martin Secker, Spotorno, Italy, 1925.
(HRC)

Rina Secker and Frieda on the balcony
of the Villa Bernarda, Spotorno, Italy,
1925. (HRC)

today. [98] We have been back some weeks. I was very ill in Mexico, and the doctors wouldn't let me sail for Europe. But now I am much better: and hope to get to England in the autumn. Meanwhile I am just "ranching."

In answer to your letter, I cannot promise to give you all my future books, to publish. The next novel, the one I finished in Oaxaca, is already promised to Knopf. I cannot withdraw. I would not have withdrawn from you, if you had showed me confidence for confidence. But you didn't.—Now, as to the future, I know nothing and can promise nothing. We will let time work out its own solution.

Will you tell your clerk to put *Questa*, not *Taos*, for my address.

And I do hope things will really brighten for you.

Yrs., D. H. Lawrence

133

Villa Bernarda
Spotorno
Prov di Genova
Italy
28 Dec. 1925

Dear Adele

Thank you for your note, & the man (woman?) about translating. The Insel Verlag—Leipsig—have the translation rights of all my books into German.

We've been here about six weeks: villa under the Castle, above the roofs of village, & the sea. It's quite nice, though the Riviera doesn't thrill me. Frieda has her daughter Barbara here, & probably the other one is coming: & I shall go off southwards, for a trip.

It's nice, now, to be in Europe again, away from the strain of America. One can relax, & laissez voguer la galère. I'm sick of being American-tightened-up.

At the present time I think the ranch is inaccessible— William Hawk wrote, deep deep *wet* snow. He & Rachel very down in the dumps, having to clear out from Del Monte, don't get on with the old man, everything gone wrong.—I don't know what we shall do about spring & our return. Frieda says she's happiest at the ranch. But as for me, I feel like staying outside that clenched grip of America for a bit. My imagination veers towards Russia, if only I can afford it. Bisogna aspettare un po!

Brett is down in Capri, seems to be enjoying it.

Hope things are going decently with you. Remember me to Thomas.

tanti buoni auguri, D. H. Lawrence

134

D. H. LAWRENCE TO CURTIS BROWN

Villa Mirenda
Scandicci
(Florence)
13 Nov. 1926

Dear CB:

I wrote to Seltzer—I'll send you a copy of the letter. Yes, he annoyed me too, with his tone!

The *Glad Ghosts* half-dozen came from Benns. Many thanks for your trouble.

What I feel about Secker is that he is so obscure, and his range is definitely, and, I'm afraid, for ever limited and circumscribed. I like him personally. I don't want to leave him. But I feel that, even for *his* sake, if I am ever to get a wider public, some other publisher will have to help break down the fence. There's that to be thought of.

I'll copy out Seltzer's letter—mine to him, I mean. I don't want to do anything, with publishers, you don't know of from me.

Yrs., D. H. Lawrence

Dear Thomas

Your letter, with Adele's, came a week ago. I don't know why it took so long.—I had, in all conscience, to ask Curtis Brown his opinion. I can't promise to come back to you, not now at least.—You say you will pay me the arrears if I come

152

back, but not if I don't: which is a sort of threat. And you know why I left you: because you left *me* quite in the dark. And Adele says I am to come back with a best seller under my arm. When I have written *Sheik* II or *Blondes Prefer Gentlemen*, I'll come. Why does anybody look to me for a best seller? I'm the wrong bird.

I'm awfully sorry things went to pieces. Blame me, if you like, for leaving you. But blame yourself, now as ever, for not knowing how to be simple & open with me.

And I do hope you will get rich one day—honestly I do.

Yrs., D. H. Lawrence

[Letter to Thomas Seltzer taken from holograph copy on original letter to Curtis Brown]

135

Hotel Beau Rivage
Bandol
Var. [France]
3 Decem. 1928

Dear Seltzer

Seligman sent me your address—I want to ask you if you will release to me the copyright of *Birds Beasts And Flowers*—which contains *Tortoises*. You may have seen Secker's *Collected Poems* of me: I want very much to rescue in America my scattered and submerged poetry, and bring out *Collected Poems* there too. I can do it if I can get the copyrights back into my own hands. I am negotiating with the Viking Press. So please say you will let me have *Birds Beasts*—the right to include it in Collected Poems—you can still go on selling your copies, when you can—and we can knock something off that old debt to me.

I think of you and Adele often, and always with affection. People are so fond of blaming one another—and they blame you for this that and the other. But I know it was neither your fault nor mine. It is just that we are neither of us in line with modern business. I don't intend to be—and you can't be. I hate modern business, and always did. You wanted to make a success in it—and it's not really in your nature. You aren't

Drawing of Frieda and Lawrence by
Bessel Kok, made in Italy during the
late 1920's. (George Lazarus)

tough enough. I can afford *not* to succeed—but you, being in business, needed to. Which makes me very sorry things went as they did. I myself know I shall never be a real business success. But I can always make as much money as I need: so why should I bother. I care about my books—I want them to stand four-square *there,* even if they don't sell many. That's why I want to rescue my poems.

How are you both? I hope, well. How is Adele? is she good and cheerful?—I was ill last year with bad bronchial hemorrhages, and am still slowly getting better. But I *am* getting better, nearly my old self. We have given up the Italian villa, which was not good for my health—and now I don't quite know what next.

You have heard of Lady Chatterley—wonder if you read it. I lost most of the copies sent to America—and now there are *two* pirated editions, I hear—so there we are, same old story. But I sold the bulk to England—and lost nothing—& put the book into the world.

Do you still have the 96 St. flat? and Carrie? and those good baked hams so shiny?—Why didn't things turn out nicer?
remembrances from us both to you both,

D. H. Lawrence

write me c/o Curtis Brown.
6 Henrietta St., Covent Garden, London, W. C. 2

NOTES TO THE LETTERS

1   This letter, almost certainly the first letter from Lawrence to Seltzer, is important in that it dates the last stages of revision in the manuscript which Lawrence sent Seltzer. Although Lawrence says "Forwarding it to you by the next mail," he very likely did not send the manuscript until 12 September, the date on the "short Fore-word" to *Women in Love*. See Cooney, "The First Edition of Lawrence's Foreword to *Women in Love*."

Lawrence is understandably bitter in this letter about England's treatment of *The Rainbow*: court action against the novel was taken a few weeks after publication in 1915 under the Obscene Publication Act of 1857. There were only spatterings of public or legal defense of the novel, and the majority of copies were destroyed in November 1915. Consequently Lawrence had been unable to find a publisher in England for *Women in Love*, his next novel, for the last two years. See Carter, "*The Rainbow* Prosecution."

Ironically, this "short Fore-word," written especially for Seltzer, would be used as evidence against *Women in Love* and Seltzer in yet another trial of a Lawrence book. See Letters 36, 38, and 39 and "Important Censorship Case," *The Publisher's Weekly*, 5 August 1922, 463-464.

2   *The Rainbow* was published by B. W. Huebsch in November 1915. See Roberts, 26-28.

3   If a "last letter" between Letters 2 and 3 was written, no record of it exists today.

4   J. B. Pinker had been Lawrence's literary agent in England since 1914.

5   Huebsch had written Lawrence on 5 December 1919 that he regretted the misunderstanding concerning his attitude toward *Women in Love* and that he hoped Lawrence could get the manuscript of the novel back. He also cabled Lawrence on 30 and on 31 December, saying he had never seen the manuscript and that he definitely wanted Lawrence's next novel. Furthermore, Lawrence knew at this time that Huebsch had been extremely circumspect in releasing *The Rainbow* in America: Huebsch wrote Lawrence in a letter of 22 April 1919 that he had withheld *The Rainbow* after its publication because of possible attacks from smuthounds and censors and that he had only recently released, in a discreet manner, copies of the novel printed four years earlier. Perhaps Huebsch had already "lost his reputation," but he had avoided any court cases and thus protected Lawrence's interests. Lawrence's gratitude is understandable.

6   The subscription forms for Seltzer's limited edition of *Women in Love* state the price as $15.00.

7   *Touch and Go* was published by Seltzer 5 June 1920. Begun in 1913 as "The Insurrection of Miss Houghton" and then put aside for seven years, work on "Mixed Marriage" had resumed in February 1920 and the novel was completed in May. It was published as *The Lost Girl* by Seltzer in January 1921.

8   *The Widowing of Mrs. Holroyd* had been published in 1914 by Mitchell Kennerley in America and in England by Duckworth. For an account of the play's performance, see Carswell, 137-145.

9   Lawrence's friend in Malta was Maurice Magnus, and he eventually wrote an "Introduction" to Magnus' *Memoirs of the Foreign Legion* (Martin Secker, 1932).

10   Robert Mountsier acted as Lawrence's American agent from 1916 to 1923.

11   Roberts does not record a Lawrence contribution to the *Evening News* earlier than 1928, and all those published were written much later than 1920.

12   Michael Sadler was the friend who sent "The Wintry Peacock" to Carl Hovey of *The Metropolitan*; the story was published in August 1921.

13   Huebsch had written Lawrence on 8 July 1920 that he was handing the manuscript of *Studies in Classic American Literature* over to Seltzer.

14   Lawrence and Compton Mackenzie were among several artists and authors who were associated with each other from December 1919 to February 1920 on Capri.

15   Lawrence's new novel was *Aaron's Rod*; he had started it in 1917 and had worked on it only intermittently.

16   Smith's and Mudies were two of the most powerful circulating libraries, and their approval was often necessary for the financial success of a novel. For a discussion of some of the changes requested, see Roberts, 47. Seltzer published the unaltered text of page 256.

17   Again Lawrence picks up on a work begun much earlier: *Mr. Noon* was started in May 1920. Never completed, it survives as a 400-page unpublished MS.

18   "Launcelot" was Edwin Arlington Robinson's *Launcelot: A Poem*; this was the first book to bear Seltzer's individual imprint. After the partnership of Scott & Seltzer was dissolved, Seltzer merely altered the publisher's device to contain a T and an S rather than two S's. See Tanselle, 389. *Woman* was by Magdeleine Marx and translated by Adele Seltzer (Thomas Seltzer, 1920).

19   *Precipitations* was a collection of poetry written by Evelyn Scott and *Blind Mice* was a book of fiction by Cyril Scott; although Seltzer did not publish these two volumes, he later published other works by both writers. See Letter 19 below and Delany, 199-200.

20　This is the first mention in the Seltzer-Lawrence correspondence of *Psychoanalysis and the Unconscious;* there may be some missing correspondence dealing with the preliminary discussions between the publisher and author of this work. Lawrence had sent Huebsch six of these essays on 29 April 1920; Huebsch wrote Lawrence on 8 July 1920 that he did not feel that he could do anything with the essays, and Seltzer could have received the manuscript direct from Huebsch.

21　Evelyn Scott, *The Narrow House* (New York, 1921), a novel; Magdeleine Marx, *Woman,* published by Thomas Seltzer, 1920, an autobiographical novel; and Cecil Scott's *Blind Mice* (New York, 1921), another novel. See Letter 17 and letter from Adele Seltzer to Dorothy Hoskins, 1 April 1922.

22　Portions of *Sea and Sardinia* appeared in the *Dial,* October and November 1921.

23　For a listing of the reviews of *Psychoanalysis and the Unconscious,* see Roberts, 52. A reaction to these reviews forms the basis for the "Introduction" which Lawrence wrote for *Fantasia of the Unconscious.*

24　No "little explanatory foreword" to *Aaron's Rod* is known to exist; furthermore, the novel set in the Venetian lagoons was apparently never completed and does not appear to have survived in any form.

25　Lawrence may have also included in this letter the manuscript of the "Epilogue" which only appears in the American edition. There is no record of the "Introduction" being printed in any periodical.

26　Lawrence had expressed concern to Martin Secker that Norman Douglas might "identify himself with Argyle and be offended." See MS, 45.

27　Lawrence's "European History" was *Movements in European History,* published by the Oxford University Press in February 1921, under the pseudonym Lawrence H. Davison. See Roberts, 48-51.

28　Kennerley had published *Sons and Lovers* in September 1913, and, according to Lawrence, had never paid any royalties. For several years this had been Lawrence's best selling book.

29　*Sea and Sardinia* and *Tortoise* were both published by Seltzer in December 1921.

30　Selma Lagerlöf (1858-1940) Swedish novelist, won the Nobel prize (1909) and was the first woman member of Swedish Academy. Knut Hamsun (Knut Pedersen) (1859-1952) Norwegian writer, also won the Nobel prize for literature (1920).

Lawrence was eventually to translate three volumes of Verga; he had first considered translating the Sicilian novelist in November. Seltzer's firm published a large number of translations: out of the 219 books bearing the Thomas Seltzer imprint, there are twenty-two translations: five of these are by Adele Seltzer and three are by Lawrence. Seltzer also published Scott Moncrieff's translations of Proust and Constance Garnett's *Complete Plays of Anton Chekhov.* For a complete listing of the books published by Seltzer, see Tanselle, 419-448.

31 Lawrence received the James Tait Black Memorial prize for his novel *The Lost Girl.*

32 There is a much longer account of Lawrence and Nylander in a letter to Catherine Carswell, 24 January 1922. See CL, 688 and Carswell, 170. Apparently Lawrence's efforts on Nylander's behalf came to nothing.

33 Compare this description of what was to become the novel *Kangaroo* to the description given earlier of a work which apparently was never finished. "I have begun a proper story novel—in the Venetian lagoons: not pretty pretty—but no sex & no problems: no love, particularly. It won't go to England at all." (Letter 24, 8 October 1921.) Richard Aldington writes in his Introduction to the Phoenix Edition of *Kangaroo*: "The writing of *Kangaroo* was an extraordinary *tour de force* of rapid composition. . . ." The similarity in description coupled with the rapidity of composition invite speculation that the Venetian setting may have been dropped, but a similar theme carried over.

34 Seltzer's alleged "reputation as an erotic publisher" was not without some justification. A month later, on 11 July, John S. Sumner of the New York Society for the Suppression of Vice visited Seltzer's office and seized copies of *Women in Love*, Arthur Schnitzler's *Casanova's Homecoming*, and the anonymous *A Young Girl's Diary* with a foreword by Sigmund Freud.
   Seltzer appears to have written a response to Amy Lowell. See below, Adele Seltzer's comment in her letter to Thomas Seltzer, 13 July 1922, and Letter 38.

35 Upon landing in America, Lawrence wrote Amy Lowell informing her of his arrival; he asked her to reply, "unless of course the new prosecution of *Women in Love* makes you feel that least said soonest mended." She replied on 16 September: "Are you really such a silly fellow as to suppose that the suppression of 'Women in Love' can make a difference to me? I think 'Women in Love' one of your finest books, and this suppression business makes me sick. Everybody knows that I am one of your chief champions in this country. . . ." See Damon, 622.

36 Joyce's *Ulysses* was published by Sylvia Beach in February 1922; a portion hd appeared in the *Little Review* in 1920, and the editors of the magazine were convicted of publishing obscenity. John Sumner of the New York Society for Prevention of Vice brought action against Joyce, as well as Lawrence. See Ellmann, 517-159. Copies of *Ulysses* could not be legally imported into the United States until 1933, while Lawrence's *Lady Chatterley's Lover* was not legal in the United States in unexpurgated form until 1959.

37 Raymond Weaver, *Herman Melville: Poet and Mystic*, New York 1921.

38 The "war experience" section of *Kangaroo* is the chapter entitled "Nightmare" dealing primarily with Lawrence's examination by the induction authorities in England in 1916 and the expulsion by the military authorities of Lawrence and Frieda from their Cornwall home in October 1917.

39 Seltzer finally secured rights from Kennerley to publish *Sons and Lovers* in 1923.

40 The only Lawrence title to be published by Seltzer in January 1923 was I. A. Bunin's *The Gentleman from San Francisco and Other Stories*, translated by D. H. Lawrence, S. S. Koteliansky, and Leonard Woolf.

41 Seltzer had published a trade edition of *Women in Love* on 18 October; he thus capitalized on all the publicity surrounding the trial.

42 "Mrs. S." is Mabel Dodge Sterne, later Mabel Dodge Luhan.

43 Waldemar Bonsels, *The Adventures of Maya, the Bee*, and René Maran, *Batouala*, both translated by Adele Seltzer.

44 Mrs. Clarke and Mrs. King were Lawrence's two sisters.

45 The Lawrences stayed with Rachel and William Hawk at their Del Monte ranch 1922-23.

46 Knud Merrild and Kai Götzsche were "the two Danes" who lived near the Lawrences at Del Monte Ranch. See Merrild's *A Poet and Two Painters* (1938). Several of Lawrence's other Taos friends wrote books about Lawrence in New Mexico and Mexico: *Journey with Genius*, Witter Bynner (1951); *Lorenzo in Taos*, Mabel Dodge Luhan (1933); *Lawrence and Brett*, Dorothy Brett (1933); and *D. H. Lawrence in Taos*, Joseph Foster (1972).

47 In October 1922, Lawrence had written a review of Ben Hecht's *Fantazius Mallare* in the form of a letter to Willard Johnson; the letter was published in a periodical published on the University of California campus, *The Laughing Horse* (reprinted in CL, 725). Although the book caused a minor scandal, Lawrence's main point in the review was that all the "naughty words and shocking little drawings only reveal the state of mind of a man who has *never* had any sincere, vital experience in sex" and that the "tragedy" occurs when "you've got sex in your head."

48 The Seltzers had arrived on 25 December and left on 2 January. See Adele Seltzer's letter to Dorothy Hoskins, 7 January 1923.

Lawrence signed four contracts with Seltzer on 2 January: *The Captain's Doll*, *Studies in Classic American Literature*, *Kangaroo*, and the Verga translations—*Mastro-don Gesualdo* and *Little Novels of Sicily*. The contract for the second Verga translation titled the work *Black Bread*; Lawrence has marked this out on the contract and substituted *Little Novels of Sicily*. "Black Bread" is one of the stories in the volume.

49 Pips was Lawrence's dog; she was also known as Bibbles. See Lawrence's poem of that title (*Complete Poems*, 394-400).

50 Katherine Mansfield was living at the Gurdjieff Institute at Fontainebleau.

51 Lawrence had articles in the February and March 1923 issues of the *Dial*: "Indians and Englishman," and "Taos." Both are reprinted in *Phoenix*.

52 The "thousands of contracts" probably included the four dated 2 January 1923.

53 Witter Bynner recounts the Stephen Graham-Wilfred Ewart episode in *Journey with Genius:*

> To Santa Fe about this time came Stephen Graham, the English writer on Russia, who was still trying to live down his repeatedly printed conviction that the Slavs would not reject their Little Father, the Czar. The Lawrences and I had met Graham previously and through him we now met his amiable, quiet friend, Wilfred Ewart, who had come from England to New Mexico for his health and with the though that its calm might cure him of a stutter.
>
> In December neither the Lawrences nor Graham accompanied us to Zuñi; but Ewart came along. During the trip, he told us that as soon as he returned to Santa Fe, he was proceeding to Mexico, where Graham was to join him; and he said that there had been talk of the Lawrences following in the spring.
>
> Soon after our return to Santa Fe, we read in the *New Mexican* a letter from Stephen Graham which reported that Ewart, in a small Mexico City hotel, leaning against the iron railing of his balcony on a holiday, had been killed by a stray bullet. It was believed an accident, that the bullet had come from a drunken celebrant. "I don't think so," said Lawrence when we discussed it. "I don't think so. I believe that it's an evil country down there." Bynner, 16-17.

54 For Adele Seltzer's reaction to *Mastro-don Gesualdo* see her letter of 5 January 1923 to Thomas Seltzer.

55 Hearst International had paid Lawrence $1,000 in September 1922 for the magazine rights to "The Captain's Doll," but they never published the story and later released it. See Letter 62 and MS, 51.

In the enclosed letter, Lawrence wrote Curtis Brown that the book appearance must follow the magazine appearance.

56 The enclosed article was probably "Surgery for the Novel—or a Bomb," which appeared in the *Literary Digest International Book Review*, April 1923, and is reprinted in *Phoenix*.

57 Gilbert Cannan, seven of whose works Seltzer eventually published, was an old friend of Lawrence's.

58 Letter 58 was also published in *The Publisher's Weekly*, 24 February 1923, p. 580, under the heading *"Women in Love* Again."

> Supreme Court Justice John Ford stated February 5 that he intended to seek the prosecution of D. H. Lawrence's "Women in Love." A circulating library recommended the book to Justice Ford's daughter. He is determined to introduce, if necessary, a new bill to the Legislature to put teeth into the present law. He said he had been informed that the present statute on the subject had been rendered powerless by an interpretation by the Court of Appeals which holds that a book shall be judged as a whole and not by any extracts or passages.

Also see Tanselle, 398.

59 Gilbert Seldes was the editor of *The Dial* from 1920 to 1923.

60 Seltzer's terms for *Kangaroo* were 15% to 5000, then 18% up to 10,000 and 20% thereafter.

61 The drawing which pleased Adele Seltzer may have been the "drawing of the riders" which Frieda mentioned in her letter to Adele (Letter 52 above).

62 Roberts reports that Seltzer's trade edition of *Women in Love* went up to 15,000 copies.

63 The early 1920's in Germany were marked by periods of severe economic inflation; both Lawrence and Frieda would regularly send money in their individual letters to Frieda's family in Germany. On 11 January 1923, French and Belgian troops occupied the Ruhr district in Germany.

64 An entry in Lawrence's diary for 26 February 1923: "Made up income tax returns." See Tedlock, 97.

According to current figures from the U.S. Bureau of Labor Statistics, Lawrence's 1922 American income of $5439.67 would be equivalent to approximately $15,000 in 1974. Note that English royalties are not included. Below is a transcription of Lawrence's handwritten tax computation for 1922.

Received 1922

Royalties				Periodicals		
Mar. 15	Seltzer	200.		Jan. 9	*Dial*	35.
16	Huebsch	263.95		July 10	*Dial*	500.
June 19	Seltzer	200.		Nov. 15	Hearst	1000.
30	Seltzer	1000.		Dec. 1	*Poetry*	80.
Sep. 5	Seltzer	200.				1615.
18	Seltzer	200.				
Oct. 18	Seltzer	500.				
Nov. 14	Huebsch	300.				
29	Seltzer	300				
Dec. 11	Huebsch	382.27				
18	Seltzer	278.45				
		3824.67				
		1615.00				
		$5437.67				

Deduct.

Mountsier's commission	543.96
Mountsier's journey	300.
Mountsier's expenses	345.31
	1189.27

			put Mountsier's figure		
received	5439.67	40			
deduct	1189.27	28			
	4250.40	2	2,043.05-300.	1743.05
exemption	2500.00	70	tax paid $70.00	
	.1750.40			

65 Adele had the manuscript of *Mastro-don Gesualdo* when she left Taos in January. See Adele's letters below to Thomas Seltzer, 5 January 1923, and to Lawrence, 7 January 1923. The first English issue of the book was published by Cape from the Seltzer sheets in March 1925. See Roberts, 70-71.

66 The book Lawrence appreciated was L. Gutierrez de Lara and E. Pinchon, *The Mexican People: Their Struggle for Freedom*, New York, 1914.

67 Lawrence wrote Huebsch that he could go ahead with a reissue of *The Rainbow* "now in the press."

68 Lincoln Steffens had sent Lawrence an introduction to Mr. Haberman and to the University Club of Mexico City. (Unpublished letter to Steffens, 14 March 1923.

69 Justice Ford had held a meeting at the Hotel Astor and denounced the "facile pens of the blasé literati who unfortunately have the entrée to prominent pages of our foremost newspapers and magazines." And on 8 March Ford began to organize the Clean Books League. See Tanselle, 398.

70 There is no record in Roberts of a Lawrence contribution to *Tempo*.

71 The "enclosed" was a letter from the American Railway Express Company requesting information about the delivery of a parcel.

72 For a further account of the sickness of Adele's sister, see Adele's letter to Dorothy Hoskins, 8 January 1924.

73 Mrs. Zelia Maria Nuttall was an archaeologist living in Mexico City; she was drawn on by Lawrence for the character of Mrs. Norris in *The Plumed Serpent*.
   Lincoln Steffens was well known for his muckraking journalism. The reference to "Judges" alludes to the activities of Judge Ford against Seltzer and *Women in Love*.

74 Louis Feipel had sent a "rather scaring list of errors in *The Captain's Doll* and *Fantasia*." Lawrence replied, "in excuse, I've had no proofs of the books printed in America except the story 'Ladybird.' " See CL, 741.

75 The first draft of the novel (later called *The Plumed Serpent*) has 469 manuscript pages.

76 The first issue of the *Adelphi* in June 1923 contained Chapter Four, "Trees and Babies and Papas and Mamas," of *Fantasia of the Unconscious*. See Roberts, 57.

77 The Lawrences arrived in New York on 19 July and remained until 17 August. For a further account of the month the Lawrences and the Seltzers spent together, see the letters from Adele Seltzer to Dorothy Hoskins: 1 October 1923 and 21 April 1924.

78 Amy Lowell had sent Lawrence his semiannual royalties from the three volumes of Imagist poetry which she had edited. Lawrence wrote her on 18 August 1923:

Thank you for the little cheque. Sending these tiny sums is a nuisance to you; don't bother to do it, give the money to somebody who is poor. See Damon, 640.

79 Lawrence and Frieda had had a serious quarrel after leaving the Seltzers; Lawrence refused to accompany Frieda to Europe and went alone to Los Angeles.

80 Henry Seidel Canby was the editor of the *New York Evening Post* (1920-24) and later of *The Saturday Review of Literature* (1924-36). Lawrence contributed a review of *A Second Contemporary Verse Anthology* to *New York Evening Post Literary Review*, 29 September 1923.

Mollie Skinner had met the Lawrences during their stay in Australia; she had written a novel, *The House of Ellis*, and sent it to Lawrence, asking for his assistance.

Prince Antoine Bibesco was of distinguished Rumanian family; he married the sister-in-law of Cynthia Asquith. Lawrence knew them both during the war years in England.

Birkindele was the name given to "Mr. Hammerslaugh's Cottage, Union Hill, Dover, New Jersey," near "Morris Plains," and "behind the millionaire Coffin's house." "Birkindele," according to Adele Seltzer, derives from the character Birkin in *Women in Love* and is probably a composite of "Birkin" and "Adele." See letter below from Adele to Dorothy Hoskins, 1 October 1923. Also unpublished letters to Amy Lowell, 3 July 1923, and to Bessie Freeman, ?30 July 1923.

81 Seltzer had been indicted by a grand jury on 18 July 1923 and later released on $1,000 bail. The case was not finally resolved until 1925. See Levin, "The Seltzers and D. H. Lawrence: A Biographical Narrative," below.

82 "Robot" is unidentified.

83 The book by Katherine Mansfield was *The Dove's Nest and Other Stories*, a posthumous collection of twenty-one stories, fifteen unfinished. See letter to John Middleton Murry, 25 October 1923, CL, 759.

84 Lawrence did not suggest the new title, *The Boy in the Bush*, to Mollie Skinner until 1 November.

85 John Macy wrote several reviews of Lawrence's works for the *Nation*, most recently of *The Ladybird* (6 June 1922), and also the Introduction to the Modern Library Edition of *Sons and Lovers* (1922).

86 John Macy's review, "The American Spirit," appeared in the *Nation*, 10 October 1923.

"Cooper" is unidentified.

87 *Mastro-don Gesualdo* had been published on 13 October 1923 and *Birds, Beasts, and Flowers* on 9 October.

Dr. George Purnell was an American dentist practising in Guadalajara; Lawrence had met him and his daughter Idella during his earlier visit to Mexico in May.

88 Part of Lawrence's bitterness and disgust toward England, as seen in letters below, might be due to the outcome of "Lawr'[s] reception feast," also known as the "Last Supper." See Moore, 380-381, and Carswell, 201-224.

89 Three of these essays actually appeared in the *Adelphi*: "On Being Religious" (February '24); "On Human Destiny" (March '24); and "On Being a Man" (September '24). "On Reading a Book" and "On Writing a Book" were apparently never written. An essay entitled "On Being in Love" exists only as a series of notes (Tedlock, 134), and "On Coming Home" was rejected by Murry and not published until 1968 in *Phoenix II*.

90 Below is another tax statement in Lawrence's hand. The figures here can be multiplied by three for a rough equivalent to the purchasing power of the 1974 dollar.

Mrs. Kameny			March 14 / 1924
D. H. Lawrence—Income tax return			
Amt. of royalties from Thomas Seltzer		3281	
Amt. of royalties from periodicals		400	
Amt. of English income		2000	
	gross total	5681	

Deductions:	for typing	175.	
	agent's fee	832.67 (Mountsier)	
	exempt	2500.00	5681.00
amount taxable		3507.67	3507.67
amount of tax paid:	amt taxable		2173.33
(one half 43.47)	amt. of tax		86.94

91 See *Max Havelaar*, Multatuli (E. D. Dekker), translation by W. Siebenhaar and Introduction by D. H. Lawrence, Alfred Knopf, 1927.

92 Dorothy Brett's design was for the dust jacket of *Boy in the Bush*.

93 The "biographical book" was probably Herbert J. Seligmann's *D. H. Lawrence: An American Interpretation*, Thomas Seltzer, 1924.

94 Ida Rauh was an actress; at one time, she was the wife of Max Eastman and later of Andrew Dasburg. The Seltzers might have known Eastman and his wife from New York publishing circles. Dasburg was an artist in Taos when the Seltzers visited.

95 L. D. Clark notes that Dr. Manuel Gamio is often referred to as "the father" of Mexican anthropology. See Clark, 36-37. The book which he sent Lawrence might have been either *Forjando patria*, Mexico, 1916; or *La poblacion del valle de Tehtihacan,* 3 volumes, Mexico, 1922. Gamio was also editor of the periodical *Ethnos.*

96 Seltzer's "infant prodigy" was Nathalia Crane, a ten year old Brooklyn girl whose *The Janitor's Boy and Other Poems* Seltzer had published in May. Her books were enthusiastically reviewed and the book was reprinted several times.

97 "The Border Line" was published in *The Smart Set,* September 1924 and "The Last Laugh" in *New Decameron,* 1925. "The Dance of the Sprouting Corn" and "Hopi Snake Dance" appeared in the July 1924 and December 1924 issues of *Theatre Arts.* Lawrence also has one drawing, "The Corn Dance," in the July 1924 issue.

98 "On the evening of 16 April 1925, a group of authors and editors gathered at the Plaza in New York to celebrate the fifth anniversary of the publishing firm of Thomas Seltzer. . . . The committee had contacted all the authors on the Seltzer list, and letters from many of those who could attend were printed in a special booklet issued to commemorate the event." Tanselle, 380. The commemorative pamphlet was titled *Thomas Seltzer: The First Five Years;* Lawrence did not attend the ceremony and a letter from him does not appear in the pamphlet.

The Seltzers &
D. H. Lawrence:
A Biographical Narrative
by
Alexandra Lee Levin &
Lawrence L. Levin

Adele Szold Seltzer. (Alexandra Levin)

*Early photograph of Thomas and
Adele Seltzer.* (Alexandra Levin)

"Thomas Seltzer and wife are here: he's a nice tiny man, I think I trust him, really," wrote D. H. Lawrence to John Middleton Murry on December 30, 1922. "Here" was Del Monte Ranch, Questa, fifteen miles from Taos, New Mexico; Thomas Seltzer, standing just a bit over five feet, was the English writer's new American publisher. Following the suppression in England of Lawrence's novel, *The Rainbow*, in 1915, no publisher would touch its sequel, *Women in Love.* Finally in November 1920, the small, experimental firm of Thomas Seltzer brought it out in a privately printed edition for subscribers only. In the period of a few years, from 1920 to 1926, the Seltzer imprint appeared on twenty Lawrence works; the firm's record for Lawrence first editions has never been equalled by any other American publisher.

Born in Poltava, Russia, on February 22, 1875, Thomas Seltzer was brought to the United States by his family in 1887. He had attended Hebrew schools in Russia, but his education was largely American. At the age of eleven he was a sweatshop worker, but his older sister, Bertha, insisted that he attend high school. After winning an initial scholarship to the University of Pennsylvania, Seltzer earned additional scholarship assistance and received his B.A. in 1897. Postgraduate work in modern languages made him conversant not only with Russian and Yiddish, but also with Polish, German, French and Italian. When Maxim Gorky, who had actively participated in the unsuccessful 1905 Russian Revolution, landed in New York in the spring of 1906, he named Thomas Seltzer his official translator and interpreter. Gorky's *The Spy: The Story of a Superfluous Man*, translated by Seltzer, was published by B. W. Huebsch in 1908; Gorky's *Mother* was another Seltzer translation.

Thomas Seltzer's journalistic experience included reporting for three Pittsburgh newspapers, writing articles for various magazines, including *Harper's Weekly*, and serving as associate

Notes to this section begin on p. 199.

editor for *Current Literature* and the *Literary Digest*. As first editor of the *Masses*, of which he was a founder,[1] he drew heavily on the work of social reformers and on the fiction of Europe, printing stories by Tolstoi, Chekhov, Sudermann, and Bjornson. For this pioneering work, Granville Hicks, in his *John Reed—The Making of a Revolutionary* (New York, 1936), referred to Seltzer as one of the intellectual "giants of the Village."

Early in his career, while on the editorial staff of the monumental 12-volume *Jewish Encyclopedia* published by Funk & Wagnalls, Seltzer met Adele Szold who translated articles written for that work by foreign scholars and contributed one of her own.[2] Adele, the youngest of eight children, was born in Baltimore on October 26, 1876. Her German-speaking parents came from the Austro-Hungarian Empire in 1859 when her father, Rabbi Benjamin Szold, became the spiritual leader of Baltimore's Oheb Shalom Congregation. Adele, whose name was always pronounced in the German manner, A-dáy-la, received a good classical education at the Misses Adams's School; at home her scholarly father emphasized education for women. After a year at the University of Wisconsin, Adele returned to Baltimore where she did private tutoring and unsuccessfully tried to raise mushrooms as a small commercial venture. Irked by Baltimore's "stuffiness," she left home and moved to New York City. Pleased with her new role as an emancipated woman, Adele, aged twenty-four, boarded for a time at a home for working girls on East 63rd Street. At Funk & Wagnalls her friendship with Thomas Seltzer, a year her senior, culminated in their marriage in 1906.

The newlyweds, unable to afford a honeymoon, went directly to their small Greenwich Village flat. Thomas, a short, slight person, was physically incapable of doing a day's worth of manual labor. A Socialist theorist, addicted to cigarettes, endless glasses of tea, and stimulating conversation, "Toby," as Adele called him (or "Tommy" to his associates), possessed intellectual acumen and a pleasant personality that more than compensated for his small size. The Seltzers' avant-garde social circle included writers, artists and musicians such as the Ryan Walkers, Gustavus Myers, the Edwin E. Slossons, and the Paul Tietjens.[3]

Since Thomas made but a fitful income from writing and

translating, Adele took on two jobs. In the morning she was social secretary to Therese Loeb Schiff, wife of financier Jacob Schiff, at her opulent mansion, No. 965 Fifth Avenue.[4] Adele's afternoons were spent as executive secretary of the Federation for Child Study on West 100th Street. In addition she reviewed books and did translations. Thomas Tanselle, in his article "The Thomas Seltzer Imprint," states that "Seltzer's first large success in translating had been Sudermann's *Song of Songs* for B. W. Huebsch in 1909,"[5] but this translation of *Das Hohe Lied*, a lengthy novel baring the corruption of Berlin society and the immorality of the ruling Prussian Junker class, was actually done by Adele. Thomas merely did the typing, but his name was given as translator in order to further his literary prospects.[6] Adele wrote to her mother and sister Henrietta on December 20, 1909, "Thomas has several orders for books, besides the Ostwald book, which has turned out to be a difficult piece of work."[7]

On December 4, 1915, Seltzer sailed aboard the *Oscar II*, Henry Ford's "Peace Ship," as a member of the Ford Peace Party's executive committee. Nearly half of the Ford group, which hoped that the war would end before the United States could be pulled into it, was made up of writers. B. W. Huebsch, the publisher for whom Thomas and Adele did translating and editing, was in the party, as was William C. Bullitt, a reporter for the Philadelphia *Ledger*, and S. S. McClure, publisher and editor of the New York *Evening Mail*. Newsman Louis Lochner was a chief organizer of Ford's party, and Rosika Schwimmer, Hungarian feminist and pacifist, was attached to the delegation as "expert adviser."[8] After a rough, wintry crossing in a submarine-infested ocean, the peace-seekers disembarked at Christiana, where Henry Ford deserted them and sailed for home. Norway was cool to the delegates, Sweden and Denmark were cordial, and the Dutch viewed them with mixed feelings. Seltzer, who sailed for home with a contingent of his fellow idealists on January 15, 1916, felt that the leaders of the expedition had been too small for the idea behind it.

In 1917 Seltzer joined the publishing firm of Boni and Liveright as vice-president and editor of their Modern Library. Albert and Charles Boni, sons of Thomas' sister Bertha, had been in the publishing business for several years. Horace Liveright joined Albert Boni in 1917 to form Boni and

Liveright, Inc. Seltzer edited *Best Russian Short Stories* and wrote an introduction to Turgenev's *Fathers and Sons.* He also translated for the firm Leon Trotsky's *The Bolsheviki and World Peace,* and two novels, *The Inferno,* by Henri Barbusse of France, and *Men in War* by Andreas Latzko, a Hungarian. These three controversial and topical books were published in the spring of 1918. The novels, intensely anti-militaristic in thrust, were coldly received in a United States throbbing with war fever. *Men in War* was banned for a time by the government, and sales of Trotsky's book, brisk for a time to the tune of 20,000 copies, were halted by the Red Scare.[9] The disparate natures and aims of the firm's three directors led to disagreements, both editorial and financial. Albert Boni pulled out, Horace Liveright became the majority owner in July 1918, and Thomas Seltzer left about four months after his nephew's departure.[10]

Seltzer then formed a publishing partnership with Temple Scott, an experienced writer, editor and agent with a thorough knowledge of the book trade.[11] Their first offering, *The Burning Secret* by "Stephen Branch," penname for Stefan Zweig, appeared in October 1919. *A Landscape Painter* by Henry James completed that year's list. *Parliament and Revolution* by Ramsey MacDonald, published in March 1920, appeared under the Scott and Seltzer imprint although early in 1920 the partnership was dissolved. "The firm is no longer Scott & Seltzer, Inc., but Thomas Seltzer, Inc.," Adele wrote to her sister, Henrietta Szold, on March 21st. "It all went very smoothly and in thoroughly gentlemanly fashion. Thomas told Scott he wanted to separate, stated his terms, Scott made no objections. . . ."[12]

Certainly a new experimental publishing firm could not have launched itself at a worse time financially. "There's a business panic; the book trade is dead," Adele informed her sisters on June 15, 1920. "The salesman in the West says if things keep on the same way, he'll starve, and he represents some of the largest houses besides Thomas Seltzer, Inc."

On June 5, 1920, Seltzer published *Touch and Go: A Play in Three Acts* by D. H. Lawrence, the then controversial English writer. In November Seltzer brought out Lawrence's novel *Women in Love* in an edition limited to subscribers only. The novel had been brought to Thomas's attention by Douglas Goldring, a young English writer who had been published by Scott & Seltzer, Inc., and by Thomas Seltzer, Inc. "You know that after the *Rainbow* Lawrence went a-begging for a publisher, and Temple Scott came near losing him for Thomas," Adele wrote to Henrietta. "It was against Scott's advice that Thomas took *Women in Love.*" [13] Goldring, in *Life Interests*, states that the manuscript for *Women in Love* had been lying around without a taker for about three years and that undoubtedly Seltzer's "enterprise in regard to it started the ball rolling again" and put Lawrence across in America. [14]

Thomas had added to his list two more Lawrence items, *The Lost Girl* and *The Widowing of Mrs. Holroyd*, soon to be joined by *Psychoanalysis and the Unconscious*, when he wrote to his sister-in-law Henrietta on March 22, 1921:

> Times are still dull. But I think I'll pull through. It's hard work, yet interesting, so I ought not complain. But it is not about the work I am complaining.
> *The Lost Girl* by D. H. Lawrence has had an enthusiastic reception from practically the entire American press, and it is selling well. *Women in Love* is generally recognized for what it is—a tremendous work. Lawrence is overpoweringly beautiful and a gigantic intellect besides. And the best critics here place him at the very top in English literature. . . .

Adele's letter to Henrietta was about Thomas and his business:

> He's really having a *succès d'estime*, even if not a financial success. One paper referred to him as a "publisher noted for the remarkable books he issues," another as "one of the few publishers who do not merely print books, but feel it their calling. . . ." I suppose if one can't have a financial success, the other sort is next best. [15]

The book trade was indeed undergoing a depression of serious proportions. Large concerns like Brentano's, who were able to pay, held on to their money; they owed Seltzer $1,800. This situation made it hard for Thomas to operate since he, being a small concern, *had* to pay as he went along in order to get any work done. The chronically struggling Seltzers, benefactors of writers, were never very far from insolvency. Thomas needed an assistant since the business had grown beyond one man. But a good assistant cost at least $5,000 per year, a sum they could not afford. Thomas was convinced that Adele was better at publicity work than any assistant he could hire, but if she came to work at Thomas' office she would have to relinquish her position with Mrs. Schiff. The crux of the problem was that they could not get along without Adele's earnings as social secretary for even one month. When Adele first came to Mrs. Schiff the $1,000 a year she earned there was excellent pay, but that was before the purchasing power of the dollar had fallen so low during the postwar inflation. The $2,500 she currently earned was actually equal to no more than $1,200, and though she worked longer and harder for Mrs. Schiff than before—she had given up the work with the Federation for Child Study—her pay was practically the same as when she started. She felt like a prisoner turning in a cage with no opening. Then, too, Adele's financial problems and her struggle to maintain a modest mode of living contrasted so sharply with the opulence of No. 965 Fifth Avenue where she worked. Before his death in 1920, Mr. Schiff had assembled a good collection of nineteenth century paintings of the French School and a fine collection of Oriental jades. The drawing room had lighted cabinets for displaying his majolica and antique porcelain. On occasion Mrs. Schiff did not know whether she had spent $40,000 or $100,000 on her charities and regular expenses. The contrast between her employer's wealth and Thomas' indebtedness was a constant thorn in Adele's side. It all seemed so unfair. Yet despite Adele's chafing under her secretarial duties there was a degree of mutual affection between her and Mrs. Schiff. She wrote to Henrietta on October 1, 1921:

> I have just got back from nearly a full week in the country with Mrs. Schiff. Since last April she's been terribly amiable, and while I was with her this time she positively made love to me, but oh! I'm squeezed out. Thomas feels this sort of thing can't go on. There *must* be a break. I *cannot* my whole life lead a life imposed upon me by others. I feel like a wild bird caught by one wing, fluttering, fluttering, fluttering, never escaping. You see it's Thomas's life I've had to lead, with the hideous economic burden he has thrust upon me. But the blame is not to be thrown on Thomas. It lies with the marriage system. It's awful that marriage makes you "one," that what

befalls the one inevitably befalls the other. Two people are *not* one. All that affinity business is rot. There are many men I could have spent a few pleasant weeks with, not one that I really would want to marry. This I foresaw when I was in my early twenties, but fear of offending you and Mamma was too strong upon me. I was born about fifteen or twenty years too late. Today it would be the easiest thing in the world for me to live the "hetaira" life for which I was meant. I feel convinced I should have made a great deal more of my intellectual gifts, such as they are, with a life less oppressed by economic care. You see, "married" to Thomas I had to feel ashamed because he had no work at first. Today if I were twenty and loved a man, I'd not marry him and not care what he did. I'd support myself and it would be up to him to support himself. At any rate, it's too late now. Thomas's burden is my burden. I must go on sharing his economic interests, and help him pay off his debts. So I have to go on living *his* life, reading the books *he* wants me to read for his business, doing *his* publicity, and doing whatever I can do to earn money, no matter whether it is at a job that I like or don't like. But for the debts, I'd throw up everything. I shouldn't care. I'd go to a farm as a maid, anything, just not to have to be a flunkey any longer.

Adele always maintained that she was born either too early or too late. She had, she said, one foot in the nineteenth century and one foot in the twentieth, an awkward stance she was never able to reconcile. She had married Thomas against the advice of her mother and eldest sister, Henrietta, who had sensed a possible clash between two such disparate personalities. Yet when Adele wrote to Henrietta inveighing against the system of marriage, Henrietta, who always thought positively, answered that Adele should put greater stress on the intellectual affinity with Thomas. Adele replied on December 9, 1921:

I am not an advocate of self-expressionism pure and simple. I am for the absence of self-repression. If self-repression is absent, then the other takes care of itself. You're right about my relation with Thomas, and if I didn't stress the intellectual affinity, it was an oversight due to the predominance of economic cares at the time that I wrote. Every day, when I see all about, yes, *all* about me, everywhere, couples unhappily mated and dragging each other down spiritually, I congratulate myself in the wonderful companionship between Thomas and me. As I grow older and my passions subside, our relation grows serener. *He* always was serene. I wasn't. If I didn't have Thomas to fly to from Mrs. Schiff, I'd go crazy. Really, I wasn't indicting Thomas. I was indicting the institution which makes you pay so dear even if you derive satisfaction from it. *Why* are our relations more serene? Because I ask less day by day. What does my asking less mean? The springing up of a fine quality of renunciation? Not a bit. It means the paralyzation of parts of my nature. That inevitably is what marriage does. One or the other, husband or wife, must submit to a para- lyzing of parts of himself; one nature or the other finally dominates. Outwardly I seem to be the one that dominates because I have my way in small matters, and because what men want are not wives but mothers, mothers who will dominate them like small boys. It's fearfully hard for me to be motherly. I can only be motherly to a dog or cat. The worst stage in marriage is when you feel yourself ceasing to be wife and turning all mother. Everything in you revolts.

Despite feeling stifled both by the institution of marriage and by her work at Mrs. Schiff's, Adele felt encouraged about the business. A month earlier, on November 8th, she had written to Henrietta:

People think marvels of Thomas that he has held his own during these fearful times. Old established businesses have gone crash, and he has kept up. But it has been a miserable struggle.

His list this autumn is stunning. Really tremendous things on it. It's a delight. The greatest delight is D. H. Lawrence. I cannot convey to you what that man means to me. Thomas feels about him just as I do. You know I've always maintained I was sorry I was born. I really don't like life. I don't like it at all. I dislike it chiefly be- cause it's got a fearful, intimate, vulgar hold on my physi- cal self, so that I can't let it go. Well, Lawrence makes me glad I lived so that I know him. I used to feel the same way when I read about the magnificent buildings of the Egyptians and saw their magnificent remains in museums. Lawrence seems to come of a super-race, not a race of Titans, but a race made of fine lightning and heavy thunder, and delicate moonshine and blazing sunlight. But he *is* a Titan; one of those giants born into the world once in many, many centuries, like Euripides or Shakespeare. To *me* he is greater than any. That may be because he is a modern. And I'm not anything if I'm not a modern. (Oh, the irony of it! Me, the modern yoked to a Queen Victoria—a Queen Victoria!) It also may be that he, coming later, has what they had plus what the world of today adds. But still I feel that had he been born in the age of Euripides or Shakespeare, he'd have been greater than either.

You should see Thomas when he comes home with a letter or Mss. from Lawrence, or even a letter from a sort of agent-friend of his, or a letter from a brilliant young South African artist who has illustrated one of Lawrence's books. I can tell the moment Thomas walks in the door by the *Schmunzeln* [smirk] on his face. "Quick," I say, what is it now? Show it to me." Then, "Isn't he a wonder? Isn't he this, and isn't he that?" We say these things to each other again and again, and for once Fate seems kind, that she has granted to the little Russian Jew, Thomas Seltzer, to be the publisher of the works of a century-marvel. And Lawrence appreciates Thomas and feels very friendly to him and writes him glorious letters. For Lawrence, before Thomas got him, suffered at the hands of publishers. He had two in America, Huebsch and Mitchell Kennerley, both of whom *cheated* him, and at the same time did nothing to promote him. He rightly feels that Thomas is the one publisher who, understanding the significance of his works, knows how to promote him.

In December 1921 Seltzer brought out Lawrence's poems, *Tortoises,* and *Sea and Sardinia,* the latter strikingly illustrated in brilliant color by Jan Juta. Early in 1922 Adele turned her energies to the work she liked best—promoting the Seltzer publications. From March 25th to April 7th an exposition was to be held at the Grand Palace in New York under the auspices of the Travel Club of America. There was to be voting on the favorite travel books; the ten receiving the greatest number of votes would be given wide publicity. Immediately Adele set to work. She had placards printed and distributed to every bookshop in the United States saying, "Vote for *Sea and Sardinia* as one of your favorite travel books." Accompanying each placard were a dozen slips for the shops to distribute. She also wrote to all the reviewers of the book telling them to vote and distribute slips. Out of the twenty-five best travel books chosen by the mailed-in slips, the ten best would be chosen at the exposition for a permanent Wanderlust shelf. Of course, there was always the possibility that the "rich" publishers might stuff the ballot box. But whatever the result, *Sea and Sardinia* was garnering invaluable publicity.

When the show opened, *Sea and Sardinia*, running far ahead of the other entries, was on the list of twenty-five books. Thomas Seltzer, Inc. had a booth with a striking display attended by attractive girls costumed as Sardinian peasants. An artist friend of the Seltzers' had made a huge, brilliant poster and a small stage, copying the picture on the dust jacket, on which little costumed dolls actually emerged from the church in the background. Plans called for a well-known lecturer to speak on Lawrence.

Mrs. Schiff had sailed for Europe, leaving Adele free to do publicity work at Thomas' office. Her letter to Henrietta on March 14, 1922, was enthusiastic:

> There's such a delightful drama in the publishing business. Here's an example from today. I didn't go to the office this morning, and at eleven o'clock Miss [Sylvia] Turman 'phones me to say—"No special business, Mrs. Seltzer. Just thought you'd like to know that Mr. Cosgrave of the World 'phoned to say that Sunday, Mch. 26, the important Sunday of Travel Week, there will appear a full page on Lawrence with three-color illustrations from Sea & Sardinia." (*Sea & Sardinia*, you see is a so-called Travel book). This whole business of Travel Week will give you some idea of what I do. But first to finish about the drama. You can tell that even Miss Turman rejoices in watching results. This Cosgrave page is one of the results of what I've been doing.
>
> In other ways T's office is an enchanting place. For one thing his employees are all so fine. Miss Turman is one of

the marvels of precocity that this generation has produced. I could write a whole letter on her alone. She loves ideas in themselves. You can see her whole being brighten and open and expand when a new and attractive idea is presented to her—an intellectual idea, I mean. Not an idea for publicity, or business. Miss Kameny, the bookkeeper, is a fine, solid, reliable, sterling sort who fairly adores Thomas. Miss Lerner, the new typist at $15 per, provides the genuine flapper element. She jumps up with a smile ready to do anything you ask of her, and if you let her, she'd get a violent crush on you. She's got a violent crush—Beatrice Stein. Do you remember her? She's the beautiful young creature that lost the use of her lower limbs from infantile paralysis, the daughter of Gerda Stein. She comes to our office regularly every afternoon to work as a volunteer. I could write a whole letter about *her*, too. And another person I could write a whole letter about is Gus [Augusta] Carey. She's such a stunning personality—I shan't even begin on her because I couldn't convey her stunningness. Everyone feels it, even Thomas. It's as though she were pervaded by a dynamic fluid missing in other people. She reads Mss. for us, tries to steer American writers to us (she knows *everybody* in the literary world), and gets articles about our books into magazines. And when I retire from the office, as I shall in a day or two, to translate *Die Biene Maya*, she will carry on my publicity work.

So the reason I haven't written to you for so long is that I've been too happy to write. I was just living. I couldn't stop to record my living.

Had it not been financially imperative that Adele devote herself to earning a living in New York, she would have liked nothing better than to travel about the country lecturing on Lawrence and giving readings from his writings. She wrote an excellent 8-page promotional pamphlet, *D. H. Lawrence: The Man and His Work*. She even jotted down in pencil random thoughts about Lawrence on any scrap of paper available. On the back of an outdated blank check is an example:

Lawrence's conversations about general topics are so alive because the reader feels that the speaker *feels* what he is saying. Other authors bring in conversation on general topics either to air their own views or to describe types. For instance, they put a socialist theory into the mouth of a socialist, an anarchist theory into the mouth of an anarchist, a poetic idea into the mouth of a poet. The thing is said for the sake of the thing said, not for the sake of the person who says it. Lawrence always keeps uppermost the *feelings* of the speaker. What the speaker says springs from the intensity of feeling of the moment. It may be an idea that he has carried about in his mind for years or has formulated aloud many times before, but when Lawrence records it, it springs from the feeling of the moment. That is why Lawrence's conversations on general topics have the drama of a fist-fight. [16]

As Mrs. Schiff was not expected home from Europe before August, Adele, accompanied by her friend, Ida Guggenheimer, wife of a New York lawyer, Jay Caesar Guggenheimer, went in July for a short rest at Camp Arcadia in Westport, Ontario, Canada. Thomas, tied to momentous events at the office, had to seek refreshment from the summer heat atop a New York bus. The heat was more than meteorological. On July 7th, the day after Adele left for Canada, John S. Sumner, guardian of public morals, raided Seltzer's office and carted off his complete stock of *A Young Girl's Diary, Women in Love, Casanova's Homecoming,* and several volumes from Thomas's private collection. Sumner was successor to Anthony Comstock, author of the New York state statute forbidding immoral works, inspirer of Boston's Watch and Ward Society, and organizer of the New York Society for the Suppression of Vice; as secretary of the Society until his death in 1915 he was responsible for the destruction of 160 tons of literature and pictures. Sumner's raid was not the first time Seltzer had felt the heat generated by the Vice Society. In a previous encounter his translation of Przybyszewski's *Homo Sapiens* for Knopf had been attacked. Knopf weakly withdrew the book without putting up a fight. But when Sumner, executive secretary of the Vice Society, declared war on the Seltzer firm, Thomas accepted the challenge. His first move was to retain an excellent lawyer, Jonah Goldstein, husband of Adele's friend, the former Harriett Lowenstein. With battle lines drawn, diverse forces across the country marshalled to Thomas's defense. Adele wrote to Henrietta on October 6, 1922:

No real fight had been put up by a publisher before. Thomas fought and won, won gloriously. The judge completely exonerated him in a statement that took him three-quarters of an hour to read, in which he spoke of the fine high literary quality of the three books attacked. Wasn't it splendid!

So Thomas has come out with colors flying, you may say tri-colors flying: a color for vindication, a color for courage, and a color for the excellence of the books he has made it a practice to publish. It was a regular cause célèbre.

Clippings have come pouring in from all over the country. Everybody is rejoicing, really. The Vice Society has become very much hated of late because it has diverged from its original object, which was merely to suppress pornographic postal-cards, and began to mess in the fine field of literature. What has come out very clearly is that it is a one-man affair and fortunately does not represent a class or body of people. There is no big sentiment behind it; there is a great deal of righteous sentiment against it. We are getting congratulations on all sides and the weak-kneed publishers are all delighted that Thomas has fought their battle for them. He is bringing a counter-suit now against Sumner of $10,000 a piece for each of the books. . . .

The favorable verdict meant a tremendous inrush of business. Everybody wanted the three "obscene" books and all of them are now quite sold out, and going into new editions.

At the trial, held on July 31st before Judge George W. Simpson of the 54th Street Court, several physicians testified on Seltzer's behalf in regard to *A Young Girl's Diary*, an anonymous work previously published in London with a preface by Sigmund Freud. Soon after the book was published by Seltzer, Adele wrote that it was making a sensation. She added:

G. Stanley Hall, Dr. Brill and some big educators are going to endorse it. *I* don't give a fig for their endorsements as educators and social workers. It's a work of art, exquisite, naive, charming. The securing of endorsements is hypocritical deference to Victorianism. But so it must be. And the endorsements will help sell the book and defend it against Sumnerian attacks. [17]

Undoubtedly the book had merit if it met the approval of such outstanding authorities as Dr. Hall, the noted psychologist and educator, whose book *The Contents of Children's Minds* inaugurated the child-study movement in the United States. Dr. Nathan E. Brill, associated with New York's Mt. Sinai Hospital and professor at Columbia, also could influence public opinion with a favorable evaluation of the work. Mary Isham, another physician, had a laudatory critique of the book in the *New York Times Book Review and Magazine* of January 8, 1922. Dr. Isham wrote in part:

> From the opening paragraph, when the author is barely eleven years of age, to the last, at fourteen and a half years, every word is of interest not only to educators and students of a more individual psychology, but to all who love the human kind.
>
> Many books containing matter like this have been written and ruthlessly destroyed. . . . Happily this fresh young thing's impulses and emotions have finally reached printed pages accessible to those interested in the innumerable variations of the plastic psyche. . . .

But endorsements had not defended *A Young Girl's Diary* against prudish Sumner who found the book distasteful because it described the curiosity of the child concerning puberty and her growing awareness of sex. Yet the wife of Judge Ferdinand Pecora, whose aide prosecuted the case, allowed her two young daughters to read the *Diary* after she found in it nothing harmful.

Other witnesses testified in Thomas' defense. Carl Van Doren, literary editor of the *Nation*, referred to *Casanova's Homecoming* by Viennese playwright and novelist Arthur Schnitzler as "the most finished piece of fiction that was published in the United States in 1921." [18] Magistrate Simpson eventually ruled that the Seltzer publications were valuable both from the literary and the scientific viewpoint. "I have read the books with sedulous care," Judge Simpson declared in his verdict. "I find each is a distinct contribution to the literature of the day." [19] The case was dismissed on September 12th.

Seltzer's triumph in defense of *Women in Love* and the other books added not only to Lawrence's literary laurels but to his purse as well. Two months later, Adele wrote to Henrietta that the world was slowly coming around to her opinion of Lawrence and his fine novel:

> All the great critics are saying that Lawrence is the towering genius of the age and the only English writer who has broken fresh soil. . . . Tomorrow Thomas and I are going to a lecture by Hugh Walpole, who is one of the men who thinks Lawrence "the towering genius." [20]

Walpole was one of the few Englishmen who thought highly of Lawrence at this time. It was the promotional efforts of the American firm of Thomas Seltzer, Inc. that spearheaded the sale of 15,000 copies of *Women in Love* in the United States in a comparatively short time, thereby spreading the reputation of its author.

"Lawrence is in this country now," Adele wrote excitedly on November 13, 1922. "He entered by San Francisco and went to New Mexico where a wealthy woman had built him and his wife an adobe villa. He has invited Thomas and me to come there and visit him and go with him to the Santo Domingo pueblo, which I take to be a great annual Indian dance."

Turning his back on the England which had rebuffed him, Lawrence, accompanied by Frieda, had sailed from Naples for the United States, with stopovers in Ceylon and Australia. Mrs. Mabel Dodge Sterne, a wealthy patron and protector of celebrities, had invited them to live at Taos, New Mexico, eighty miles from Santa Fe. After less than three months at Taos, Lawrence, stifled by his would-be Egeria's desire to monopolize his life, retreated to Del Monte Ranch, Questa, some fifteen miles or so distant. Adele wrote to Henrietta on December 6th:

> The most, most wonderful thing that could happen to me has happened. . . . like the crown and apex of my whole existence. Guess! You know what I think of D. H. Lawrence—that he's Chaucer, Piers Ploughman, John Bunyan, Fielding, Shakespeare, Goethe, Schopenhauer, Nietzsche rolled into one, modernized and added to. Above all he's English, the kind of English I've always romanced about, not the Kiplingesque Colonial English,

whom I've always detested. . . . Thomas and I are going to his log cabin to spend a week with him. Mrs. Schiff gave me leave. . . . Thomas contemplates riding lessons!!! Isn't that too amusing? Altogether *his* attitude toward Lawrence is killingly funny. He carefully, most tidily, most scrupulously keeps L's letters in a locked drawer in the office. I have come upon him unawares when he has opened the drawer and is tenderly fingering the piles. He won't let me touch a letter unless I have just washed my hands.

In regard to Lawrence's letters to Thomas, it may be of interest to note here that Thomas carefully preserved them through thick and thin until near the end of his life. After Adele's death, when he came to Baltimore to live for a time with his sister-in-law, Bertha Levin, he gave her the letters as a cherished legacy.

Adele's letter of December 6, 1922, continued:

Once or twice I wanted to write Lawrence a line, and Thomas wouldn't permit me to. He handles Lawrence himself as delicately as he does his letters and treasured Mss. But Lawrence does seem to be a most delicate personality, with the finest, oh, the very, very finest feelings, and one *is* dreadfully afraid of overdoing with him. . . .

But to return to this experience of meeting him personally. It's more to me than if I were told I could spend two weeks with Shakespeare. Shakespeare has not had my modern experiences. Lawrence is the supreme expression of the modern soul (psyche one should say, to be truly modern).

Three days before Christmas the Seltzers started for the West. Taos, and especially Ranchos, a small village two miles from Taos, were a revelation to Adele. She had been prepared to see adobe dwellings, but was surprised by its special form of beauty, not one borrowed from the Old World, although reminiscent of Spain. Adele wrote to her three sisters on January 16, 1923:

We stayed one night in Taos, then the Lawrences took us out in an automobile to a ranch which they have leased for three months and on which they are having live with them, though in a separate cottage, two Danish artists,

Norse gods these are, mates of the Norse goddess, real Siegfrieds. Lawrence has good taste in human beings. He is altogether simple and approachable, too much so, like all great people, that is why he has to guard himself by staying in remote places. He would be overwhelmed in a city like New York unless Thomas undertook to act as a watch-dog.

It is difficult for me to convey the "psychology" of our relation. As none of you is really intimate with Lawrence's works you could not possibly have gathered an idea of his character as I did beforehand. His wife told me it was quite miraculous that I knew him as I did and understood his works into the very subtlest details. There is no doubt that Lawrence is ahead of his time. The subtleties are bound to get by most people and will not be understood except by the next generation. At the same time it is quite startling to see how some young people of today already do understand him.

There were no conveniences in the five-room cabin occupied by the Lawrences. They chopped their own wood, hauled water from holes broken in ice near the house, and made their own fires. Lawrence relished good food and liked to cook. He prepared the main dishes and was particularly adept at making desserts. "I like living that way," Adele wrote, "especially when part of the program was a daily horseback ride." She was thrilled to gallop across the open country with Lawrence.

The Lawrences and their guests spent much of their time in the one fair-sized room which had a fireplace on one side and a table on the other.[21] Lawrence and Thomas, seated facing each other across the table, would have serious conversations on a variety of subjects. Apparently Lawrence found in quiet, almost shy, Toby a restful influence plus a personal and intellectual sympathy. While the men talked, their wives sat in front of the fireplace, Adele reading and Frieda knitting a skullcap for her husband. On one occasion Frieda asked Adele if she really thought Lawrence great. "Yes," Adele replied, "in America they think him a towering genius, but I think he has gone to the end of his theme in Aaron's Rod. He must become more universal in his theme. It is yet too subjective." At that moment Adele overheard Lawrence say, "Thomas, you are the only one who gets the core of me." "Lawrence," Adele asked, "what do you consider the core of you?" Lawrence turned on her ferociously with: "Something you two females couldn't understand. You couldn't understand, Adele, any more than Mountsier"—referring to Robert Mountsier, an American journalist and Lawrence's agent in the United States. Frieda, feeling that her husband had insulted their guest, said, "Lawrence, you must take that back." Lawrence ignored his wife's request and with a toss of his head, answered, "I'll tell you what the core of me is. The core is domination of the male. That's something you two females couldn't understand, and you can put your two heads together until they crack like nuts." Adele refused to let this pass. "We would be glad to accept the domination of the males if you didn't sputter so much about it," she parried. Lawrence turned, thrust out his head—a characteristic mannerism—turned pale, and stalked from the cabin. It was four hours before he returned.

Shortly after New Year's, Adele returned home while Toby journeyed to Los Angeles. He had received a Hollywood offer of $10,000 for the screen rights to *Women in Love,* but he hoped to receive more. In the end the deal fell through. Adele wrote of her recent experiences to her sisters on January 16, 1923:

> Here I have been back in New York ten days and the spell of the visit of D. H. Lawrence is still upon me. He is the remarkable person that I had expected. And as for his wife, she is a Norse goddess. Both of them are people full of electricity, always giving off sparks. Of course, Lawrence especially so. . . .
>
> The best thing I believe that came out of it all is that Lawrence seems to have great confidence in Thomas. This means very very much because Lawrence had been so badly treated by his earlier publishers that we were very queasy about it. I think we need have no more qualms. I think Lawrence means to be absolutely loyal to Thomas. I simply cannot get over the wonder that we are the publishers of this greatest genius of our age and that we are his publishers not by having snatched him away from somebody else but because he really needed us, because we came at a time when he could not get any other publisher.

Adele's exuberance was short-lived. First, she had to return to her irksome job as Mrs. Schiff's social secretary, and secondly, censorship was still a significant threat. Justice John Ford of the New York State Supreme Court was horrified when he came home one day and found his daughter reading *Women in Love*, a book recommended to her by a clerk in a circulating library. He decided to dig up the case dismissed by Judge Simpson. Thomas Seltzer was indicted by a grand jury for publishing "unclean" books on July 18, 1923. The grand jury found only *A Young Girl's Diary* and *Casanova's Homecoming* objectionable, *Women in Love* having been exempted from the case. The new trial was to be by jury, and Seltzer was released in midsummer on $1,000 bail.[22]

The Lawrences, following a sojourn in Mexico, arrived in New York that July. Since Lawrence hated the city, the Seltzers rented for him a cottage in a remote section of the New Jersey hill country near Morris Plains. The Lawrences asked Thomas and Adele to join them there.

For an entire month the two couples shared the secluded cottage which they dubbed "Birkindele" after Rupert Birkin, a character in *Women in Love*, who was obviously Lawrence himself. Here Lawrence was occupied with proofreading—five Lawrence items appeared on the Seltzer fall list. Adele, too, was busy translating *Dr. Graesler*, a novel by Arthur Schnitzler. In honor of Adele's work, Lawrence humorously nicknamed a kitten which played around the cottage "Schnitzler" or "Schnitz." Adele had been a pet lover since childhood; her early passion for dogs had given way to one for cats which were better apartment dwellers.

As at the Del Monte Ranch, Lawrence did a major portion of the cooking. Frieda hated to wash dishes, so Adele and Lawrence usually undertook that job. "He did even that with a grand sublimity," Adele recalled later. "There was a great deal of the feminine in him, despite his virility." The Lawrences incessantly bickered about intangibles which sometimes created an unpleasant atmosphere at "Birkindele." But Lawrence was "utterly happy with Frieda" and needed her presence despite their frequent fights.

Lawrence occasionally accompanied Thomas when he commuted to his New York office via the Lackawanna railroad. Adele remembered that even here Lawrence had a remarkable effect on people:

189

His presence could be felt in any crowd. I remember when he used to travel on the D. L. and W. with commuters from Morristown into New York City that the entire coach was alert when he entered. This was not due to any histrionic mannerisms, for Lawrence was essentially at all times the well-bred, poised outwardly calm Englishman. It was some inner greatness which affected others. [23]

Although Lawrence disliked the crowds of the city, he enjoyed good company. Thomas arranged a luncheon at which Lawrence met William Rose Benét, Christopher Morley and Henry Seidel Canby. [24] At another luncheon Lawrence was introduced to critic Lewis Gannett, writer John Macy, humorist Franklin P. Adams, and Osward Garrison Villard, editor of the *Nation*. Lawrence did not like Villard whom Seltzer overheard attempting to draw Lawrence into a discussion of the political ramifications of President Warren G. Harding's sudden death the day before. Lawrence turned away, obviously disgusted, muttering something which sounded to Thomas like "Silly ass!" [25]

The Seltzers gave dinner parties for the Lawrences at their New York flat, and entertained them in the city. Adele's cousin, Mrs. Bernardine Szold Fritz, recalled, in an interview on July 26, 1974, one occasion when the Seltzers entertained Lawrence and a party of eight at the Algonquin Hotel, a popular rendezvous for artists and writers. Mrs. Fritz was at that time Mrs. Otto Liveright, sister-in-law of Thomas' former colleague at Boni and Liveright. She said:

> I remember exactly the round table. As you came in it was just a little to the left of the door. Along the wall there were booths, and the first big round table was their table, and there was not anything singular to me at all except that practically everybody I knew found some reason to stop at the table that day and ask a question of Thomas. Ordinarily they would have passed right on, but Lawrence's face was so well known that as people entered at the door they sort of jumped with shock to see him there, and they immediately thought of something to ask Thomas, so that they would have a chance to go around saying, "Guess who I just met?" And that was my first introduction. He said *very* little.

The numerous dinner parties given by the Seltzers for Lawrence were kept small out of deference to Lawrence's aversion to large groups. The guest list usually included only those few people who agreed with the distinguished author and felt themselves in the presence of a forerunner in the world of literature. Lawrence and Seltzer during this time "seemed very amiable with each other," according to Mrs. Fritz:

> They talked a great deal about writing, and Lawrence talked a great deal, when Lawrence did talk, about the excessive Puritanism in this country which he thought was even worse than in England because, he said, in England many people acknowledged that they were conservative about sex . . . whereas in this country he felt it was on people's minds all the time. And when they talked about it they did so in terms that were snide or vulgar rather than in terms of creativity and beauty. [26]

In January 1924, Justice Robert F. Wagner called Thomas Seltzer to face jury trial over Schnitzler's *Casanova's Home-coming.* Seltzer's growing financial troubles (he had lost $7,000 during the year) combined with his worries over the case of the People *vs.* Seltzer made this year a particularly difficult one for the Seltzers.

Meanwhile, Lawrence, who had followed Frieda to England in December of 1923 after a violent quarrel, had tired of Europe and decided to return westward. Thomas' communications had become infrequent, and Lawrence's suspicions about the shaky state of the business grew. Instead of "a nice tiny man" Thomas now became, in Lawrence's letters to friends, "miserable," "hateful," and "up to tricks." Lawrence had turned against previous publishers for one reason or another, and, as Tanselle points out: "Lawrence was always suspicious of publishers and demanded strict and businesslike accounting of them, but the kind of publisher he was naturally drawn to (and the kind that would accept his work) was often not very businesslike." [27] Certainly Thomas was unbusiness-like. Congenitally unable to do anything on time, an East European trait which often had Adele, who was accustomed to Western promptness and efficiency, beside herself, he continually put off writing important letters. Actually, it was a wonder that anything got done at his office, and what did get accomplished was due largely to Adele.

When the Lawrences, accompanied by Dorothy Brett, arrived at New York aboard the *Aquitania* on March 11th, Thomas, despite not having been informed of their schedule (an intentional slight by Lawrence), was waiting in a near blizzard to welcome them and take them to his New York flat. As the Seltzer apartment was too small for five persons, Thomas and Adele camped at the office, Lawrence slept at a nearby hotel, while Frieda and Dorothy Brett occupied the apartment for a week. At week's end the Lawrences and Brett left New York for Taos and the Del Monte Ranch. Lawrence's attitude toward the publisher who had risked a great deal had soured—as it had toward many of his friends and associates at one time or another. Although hampered by a lack of operating funds, a chronic problem, Thomas scraped up as much as he could for the Lawrences' trip west. He still hoped to be able to pay Lawrence eventually all royalties due him.

Early in 1925 the court case against Seltzer was finally settled. Plagued by financial losses and the prospect of additional debilitating expenses, Thomas felt himself unable to face prosecution. After copies of *Casanova's Homecoming* and *A Young Girl's Diary* were withdrawn from circulation and the plates destroyed, Sumner withdrew his suit.

On April 16, 1925, a testimonial dinner was tendered Seltzer by friends—"The Committee." The group of forty-five persons, headed by Mrs. Rebekah Kohut, a friend of the Szolds from Baltimore days, included Oswald Garrison Villard and Mark Van Doren. The toastmaster was Glenn Frank, editor of *Century* magazine, and later president of the University of Wisconsin. A souvenir booklet, *Thomas Seltzer: The First Five Years*, contained thumbnail sketches of seventy-four of his published authors, laudatory letters from prominent persons unable to attend the dinner, and Herschel Brickell's column, "Books On Our Table," reprinted from the New York *Evening Post* of April 20, 1925. After quoting some of the evening's speakers, including Carl Van Doren and Padraic Colum, Brickell wrote:

> Mr. Seltzer thanked his friends and said that the publisher who takes his profession seriously can become an important factor in conserving good taste. He does not have to reach millions and hundreds of thousands, like the newspapers, popular magazines, motion pictures, and

radio. He can be contented with appealing to tens of thousands or even to merely thousands. Therefore the publisher of good books furnishes the sole means of escape from jazz and the vulgarizing influence of a totally literate democracy.

About the time that the dinner was held, D. H. Lawrence had begun to break with Seltzer, leaving him for Knopf. Seltzer's long drawn-out litigation had left him financially drained and unable to pay his authors what was owed them. Seltzer's list for 1926, the last year he published regularly, had nothing of D. H. Lawrence, a name which had brightened his offerings since 1920. Yet in that period Seltzer brought out more Lawrence first editions than any other American publisher as well as the first book about Lawrence, Herbert J. Seligmann's *D. H. Lawrence: An American Interpretation*. Scott & Seltzer and Thomas Seltzer, Inc. had published some 219 works. After its collapse, the Seltzer business was taken over by Thomas's nephews, the Boni brothers.

Despite the business break with Lawrence, the Seltzers again entertained him and Frieda in September 1925, just before Lawrence left America for the last time. New York had been hot and humid, and Lawrence had run about seeing people, including his new publishers, the Knopfs. For the Seltzers, the visit was an unhappy one. Dangling on the brink of bankruptcy, they were hurt that Lawrence, who had once said, "Thomas, you are the only one who gets the core of me," would leave them in their hour of need. Thomas felt betrayed.

Adele had been corresponding since 1922 with Mrs. Dorothy Hoskins, a literary agent who kept an eye out for likely material for the Seltzers. Mrs. Hoskins, who lived in Texas, must have asked for a sample of Lawrence's handwriting, to which Adele replied on February 10, 1926, that since Thomas had lost his "bridal feeling" for Lawrence, he was willing to part with a long letter to Adele, which Adele enclosed. A year earlier Thomas would have refused to part with even an envelope addressed in Lawrence's handwriting.[28]

During the next several years Adele worked hard and denied herself all but bare necessities in order to pay off Thomas' creditors. On many occasions she smarted from the insensitivity of certain friends who criticized her shabby clothes when she was making a deliberate sacrifice for what she regarded as her moral duty.

The Seltzers explored a number of avenues to hoped-for solvency. Both did some translating, and Adele continued as social secretary to Mrs. Schiff. A tea room venture fell through for Adele. In March 1927 she was being considered by Adolph Ochs, publisher of the *New York Times*, as editor of the works of Isaac M. Wise, a pioneer of Reform Judaism in America; this, too, came to nothing. The promise of some publicity work elicited an enthusiastic note from Dr. Alexander Kohut, author of a monumental dictionary of the Talmud, and his wife Rebekah: "We are so happy to hear of your good fortune and I, for one, heartily rejoice over the failure of the Tea Room idea. It would have been so pitifully anti-climactic for a woman of your rare spirit and dignity. No, you are far better suited for the role of an 'intelligencer'—for that is both euphemistically as well as etymologically the function of the publicity expert. I predict great success for you—and only the good Lord knows how much you deserve it—you sweet, lovely, patient, long-suffering creature . . . you are in your native element in this new venture and will make of it, with your inimitable grace and talent for doing things right (artistically and morally right!) a really great adventure. May all the seven heavens prosper you!" [29]

Unfortunately this work did not last long, so when Mr. Samuel W. Craig, formerly with the Literary Guild, tried to organize The Book League of America, Adele called on him and asked if he saw room for her husband in the new project. Mr. Craig did—Thomas's reputation as an excellent editor was well-known—the two met and took to each other immediately. Money was raised, subscribers enlisted, and The Book League of America, which offered twelve new books and twelve classics a year, was off to a hopeful start. The board of editors of its monthly magazine included such distinguished names as Edwin Arlington Robinson, Van Wyck Brooks, Gamaliel Bradford, Eugene O'Neill, and Alice Roosevelt Longworth. Among the contributors were Stuart Chase, Joseph Wood Krutch, Mark Van Doren, Norman Thomas, Langston Hughes, Bertrand Russell, John Macy, Clifton Fadiman, Howard Mumford Jones, Norman Hapgood, Padraic Colum, and Thomas Hardy. Seltzer, who served as secretary of the League, had no financial responsibility but was in charge of making a deal with the Macmillan Company and getting out twelve hard-cover classics yearly. He also contributed a

194

number of articles to the monthly magazine and wrote unsigned pieces for the front pages in the nature of promotional introductions. One issue of the *Book League Monthly* contained Seltzer's article "The Core of D. H. Lawrence" in which he referred to his former friend as "the great literary figure of the age." Seltzer wrote:

> It was in the character of prophet that Lawrence spoke of his core, a character which I am convinced that Lawrence the poet and novelist utterly repudiated. I have never met another author in whom two contrasting elements revealed themselves as such distinct and separate entities, constantly at war with one another. He was well aware of these two conflicting traits of his nature. He was fond of saying, as he put his hands horizontally across his lips: "Here, you see, there are two Lawrences, the one of the soft fair hair on my head, and the one of the rough red hair that makes my beard, and you can't combine them into one. There is no use trying."
> . . . In his role of prophet he often literally imagined himself a Christ come to preach a new gospel to the world. At such times his magnificent writings, by which alone he will remain known, meant nothing to him. . . . [30]

The Book League appeared to be sailing in serene waters until the Literary Guild claimed that Craig had helped himself to lists of its subscribers which he was circulating to get subscribers for the Book League. The matter was put into the hands of lawyers and settled out of court. Craig left and bankruptcy loomed until a buyer, Tom Stix, was found. Adele wrote to Henrietta on July 30, 1929, concerning the Book League, "It is not yet successful and Thomas is drawing a salary of only $50 a week. . . . But he is to blame. He did not, as usual, guard himself at the right moment. However I cannot censure him. We Szolds haven't the worldly trick, either, of guarding ourselves, or advancing ourselves. And *my* propensity for trusting others is absurd." Isaac Don Levine, managing editor of the Book League, recently recalled in conversation that when the operation was foundering that he and others worked for no salary because there was such a great "esprit de corps." Everyone, he said, liked Tommy Seltzer.

During the Depression Adele connected herself with an agent for whom she read books and recommended those suitable for publication. When Mrs. Schiff died in 1933, leaving Adele a legacy in recognition of her twenty-seven years of faithful service, she bought a 200-year-old farmhouse in Easton, Connecticut. Here she delighted in rural living, archeological digging, writing a book about her adored cats—it was never published—and having the old house restored in the Colonial manner. The huge, old-fashioned barn, loaded to the roof with thousands of books, housed Thomas's large desk, publishing memorabilia, and the painting of D. H. Lawrence done from life by Kai Götzsche, the Danish artist they had met while staying on the ranch with Lawrence and Frieda. Lawrence had given the portrait to Adele as a present in happier days.

Despite Mrs. Schiff's legacy, life at Sweet Cicely, as Adele named her house, was still a struggle financially. Funds had to be stretched to help support Thomas's old father, who had emigrated to Palestine, and a brother of Thomas. Adele tried to make ends meet by finding another position for her black cook, Carrie Payne, and doing her own housework. After the Depression set in Adele had no luck trying to place Carrie, and she wrote to Mrs. Felix M. Warburg, Mrs. Schiff's daughter, hoping she could help. "Perhaps the recent appearance of a book by an English earl's daughter will help," Adele explained to Frieda Warburg. "That same earl's daughter, the Viscountess Brett, lived for a week or so in my apartment. In her book on Lawrence she recalls the episode (which I had about forgotten) and praises my Carrie for her cooking." [31]

On January 11, 1934, Adele wrote to Henrietta, "Thomas has entered not into combination or association with a publisher, but a sort of collaboration in bringing out two books." The previous month Thomas's imprint had appeared on a book by John Middleton Murry. But the pleasure of seeing the Thomas Seltzer imprint once more was offset by expenses incurred—his railroad fare, his lunches in the city, and his small investment in the new venture. Adele had taken a position as secretary to Mrs. Warburg, but the $125 per month she earned scarcely maintained the household. In addition, Thomas developed a stomach ulcer which meant doctors' bills. Thomas's ulcer was improved by treatment and diet when Adele wrote again on November 13th, "But he still catches cold easily, remains poking indoors, goes to bed late, gets up late, does nothing with his days, and I doubt if anything develops in his business." The business was again entirely in his own hands—at least what was left of it. "Orders dribble in," Adele continued, "and I do believe that if Thomas went after things he'd land something good. But . . . !" Thomas was a broken man, unable to struggle more.

In March 1938 Adele sailed with Bertha Levin to visit their sister Henrietta. Miss Szold was in charge of settling in Palestine thousands of adolescents who had escaped from the holocaust of Hitler's Germany. During the extended visit, Adele became seriously debilitated from the effects of amoebic dysentery, a condition which the doctors seemed unable to cure. She wrote to Thomas from Jerusalem on July 15, 1939, "You are my home, Toby. I come to roost and to rest with you." Late in November she sailed for home. She died on March 16, 1940, from bacterial endocarditis. Adele's last literary effort, a long, informative article on Palestine, was published posthumously in four consecutive issues of *Opinion*, a monthly magazine.[32] Thomas sold Sweet Cicely and moved into bachelor's lodgings in Brooklyn. A lonely, defeated, childless widower, he survived Adele three and a half years, dying on September 11, 1943. The headline of his obituary in the *New York Times* emphasized his winning the censorship case brought by Sumner twenty-one years earlier.[33]

A great and eclectic lover of the literature of all nations, Thomas Seltzer had sought to educate the American public up to his standards in spite of overwhelming obstacles. Isaac Don Levine, a foreign correspondent for fifty years and whose book *The Man Lenin* Seltzer published in 1924, recently said that "Thomas Seltzer was a real pioneer in the publishing field, and in my belief remained a dedicated and idealistic publisher to the end, unlike others to whom publishing was a money-making business. He was a starry-eyed dreamer, as honest as daylight; he would never have cheated anyone."[34] And Thornton Wilder recently wrote of the Seltzers, "I knew them and knew well thereafter of the distinction of Thomas Seltzer as a publisher and would have been proud to be published by him . . ."[35]

Certainly a publisher whose list includes works by John Middleton Murry, Anton Chekhov, Stefan Zweig, Gilbert Murray, Marcel Proust, Ford Madox Ford, e. e. cummings, Edwin Arlington Robinson, Henry James, Mark Van Doren, and D. H. Lawrence deserves recognition. Many of the authors Seltzer promoted, today important names in the fields of literature and criticism, were then not yet established. Thomas Seltzer lost money on most of his writers, but in the process he gave many of them a foothold to fame and further enriched our literary coffers.

NOTES

1 Theodore Peterson, *Magazines in the Twentieth Century* (Urbana, Illinois, 1964), p. 422.

2 Vol. III, p. 95.

3 Ryan Walker (1870-1932) was a free-lance cartoonist who contributed to *Life, Judge, Bookman, New York Times*, etc; his wife, Maud Davis Walker, was a writer. Historian Gustavus Myers (1872-1942), wrote a number of exposés in the muckraking period of American literature. In his 3-volume *History of the Great American Fortunes* he shattered any idea that the acquisitors had come by their wealth honestly. Kansas-born Dr. Edwin E. Slosson (1865-1929), literary editor of the New York *Independent*, in his later years devoted much time to defending freedom of scientific teaching against Fundamentalist laws forbidding the teaching of evolution in schools. His wife, also a writer, was the first woman to receive a Ph.D. from Cornell, and for several years was the only prison chaplain in the United States. Paul Tietjens (1877-?), pianist and composer, wrote music for the extravaganza "Wizard of Oz" which starred Fred Stone. His wife Eunice (1884-1944), from whom he was divorced in 1914, wrote a number of books, was a war correspondent in France for the Chicago *Daily News*, and was on the staff of *Poetry* magazine, reviewing D. H. Lawrence's *Amores* in Feb. 1917.

4 Adele to Bertha Levin, Dec. 20, 1909: "I had a strenuous morning at Mrs. Schiff's disentangling the intricacies of her Emanu-El Sisterhood accounts. They kept me until one o'clock. So she asked me to stay for lunch, especially as a Miss Buchman was coming for whom she is arranging two 'musical readings,' and for whom I am sending out invitations. So I stayed until three o'clock to get Miss Buchman's difficulties straightened. My head was aching by this time . . ." (Letter in possession of A. L. Levin).

5 *The Papers of the Bibliographical Society of America*, LVIII (1964), p. 387. Tanselle lists a number of other translations done by Thomas Seltzer.

6 Adele to Bertha Levin, Dec. 20, 1909: "Thomas came home with the news that the Song of Songs is going into a second edition. Somebody told Mr. Huebsch today that Roland Holt of the firm of Holt & Co., said, "Well, *that* translation *we* would have been willing to take."

7 Letter in possession of A. L. Levin. Mrs. Szold and Henrietta were traveling in Europe and Palestine, and the Seltzers were occupying the Szolds' apartment while they were away. The "Ostwald" book, published in 1910, was *Natural Philosophy* by Wilhelm Ostwald, the German physical chemist and natural philosopher (1853-1932), who received the 1909 Nobel Prize in Chemistry.

8 Burnet Hershey, a cub reporter for the *Brooklyn Eagle* and who was along, wrote in his *Odyssey of Henry ford and the Great Peace Ship* (New York, 1967) pp. 193-94, that Thomas Seltzer was considering writing a biography of Nobel at the time and was "full of the subject." When one of Ford's admirers suggested that *he* might be a candidate for the Nobel award, Ford, according to Seltzer's recollection some years later, replied: "*Me* get this peace prize? Heck, I'll *give* one of my own."

9 Walker Gilmer, *Horace Liveright—Publisher of the Twenties*, (New York, 1970), pp. 16-17.

10 *Ibid.*, pp. 18-19.

11 Tanselle, pp. 382-89.

12 Unless otherwise indicated, Adele Seltzer's letters quoted in this sketch, and one letter from Thomas Seltzer to Henrietta Szold, are in the Zionist Archives, Jerusalem, Israel. For a more detailed treatment of the Seltzers and Szolds see Alexandra Lee Levin, *The Szolds of Lombard Street* (Phila., 1960), and *Dare To Be Different* (New York, 1972).

13 December 9, 1921.

14 (London, 1948), p. 86.

15 Undated, but Henrietta Szold noted on it that it was received at Jerusalem about April 5, 1921.

16 In the possession of A. L. Levin.

17 December 9, 1921.

18 *New York Times*, July 19, 1923.

19 Quoted in a publicity advertisement of Thomas Seltzer, Inc. and enclosed in Adele's letter of Oct. 6, 1922.

20 November 13, 1922.

21 Much of the following discussion is taken from an informative interview conducted by reporter Anne Whelan with the Seltzers which appeared in the *Bridgeport Sunday Post* (Bridgeport, Conn.), Feb. 27, 1938.

22 Tanselle, pp. 398-401.

23 Whelan interview.

24 See Henry Seidel Canby, *American Memoir* (Boston, 1947), p. 325: "Lawrence's lean, ascetic face, with its sparse red beard, his burning eyes, his dogmatism, gave me a vision of what Savonarola may have been like. I spent an afternoon with him once, coming away with an impression of a will stronger than a reluctant body."

25 Whelan interview.

26 Mrs. Bernardine Szold Fritz, of Beverly Hills, Calif., was interviewed by Dr. Lawrence L. Levin at her home.

27 Tanselle, p. 392.

28 Letter at University of Texas Library.

29 August 25, 1925. The Kohuts lived at 1 West 70th St., N.Y.C. Postcard in possession of A. L. Levin.

30 April 1930, p. 290.

31 From Box 92A, Route 2, Danbury, Conn., Oct. 30, 1933. Carbon copy in possession of A. L. Levin.

32 October 1940-January 1941.

33 September 29, 1943.

34 Interview at his home, Waldorf, Md., August 19, 1974.

35 Thornton Wilder, Edgartown, Martha's Vineyard, Mass., to Alexandra Lee Levin, Baltimore, Md., October 1, 1974.

The Letters from
Thomas & Adele Seltzer

Thomas Seltzer, Inc.
Publishers
5 West Fiftieth Street, New York

Mr. Robert Mountsier
417 W. 118th Street
New York City

October 4, 1920

Dear Mr. Mountsier:

Can you call to see me? Please ring me up for an appointment. I want to speak to you about *The Lost Girl*, which I am anxious to publish by next January, if possible. I understand that Secker is publishing it this fall. If it if to be brought out next January, the work on it ought to be begun at once.

Yours sincerely, Thomas Seltzer

Thomas Seltzer to Robert Mountsier

Thomas Seltzer, Inc.
Publishers
5 West Fiftieth Street, New York

Mr. Robert Mountsier
417 West 118th St.
New York City.

Nov. 29, 1920

Dear Mr. Mountsier:

Please call to see me tomorrow, Tuesday, at eleven in the morning or at about half past three in the afternoon. I cannot understand Secker's behavior. I think we shall have to do some cabling in an effort to stop him from continuing his peculiar actions.

Yours sincerely, Thomas Seltzer

Thomas Seltzer to Robert Mountsier

Thomas Seltzer, Inc.
Publishers
5 West Fiftieth Street, New York

Feb. 9, 1921

Dear Mr. Mountsier

Can you drop in to see me to-morrow, Thursday, or ring me up?

Sincerely yours, Thomas Seltzer

Thomas Seltzer to Robert Mountsier

Thomas Seltzer, Inc.
Publishers
5 West Fiftieth Street, New York

Mr. Robert Mountsier
c/o American Express Co.
11, Rue Scribe, Paris

June 17th, 1921

Dear Mr. Mountsier:

You ought by this time to have had several letters from me. But what with printers' strikes and binders' strikes and the hard times, I hardly get an opportunity to attend to my correspondence. So you will forgive me, won't you?

Your sister was at my office the day before yesterday and gave me some poems and the MS on Sardinia.

I don't think you will have to curse me about the picture cover of *Tortoises*. I will have it done properly, don't fear. The trouble is the difficulty of getting any work done at all now. The spring lists of publishers have been badly cut into by strikes and as a result there are very few books published this season. But perhaps this is not an unmitigated evil since it helps us sell the older books.

The Lost Girl continues to sell, not rapidly, but steadily. Of our second edition of 3,000 we have 1500 left, which means that a little over 4,000 have been sold. But the reputation of *The Lost Girl* seems to be growing. I am keeping right on with publicity. Over 12,000 of the enclosed circular have been printed and most of them distributed.

Of *Psychoanalysis and the Unconscious* about 700 copies have been sold so far, which I consider rather good. Most of the reviews show a puzzlement. The critics don't seem to get Lawrence's meaning. I don't want to trouble Lawrence with the reviews but when I get a permanent address from you I will send them to you. I want you to read them. It may be a good thing for Lawrence to reply to the most important ones, as, for example, Llewellyn Jones' who is favorably disposed to Lawrence's work and whose criticism, though showing a surprising lack of intelligence, is, I am sure, honest. On the other hand, I think Lawrence ought to completely ignore Mencken.

Women in Love also continues to sell steadily, but I don't think we have sold more than about fifty since you left. I shall give you exact figures of the amount sold to date in my next letter. When this edition is sold I shall begin to plan a new edition immediately.

The price of books has not gone down much or hardly at all. If conditions keep on as they are I don't see how I can make the price of *Mr. Noon* less than $1.75. In fact, I don't think that it will make any difference in the sale even if the book is $2.00. However, I shall do my best to make it no higher than $1.75.

I have done some thinking about the wisdom of publishing *Mr. Noon* in the fall. The more I think of it the more I am convinced that if *Aaron's Rod* has the possibility of a popular success, that is, if we believe it has a chance of selling at least as well as *The Lost Girl*, and if it is really unobjectionable, then *Aaron's Rod* ought to be the next novel for us. To have another novel against which there is no definite objection follow *The Lost Girl* would give Lawrence a very strong position here. After that we need fear no antagonism. *Mr. Noon* may arouse a storm of protest which we could stand very well after a second success like *The Lost Girl* but not so well before. So I would very much like to see the MS of *Aaron's Rod* before we decide. All of this of course if *Aaron's Rod* is completed in time for fall publication. If not, our course is clear. Fate will then have decided for us that it shall be *Mr. Noon.*

I have so far received replies from Arnold Bennett, May Sinclair and W. L. George. The letters from Bennett and May Sinclair are very satisfactory.

Arnold Bennett:

"I am glad of the opportunity to express my opinion that Mr. Lawrence is the foremost of the younger British novelists and beyond question a genius, and that I have a very great admiration for his work. I greatly admire *The Lost Girl*, which in my opinion, is a novel of great beauty, distinction and force." He says this is not for publication in England. So of course we must respect his confidence.

May Sinclair:

"I have the greatest possible admiration for Mr. D. H. Lawrence's work. I think he is one of the very few novelists of this decade who will live. I consider the suppression of *The Rainbow* a crime—murder of a beautiful thing—dishonoring to everybody concerned in it. And I would be delighted to contribute to your 'symposium' but for two reasons: 1—I am writing a book on metaphysics which will demand my undivided attention for some little time; 2—I shall be writing an appreciation of Mr. Lawrence later on which will be included in a volume of similar essays, and I must not forestall that. I am glad to hear of the success of *The Lost Girl* in your country."

In the event of anything happening in England with *Women in Love,* I shall of course do my best here in support of Lawrence. We will, I think, be able to accomplish a great deal.

By all means let me have definite information about *Movements in European History.* I will publish it as soon as possible if the American rights are not preempted. But I would like to publish it under Lawrence's own name.

A letter from James B. Pond of the Pond Bureau asks whether Lawrence could be got to lecture in this country. He thinks Lawrence will get big audiences here.

Twelve copies of *Psychoanalysis and the Unconscious* were forwarded to Curtis Brown immediately upon receipt of your radiogram. I am afraid that through some error the copy for

Miss Lydia Tyler was not forwarded promptly. I am sorry.

A note from Miss Amy Lowell a few weeks ago—asking for Lawrence's address. So evidently she is all right about Lawrence.

The new edition of *The Rainbow* is still being talked about a lot but not yet in sight.

As the season is late and it was impossible to publish *Tortoises* before, we shall have to postpone it to the fall. Earlier publication is now out of the question for we could get no sales on it. I do wish *Sons and Lovers* were released for us. The pity of it. It is selling continually. What Mitchell Kennerley is about I have no idea. His edition seems to be exhausted. The Sunwise Turn, for example, who had been getting the book from him right along ordered five copies from me some three weeks ago because at Mitchell Kennerley's they were told that they were temporarily out of stock. I think the sooner action is taken on this the better.

Brentano's June Book Chat has not yet made its appearance. It will have a splendid article on Lawrence by Sherwood Anderson which I hope will be largely reprinted in the newspapers.

Glad to hear about Lawrence writing the text for a children's book. Do you think that we can get the American rights?

Send me stories and poems, the lighter the better. I may have a chance to sell them at a good price.

I still owe $50 on *Psychoanalysis*. I am having the devil of a time with collections. The times are as hard as can be. Everybody feels the strain. But be sure I shall take care of you and Lawrence before anybody or anything.

I am going to write to Secker and quote him a price for 100 copies of *Women in Love*.

With best wishes for a jolly and interesting trip for both of you,

Sincerely yours, Thomas Seltzer

Women in Love

One omission occurs on p. 384, line 7 from bottom, after the sentence: "Like a child at the breast, he cleaved intensely to her, and she could not put him away." The sentence omitted is: "And his seared, ruined membrane relaxed, softened; that which was seared and stiff and blasted yielded again, became soft and flexible, palpitating with new life."

209

I cannot for the life of me remember the second omission. I know it is slight, quite slight. I will get it soon by application and will let you have it. I think both are in Secker's edition.

Thomas Seltzer to Robert Mountsier

Thomas Seltzer, Inc.
Publishers
5 West Fiftieth Street, New York

Mr. Robert Mountsier
c/o Frau Baronin von Richthofen
Ludwig-Wilhelmstift
Baden-Baden, Germany

July 16, 1921

Dear Mr. Mountsier:

Many thanks for your letters. I hope you have received mine of June 17th which is a reply to two or three of yours.

I am greatly disturbed that I have not yet received the manuscript of *Aaron's Rod.* You seem to think I have it. If it was sent to me it must have been lost. By all means I want to publish it before Secker does. But I ought to have the manuscript by now. Even so it would be necessary to hurry its manufacture in order to bring it out in September.

But I am thinking of something else. From present indications there is a possibility that *The Lost Girl* will reach its largest sale in the fall. In that case it would be folly to bring out another novel for it would only create confusion and, I am afraid, be harmful to the sale of both. If the matter could be held in suspense for some time, that is to say, if you could keep Secker from publishing it before we are ready to, I would get *Aaron's Rod* printed at once so that we can publish it any time we want. This is the best way. I hope it can be done.

I prefer to bring out *Mr. Noon* in one volume.

The Wintry Peacock they tell me will be published in August. I secured two copies and sent one to Michael Sadler in London and the other to Lawrence, not c/o Cook & Sons, Florence, but to Baden-Baden, because I just received a letter from Lawrence telling me that that address is the safest. I hope it is all right.

Business is extremely dull, practically dead. They say that we have reached the limit and from now on there will be an improvement. Let us hope so. But Lawrence's books are going very nicely. I feel pretty sure that were the times normal we should have sold about 10,000 or 15,000 of *The Lost Girl* by this time and twice as much as we have of *Psychoanalysis and the Unconscious*. As it is, *Psychoanalysis* is now about 700. I am sending you a detailed statement for each title up to June 30 and the amount that will be due for payment on September 30. The $50 balance on the advance for *Psychoanalysis* was paid a couple of days after my last letter to you.

The Lawrence boom is growing. There is hardly a literary page we pick up that has not some mention or other about *The Lost Girl* or some other recent book.

The business situation has somewhat upset publishers. In the middle west they have stopped buying books entirely. Publishers' travellers, who as a rule would by now have covered that territory and be back with their fall orders have not yet started on the road. You see how confusing this is. It means a delay of over two months as the buyers will be taking their vacations through July and August. As a result the publishers' lists are all uncertain. Of course I am also affected by this situation. I am behind with all my fall books including *Tortoises*.

The book on Sardinia with the illustrations Lawrence proposes would be very good for Christmas but I doubt whether it can be gotten ready in time for this year. I shall do my best.

I don't remember if we agreed on a royalty of 10% or 12½% on the first 2,000 copies of *Psychoanalysis*. It ought not be more than 10%. It can't be done. Please don't insist on it. I am spending money freely on publicity for Lawrence. We are accomplishing a good deal. This is worth more than a little bit higher royalty. I want to continue to do it and you must help me. It isn't a question of driving the hardest bargain one way or the other. It is a question of what is best for all of us.

The Rainbow is out at last. The paper is rather nice. I don't care much for the binding.

I'd like to buy some 150 sheets of *The White Peacock* from

Duckworth. If we kept Duckworth's imprint on the title page I don't think it would lose us the copyright. There is a slight demand for it now which I could stimulate somewhat, but not enough to justify making plates.

I sent Secker a quotation for 100 copies of *Women in Love.* Some copies of his edition have been smuggled in. I took very strong measures and I don't believe the book will be imported here to any great extent, but it is bad enough as it is. This cheap English edition is very troublesome because we won't be able to publish it at any time for less than $5 and the fact that there exists in England an edition that can be sold here for $3 at a profit, is a great drawback. I do wish it were possible for us to publish this book in a regular $2.50 edition. I think it would have a considerable sale.

Let me know as soon as possible about the history and also of any further developments in regard to the children's book. If Lawrence comes to an agreement with the Oxford Press be sure to keep the American rights for us.

You mean *Eternal Maiden* by E. T. Harré which was published by Mitchell Kennerley in 1913. It is out of print now. I will try to get a copy for you at no higher price than the original.

By this time I suppose you have joined Lawrence and have had your tramp. Where are you now?

With best wishes,

Sincerely yours, Thomas Seltzer

212

Thomas Seltzer to Robert Mountsier

Thomas Seltzer, Inc.
Publishers
5 West Fiftieth Street, New York

Mr. Robert Mountsier
c/o American Express Co.
11, rue Scribe
Paris, France

August 20, 1921

Dear Mr. Mountsier:

This is just a brief note to tell you the essentials as my bookkeeper is away on her vacation and Miss Turman is leaving in a day and I am in the midst of such a pile of work that I don't know where to begin.

1—The Juta pictures have just been rescued from the Custom House after a lot of red tape, covering more than a week.

2—The Dial has not received the manuscript of *Sea and Sardinia.* To-day, as soon as I got the illustrations, I sent them over with my manuscript of *Sardinia* to Gilbert Seldes (Thayer, you know, is in Europe now) and expect a decision from him within a few days. I think the Juta paintings very good. They will make a striking book. Of course, if you insist on 15% royalty, the price of it will be sky high. I hope they will pay it.

3—*Tortoises* will be ready about the middle of September or, at latest, the end of September, a very good time to bring out a book. The cover design, I believe, will be entirely to your liking. I am taking great pains with the book to make it good looking. But the price will be $1, not $.75.

4—I don't think there is any likelihood of Mitchell Kennerley selling *Sons and Lovers* to Knopf. Knopf, you know, was once employed by Kennerley, and there is no friendship wasted between them. Wherever Knopf worked he is not a favorite. If I find that there is anything on foot I shall certainly get an injunction, if possible. It is an outrage as it is. In spite of the fact that not only is nothing being done for the book but everything against it, apparently *Sons and Lovers* is selling,

213

and why Lawrence should not be getting the royalties due him is beyond my comprehension. Furthermore, it is high time that Lawrence's books be published under one aegis.

5—I didn't know I had signed up a contract to pay so high a royalty on *Psychoanalysis and the Unconscious*. I must have been asleep. Or was it your persuasiveness? If so, am I to pray that you remain away from New York as long as possible? If there will be a second printing I shall of course make the corrections to which Lawrence calls my attention. In the meantime I will have an errata slip printed and tipped in with the next binding order.

6—I shall shortly deposit in your bank $300 or $400 in advance for what is due you for *The Lost Girl* and *Women in Love* on October 1. So that after the first of September you can safely draw on this amount which I will depost to your joint account, should you need to.

7—*Psychoanalysis and the Unconscious* is turning out to be a big success—shall I say, morally speaking? The queer thing about it is that real authorities like Buermeyer and Grace Phelps, and the better critics like Hackett, consider it a great work, and the only people who talk nonsense about it are the ignoramuses. So that *Psychoanalysis and the Unconscious* has decidedly enhanced Lawrence's reputation. You know what my opinion of the book is. I have always though that it was a very important and striking contribution. I am sending Lawrence all the reviews of it as he writes me that he will make a peppery reply to his critics, of which I am mighty glad.

8—I am looking forward to the book by Wassermann you are sending me and the book that will show me the superiority of Austrian printing. I know it is superior. I wish I could do my book work either in Austria or Germany.

9—If possible, I will try to have *Sea and Sardinia* ready for the Christmas market. I think it has a good chance. I am sorry there has been such a delay in getting the illustrations. Curtis Brown asks me for a quotation on sheets and color plates. I shall await word from you before I do anything in the matter.

10—From what Lawrence writes me I gather that I will have the manuscript of *Aaron's Rod* within not more than a week. I am definitely determined to bring it out this fall. I will not have Secker's edition imported here and sold by the hundreds.

11—*The Lost Girl* is still selling nicely and *Women in Love* is doing well considering the times. I don't think we will have any copies left after January 1, and then we will begin to think of a new edition. It cannot do any harm for Lawrence to send me 100 sheets with his signature for *Women in Love*. I doubt whether we could get more for the book than $15 net, even with the signature, inasmuch as the price is already so very high and the English edition does interfere. But it will be easier to sell the book with Lawrence's autograph. Whatever extra I get for the book, I will divide equally with Lawrence. That is to say, if I get $5 more for the book, Lawrence will get $2.50.

12—The new printing of *The Rainbow* is all sold out and is now already commanding a higher price. They are selling it from between $7 to $10. No doubt very soon it will sell for $15. This is an indication, I think, of what *Women in Love* would sell if the price of it were $5. I do wish we had in our hands *The Rainbow, Sons and Lovers*. Then I think I would also bring out *The White Peacock*. Let us work to that end with all our energy. It must be done in some way, the sooner the better. I am to see Mr. Ruben of Stern and Ruben some time next week and then I will write you what he thinks is best to do with regard to *Sons and Lovers*. I talked to him over the phone to-day and he told me Kennerley claims that he did pay some royalty on the book to Lawrence. I don't know exactly how he found out that he claims it since he told me that Kennerley had made no reply to his numerous letters.

13—Grand surprise! About ten days ago the assistant managing editor of the Brooklyn Eagle called me up and told me he wanted to run *The Lost Girl* serially in the Brooklyn Eagle. I immediately cabled to Lawrence. As I have had no reply I suppose the cable did not reach him. I am sorry. I hope we are not going to lose this opportunity. I had not meant to let them run it at once as this would interfere with the sale of the book, but I do want to contract with them for some future date. I don't think we can get much money for the second serial rights. They don't pay much as a rule, but the Brooklyn Eagle is a good, old, conservative organ and it would mean a great deal to us in the matter of publicity. The editor told me that when a serial runs in the Brooklyn Eagle there is usually a demand for it from other papers.

14—Secker changed his mind about *Women in Love* and ordered only 50 copies, not 100. I suppose you have made arrangements with him about royalties on this.

15—The Medici Society seems to have a very good organization for that sort of thing here.

16—What about the history? My proposition is 10% for the first 2500, 12½% for the second 2500 and 15% above.

I think I have covered the most important points.

With best wishes,

Sincerely yours, Thomas Seltzer

You all did seem to have such a good time drinking Meersburger.

T. S.

Thomas Seltzer to Miss Mountsier

Thomas Seltzer, Inc.
Publishers
5 West Fiftieth Street, New York

Oct. 20, 1921

Dear Miss Mountsier:

Here is the galley proof of Sea & Sardinia. Some passages that might have given offense have already been excised. Please strike out anything else you think necessary. This is to be a gift book in general and a Christmas gift book in particular and must be absolutely unobjectionable.

We are late with this publication. So I hope you can read the proof and make the necessary eliminations quickly, so that we can return it to the printer before the week is over.

It is very kind of you to do this for us, and I am greatly obliged to you.

Yours sincerely, Thomas Seltzer

Adele Seltzer to Robert Mountsier

Thomas Seltzer, Inc.
Publishers
5 West Fiftieth Street, New York

Mr. Robert Mountsier
417 W. 118th Street
New York City

January 3, 1922

My dear Mr. Mountsier:

Would you care to have a seat in our box at the Liberator Ball on January 13th?

Mr. Seltzer is going to have a book display there and is going to feature Lawrence. We thought you would be interested, and perhaps might enjoy the ball into the bargain.

Would you please give me Mr. Pillard's address? Mr. Seltzer would like to invite him to the ball too. Do let me have it promptly because there is not very much time.

Sincerely yours, Adele Szold Seltzer

Adele Seltzer to Dorothy Hoskins

Thomas Seltzer, Inc.
Publishers
5 West Fiftieth Street, New York

[1 April 1922]

Dear Mrs. Hoskins:

Indeed I did receive your several communications—a long, breezy letter, the dialect verses, and the Texas pecans. For which my more than warmest thanks. Thanks, indeed, are not adequate. Just what *is* adequate, I don't know. Returning in kind wouldn't be adequate for two reasons. I can't produce the "kind" to return in, and even if I could, it would seem like trying to "get even." So I am helpless. I can merely be poignantly grateful that thousands of miles away there is a dear friend who enriches and adds color and intensity to my life.

I haven't tasted the pecans yet, but I *have* read the Mammy Goose. The verses and illustrations seem very charming to me, very indeed. But there's a "but." Many questions arise in my mind. You say Southern people would read the book. This is not much of an inducement. The South can practically be discounted as a market for books. Then how about the North? There would be no prejudice on account of color, yet some mothers may object to dialect of any sort for their youngsters. However, there are the Uncle Remus stories. These verses would be better if they were not verses, but stories. As an imitation of Mother Goose, they haven't got the proper merry rhythm:

> Jack, be nimble
> Jack, be quick,
> Jack, jump over the candlestick.

That adorable old-fashioned light swing and rapid trot which snatches you up on on to the broom-stick, and over the moon, and away with the spoon, and out bobbing on the sea with the men in the tub. But this point of view of mine is too classical. Though I would be satisfied to bring my children up (if I had children) on a few sappy classics, the rest of the world, the multitudinous rest, is not so eclectic. Therefore, the Mammy Goose verses are going to be given for reading to several readers, each with a different point of view. One runs a successful children's book-shop, another is a modern young woman who has written two books in child study, is chairman of a committee that every year makes a selected list of children's reading, and has written one or two monographs on children's reading, another is a girl who has made a specialty of story-telling to children in settlements, another is this girl's mother, and still another is a regular Mss. reader whom we have recently taken on. She, too, is rather an expert in children's literature, having brought up three children of her own according to most approved modern methods, and having made a study of the whole field of child-education.—I began by saying that the verses are charming. They are. They bring out the rich lovingness in the colored people that makes me so fond of them. The "mammy" is just the dear those old mammies are. And each poem has a delightful theme. I still think that if the themes were worked out in storyform à la Uncle Remus, instead of the rather lumbering metre, it would be better. On the whole, the impression remains one of charm. The illustrations are delightful. No doubts about them of any sort. How much easier the pictorial art seems than the literary art! I think I know why. The intuitional element *must* predominate in the pictorial art, and therefore *does* predominate. In writing there must be an admixture of the intellectual or mental. And the whole difficulty is keeping the proper balance between mind and intuition. I love Lawrence as I do because of his pure strong unspoiled intuitions. And how I *do* love him!

What do you think of this little satire on *Sea and Sardinia?* A friend of ours wrote it for fun. He really likes the book.

The reason I haven't written you before *is* "Sea and Sardinia." I've been tremendously busy "pushing" it. There's a travel show here now. People were to send in votes for the best 25 travel books; then at the show itself now they are voting for the 10 best out of the 25 for a permanent Wanderlust shelf. Sea & Sardinia got on the list of 25. I don't know yet about the ten. We have a booth at the show, and someone must be in attendance all the time. Our display is very striking. An artist friend made a huge, brilliant poster, and also a little stage copying the picture on the jacket. Little dolls dressed in the costume actually emerge from the church in the background.

How tragically amusing that about Mr. Eager's journals! And how particularly interesting in connection with the Widow's Cruse. From the clippings one does absolutely gather that Mrs. Eager is a true Florence Pome—from the clippings taken in conjunction with the cremation of the journals along with *other* trash! And now that the journals have been cremated I am almost more eager to see them, though what you had said of them whetted my anticipations considerably.

No need, is there? to urge you to keep us in mind. Go on scouting for us. Tell us of anything you think marketable. Don't assume we're too highbrow for anything. One needs "best-sellers" to enable one to publish the classical stuff.

That about mental and intuitional reminds me of what I had been meaning to tell you of my feelings about Magdeleine Marx. I think she, too, has right and powerful intuitions, but she spoils them, yes spoils them. She allows barren mental processes to sap the juice from them. She is too eager to reduce them to formulas and creeds. She dogmatises them. As someone very cleverly said, "She is like a plank in a platform." Her dogmatising may proceed from youth and from her ardour for Socialism. But if it isn't knocked out of her now, it may go on and harden and crystallize. I wish she'd come to America. I'd like to put it to her squarely: Does she want to be an artist or an advocate? If an artist, then she must give up special pleading and dedicate herself to glowing life. If an advocate, then she must give up fiction. (Between you & me, I don't *mean* this, not carried out to its logical conclusion. I don't *want* her to give up fiction. As it is, *with* her dogmatising she produces far, far better works than anyone in America.

That club page of yours! You sent me a sample long ago, and I had been meaning to express my wonder and admiration. I couldn't do it, just couldn't. I'd rather hang clothes on a wash-line. *Rather?* Well, more than rather. I *love* hanging clothes on a wash-line if the line extends over a back-garden in the country, not an alley-way in the city.

The enclosed leaflet on Lawrence is a specimen of my work. *If* I weren't connected with Thomas Seltzer, I'd like to go about the country lecturing on him and giving readings from his works. Unfortunately it is so hard to secure The Rainbow & Women in Love, the former because it is out of print, the latter because it is so expensive. Have you read either or both? I can *lend* you copies of both, if you want them. There are parts in each that are more beautiful to me than anything in the entire range of literature going all the way back to Euripides. To use something like Lawrence's own singular metaphors, it is as though he were connected at the core with the mysterious navel of the universe, some old intimate hot blood connection with the very sources and springs of life. My, how I love his works!

Thomas & I both liked and enjoyed your review of A Widow's Cruse.

You will hear from me again when I have tasted the pecans.

Yours, Adele S. Seltzer

Thomas Seltzer, Inc.
Publishers
5 West Fiftieth Street, New York

April 8, 1922

Mrs. Dorothy Hoskins
306 Burr St.
Oaklawn, Houston, Texas

Dear Mrs. Hoskins:

The pecans were tasted an hour or two after I wrote you my last letter. The quantity has been considerably diminished since then. They are perfectly delicious. It makes me feel greedy to eat nuts that I myself don't shell. And I carefully refrain from consuming as many at a time as I am tempted to. This just has to be a hasty letter of thanks. There is lots ahead of me to do today.

Cordially yours, Adele S. Seltzer

Since the above was written a letter from you came. Our lend-about copy of *Women in Love* is in someone else's hands just now, and may not be free for another three weeks. In the meanwhile, don't you want *The Rainbow?* Have you read that? It should be read first, because it plants the childhood of Ursula, who is one of the four main characters in *Women in Love*. And *Women in Love* should be read before *Aaron's Rod*, though the characters are not the same. Lawrence himself regards these three books as a trilogy. To anyone who has a profound instinct in these matters, it is very obvious that in the trilogy he expresses the emotional conflicts of young people (especially himself as a young man). At first they are chaotic, unclear, hazy, almost incomprehensible. *Aaron's Rod*, demonstrating Lawrence's own emergence into maturity, sets forth the conflict in great clarity, almost precision.

The man's a god! We have another work of his, *Fantasia of the Unconscious*, that ought to produce a revolution in our thought.

No, I have not read the Midget book. Ought I? I have not
even heard of it. Tell me about it.

Yours, Adele S. S.

Thomas Seltzer to Robert Mountsier

Thomas Seltzer, Inc.
Publishers
5 West Fiftieth Street, New York

Mr. Robert Mountsier
c/o Walker
Elizabeth, Pa.

May 25, 1922

Dear Mr. Mountsier:

Thank you for your letter of May 22.

Our Eleven Billion Dollars
All the reviews so far have been extremely favorable, and I
have heard favorable comment from various people. It has
established you firmly as a financial expert. I am placing an ad
in the Library Journal, in the Times, the Nation and in
Publishers' Weekly. I also expect to print a circular, as we
have enough reviews now to make a good showing, and have
them distributed ourselves by mail and also through book
jobbers and book dealers. The book should be adopted as a
text book in economic classes. I wonder whether you can help
us in this? The sales so far have been few and far between, but
then scarcely anything sells just now.

I should like to keep the pamphlet containing the list of
special libraries for another week.

Fantasia of the Unconscious
I will publish this by the end of August, and *Studies in
Classic American Literature* the first week in October.

Dregs.
Guilty. Haven't yet read it. But I promise solemnly to read it
before the end of next week and act on it.

Sea and Sardinia and Secker.

Can't do anything with Secker as he will not buy the bound copies and I don't see my way to printing a second edition before we have sold at least half of our first edition. Moreover, Secker has not yet paid us the bill, long past due, for *Women in Love*. We can't get a check from him, nor can we get him to say anything about it.

The Captain's Doll.

Hapgood had accepted *The Captain's Doll*. But he wants to run it in one issue, and therefore must cut it down to about 2/5. He thinks, and I think he is right, that a story of this character cannot run for three months for readers of his class. We may be able to get $1500 for it, or at least $1000. I shall try for $1500. He means to run it in October but says he will make an effort to do it sooner, if that will help me. If it were possible to communicate with Lawrence, I am of the opinion that we ought not to permit it to be cut so much without Lawrence's consent. But as it is, I believe we shall have to make up our minds ourselves. Apart from the money, it will do Lawrence a lot of good to appear with so excellent a story in a magazine with so large a circulation. I am strongly in favor of selling it to them. Let me know at once what you think.

The Ladybird.

I don't think any magazine will take this, except perhaps The Dial.

It seems as though we wil be able to publish all three stories in the fall, of which I am very glad.

Perhaps you had better telegraph me about *The Captain's Doll*.

Aaron's Rod continues to have a fair sale. It has also received very favorable reviews together with big knocks. One man writes a long review of three columns, saying that on reviewing *Women in Love* he had ventured the opinion that Lawrence is the greatest writer writing in the English language at present, and that this book bears it out.

We have also had some good reviews of *Tortoises* recently.

I gather from the Times review by Galsworthy of Edward Garnett's *Friday Nights*, that he has in it an extremely favorable article on Lawrence.

What are you doing now? Are you writing anything? If you hit upon a popular subject for your next book, I am sure it will be a success.

Sincerely yours, Thomas Seltzer

Are you getting the reviews of your book? If not we'll send you what we have.

Adele Seltzer to Dorothy Hoskins

Thomas Seltzer, Inc.
Publishers
5 West Fiftieth Street, New York

May 25, 1922

Mrs. Dorothy Hoskins
306 Burr Street
Oaklawn, Houston, Texas

Dear Dorothy:

By this time the promised copy of *The Rainbow* has gone off to you. I only just got our lend-about copy back from the last borrower. I hope you love it as much as I do. Oh, it is so beautiful.

I am almost done with *Memoirs of a Midget*. In my next letter, I will go into effusions over that. In the meantime, just fond greetings.

Cordially yours, Adele S.

Thomas Seltzer to Robert Mountsier

Thomas Seltzer, Inc.
Publishers
5 West Fiftieth Street, New York

Mr. Robert Mountsier
c/o Walker
Elizabeth, Pa.

June 12, 1922

Dear Mr. Mountsier:

Just a word now. I have worked day and night for the last two weeks, and so was unable to keep as up to date with you as I should like to have done.

Your book continues to get good reviews.

Enclosed is a letter from Mr. Burton of McCall's Magazine.

I am bargaining with Hearst's International. One thousand dollars sure. I am holding out for more, but I doubt if we can get any more.

Please send me MS of *Studies in Classic American Literature.* I have none of the essays in the office. I should also like to have the MS of *Birds, Beasts, and Flowers.*

Tonight I expect to read more of *Dregs.* I read some more, but it was really impossible for me to finish it. It was not neglect. I used every spare moment. After chapter four the style gets to be very poor; it's not even grammatical.

Sincerely yours, Thomas Seltzer

Thomas Seltzer, Inc.
Publishers
5 West Fiftieth Street, New York

Mr. Robert Mountsier
c/o Walker
Elizabeth, Pa.

June 17, 1922

Dear Mr. Mountsier:

I am sending you enclosed a check for $200.00 on account of royalties due to D. H. Lawrence up to January 1st. Within the next week or so I hope to be able to let you have the balance. On September 1st, there will, of course, be a considerable amount due to Lawrence on royalties for *Aaron's Rod* up to June 1st. If Lawrence needs it, I shall do my best to pay all or whatever is possible before that date.

The Hearst matter should have been clinched this week, but Hapgood suddenly left for Washington and will not be back before next Tuesday. I shall try to wind up the sale next week. I think they pay on acceptance.

We have sent out a number of letters to influential people this week about your book and sent a few copies to persons in high places, such, for instance, as President Harding, M. Jusserand and Coudert. Mr. Charles read your book and is mad about it. He is pushing it for all he is worth. In time, I believe, we will get the highest sale possible for it. Whether this will be large or small, I don't know.

I received a letter from Curtis Brown of London complaining about the price I asked for the sheets and instancing the lower prices quoted to them by American publishers for regular sized novels. They forget that the cost of 20 plates is a considerable item which does not enter in novels. However, I shall see whether I can't quote them a lower price. They ask for a quotation on 500 and 1,000.

So far it has not been moving at all. We get an order for a copy or two occasionally, no more, which considering the splendid reviews it has received puzzles me.

I am very much interested in Bunin's book and will write

you further about it in a couple of days. I saw a copy of the English edition in a book store here. They had only one copy which had been sold in advance. The English binding is very pretty, but it is a small volume which can't sell for more than $1.25, so I am trying to figure out where I will come off. The price is not high for an ordinary sized book but for so small a book it is rather steep, considering that they are short stories, the hardest thing to sell. I like the binding so much that I am thinking, if I take it, of the possibility of importing it bound with our imprint. Will you please write them and ask what they would charge for 520 copies bound and for 1050?

I hope you have recovered completely from your accident.

Sincerely yours, Thomas Seltzer

Thomas Seltzer to Robert Mountsier

Thomas Seltzer, Inc.
Publishers
5 West Fiftieth Street, New York

Mr. Robert Mountsier
c/o Walker
Elizabeth, Pa.

June 22nd, 1922

Dear Mr. Mountsier:

I have your two letters of June 19th. I have asked for an estimate from the printers for 500 and 1,000 copies of *Our Eleven Billion Dollars.* As soon as I get it, probably tomorrow morning, I will write to Curtis Brown. I hope to be able to give them a much better price, for I am eager to have the book published in England even if I have to sell the sheets at cost.

The enclosed letter from Mr. H. N. Lawrie will interest you. I think it advisable for you to put yourself in touch with him. If you can appear as a witness before the committee, it ought to help the book considerably.

There is a great deal of interest in *Our Eleven Billion Dollars* in various quarters. The book may start some day. It isn't ephemeral, and events may shape themselves at any moment so that it will *become known* as vital instead of merely *being* vital.

I shall see what can be done about syndication. When it begins to make some noise, then is the time to try. But not before we have something with which to hit the editors on the head.

I don't take much stock in the reviews of the Literary Review. Mr. Canby has an uncanny faculty for getting the wrong reviewers in almost every instance. As for himself, he tries very hard, poor fellow, to be up-to-date, and for this we must give him credit. His article on Lawrence is, of course, absurd. Nevertheless, it helped a good deal.

The arrangement for you to keep the British rights of your book, exclusive of Canada, suits me all right.

There was an error in my previous letter to you in reference to royalties on *Aaron's Rod*. I meant, of course, July 1, not June 1st, and October 1, not September 1st. Yes, there will be $500 due as advance. But there will be a good deal more due also by September 1st.

I have sold *The Captain's Doll* for $1,000 and a check is coming in a week or so. The next story we sell to Hearst I feel pretty sure we can get more for. Had a talk with John Peale Bishop about *The Lady Bird*. They would be only too glad to take a story by Lawrence if they could get one about 3,000 words long. But I gave him the MS of *Ladybird*. He may reduce it to 10,000 words and run it in three issues, September to November. If Vanity Fair doesn't take it, I don't believe any other magazine will, except The Dial. It is superb, but not popular enough for a magazine like the Red Book.

There is a very popular show now on in the Neighborhood Theatre in which a girl reading a book says to her sweetheart who speaks to her: "Don't interrupt me. I am in the midst of one of the most passionate passages of D. H. Lawrence." This, they say, always brings the house down.

Lawrence expected to cable me his address on his arrival in Australia. I have received no cable and I do not know his address.

A copy of Mr. Lawrie's testimony before the Banking and Currency Committee was received in this office yesterday and immediately forwarded to you by registered mail.

Just received an editorial on your book from the Omaha Bee with a very complimentary letter from the editor, congratulating me on the excellence of our publications in general and on your book in particular. As he enclosed a letter for you which he asked me to forward, I suppose he is sending you the editorial. If not, I will send you our copy. This is the kind of publicity I like. From all appearances the book ought to make its way.

Received also letter from the President's secretary promising to bring your book to the President's attention.

Sincerely yours, Thomas Seltzer

An auditing statement June 30 to Dec. 31, 1921. I want to speak to you about royalties on "Psychoanalysis and the Unconscious" and "Tortoises." It is impossible for me to pay 15% on the first 5000 of these books as you can see for yourself. You know I am reasonable, and you also know I have no money to lose.

T. S.

Thomas Seltzer to Robert Mountsier

Thomas Seltzer, Inc.
Publishers
5 West Fiftieth Street, New York

Mr. Robert Mountsier
c/o Walker
Elizabeth, Pa.

June 29, 1922

Dear Mr. Mountsier:

I am sending a check today for $1,000 to the Charleroi Savings and Trust Co.

I have given Curtis Brown the following quotations for *Our Eleven Billion Dollars*:

> 1,000 flat sheets at 30 cents a copy
> 500   at 35 cents a copy
> exclusive of author's royalty.

If John Lane accepts this offer, we will print the book for him using not quite as expensive a paper in the American edition but good enough, quite satisfactory. We are sending a sample of the paper to England. If he kicks about this price, then there is nothing to be done. I have never seen an English publisher make so favorable an offer, though when sheets are imported from England we have to pay a duty, while they get theirs free of duty.

Thank you for the copy of Bunin's stories. I see that the book is even smaller than I had thought. It is only about 80 pages. It would be foolish to import it. Setting it up here would be as cheap, perhaps even cheaper. And the advantages of manufacturing it here are great. We can distribute a larger number of review copies; the dealer considers a home-made book as more important, and there are various other advantages. I will pay a royalty of 10%, but no more. No advance.

Fowler, I understand, is an ex-congressman and is now engaged as a financial expert and is very close to the administration. The President seems to rely a good deal on his opinion in financial matters.

Bishop of Vanity Fair returned *Ladybird*. He can't reduce it enough to run in one issue and he does not see how the story can be broken into parts. However, he wants shorter stories by Lawrence. I think that among the stories I gave you there are some I have not yet read. If any of these have not been published in English magazines, please send them to me.

Fantasia of the Unconscious will be published early in the fall. Also *Studies in Classic American Literature.* I think it is rather late for *Dregs* this fall. Our traveller has covered most of the territory already and we can't get the best results for the book this fall.

As for *Sea and Sardinia*, Miss Kameny has been away the whole week. But I don't see how I can pay a higher royalty than 10%. Even without any royalty the loss is considerable, several hundred dollars. If we had sold the whole edition, I could have just managed to pay 15% since Lawrence has to pay Juta. But as it is, I think it only fair that the loss should be reduced by a smaller royalty, and 10% is a very good royalty.

This is an awful day, awfully muggy. I am swamped with work and my head is spinning round. I don't know whether I have covered every point. If not, I will do so some other time.

Yes, Seldes is in New York, unless he just left. The Dial

people seem to be very much alive. They are offering *Aaron's Rod* as a premium and I think they will do well with it.

Sincerely yours, Thomas Seltzer

Adele Seltzer to Thomas Seltzer

Camp Aradia
Westport, Ontario
Canada

Thursday, July 13, 1922

Dearest Toby:

The damn mail arrangements here! Caesar was only fooling when he said I had walked and not written. You should receive a letter from me daily, and I made extra special efforts that you should receive a letter from me Monday because it was the letter about Mirrors. I sent the Ms. at the same time marking it Ms. Rush Important. On Friday Ida heard that the next day (Saturday afternoon) a farmer's wife in the neighborhood was going to motor to a large town nearby from which mail goes more frequently & promptly than from Westport. So Saturday noon Ida & I tramped with the letter & Ms. to the farm just so you should receive them the first thing. Monday. And the dictionary hasn't come. If the dictionary doesn't come, I don't translate Barbusse. I only hope the proof of Maya is not delayed. I wrote Mr. Irving to send it first class & mark it first class Rush Imp. By this time I should have received some Maya, ought n't I? I asked Mr. Irving to let me have it in sections, not all at once.

Well, the *Relativitätsroman* won't do at all. I reject it absolutely. I *do* think Alfred Goldsmith would be amused by it in spots. But it has no plot, no suspended interest. It is a rather commonplace Utopist novel—attempts something like Bellamy. The Utopist part is positively revolting, and what love episodes there are, are not pleasing to Americans. Caesar will be returning to N.Y. about July 24. Shall I hold the German until then & let him take it back to N.Y. I wish you or I had had sense enough to arrange for him to bring some Maya proof. It's hard to realize beforehand that mail arrangements can be so wretched. Just think—a letter posted by you Monday night does not reach me until Thursday morning.

I should be happy to read Mss. for you here, but I'd like to make sure that the mail is safe enough to entrust Mss. to it. I have no proof yet that it is unsafe, only that it is slow, inconvenient & irregular. If Mirrors reaches you Tuesday, we can conclude, I suppose, that matter sent 1st class registered is safe.

Amy Lowell! Vile! You remember, don't you? that I took a violent dislike to her. I don't think she's done you any harm with Lawrence, rather inspired a fellow-feeling for you in him. I'd love to see what you wrote him and—her! Perhaps it's a tribute to your importance in the world of publishing and letters that you are suffering the "slings and arrows of outrageous" humanity. When one crawls about a modest little worm, the world steps on one; when one struts and flaunts brilliant plumage the world shoots from unsuspected coverts. You're a gorgeous "erotic" bird now. See?

About sending The Nation. Thanks for the offer. Ida says to wait until Caesar comes. He may have made arrangements to have their Nation mailed here.

So far I have done practically no tramping. Ida loafs along; she doesn't walk. I can go a short distance with a loafer. More than that is a fret to my nerves. Altogether I have an easily fretted disposition. I suffer so, really genuinely suffer, from what nearly everybody I know except you and my family does to me. I call it grabbing at my vitals. It must be something like Lawrence's suffering from possessive women. He feels his integrity impaired. So do I feel mine. I have no defenses against prying questions or prying conduct in general. I suffer that there is practically steady, running comment on every act. When I retire to my room for privacy, all I can do is use the hour or two to dress my spiritual wounds, so to speak. They never have a chance really to heal. If I wake up during the night, as I have regularly since I have been here, it is to suffering, really Toby, real suffering. I can't do anything about it. In fact, I must pat myself on the back & say I am fine, for though everything in me rises in furious revolt, my outside betrays nothing but serenity, contentment and complete approval. Matters will change infinitely for the better when you menfolk are here. There is only one person left in the world in whom I have faith, Aline. I *don't* think she'd make me suffer. We human beings don't seem to be meant for each other. Even when we are not criminal, or abominable like Amy Lowell, but generous, fine, noble, honorable, lovable, we have such power to hurt. *Is* my suffering petty? Tell me. You know, it's very much like the feeling with which Mrs. S. inspires me and absolutely the same feeling as I used to get from Anita Black.

Don't magnify this. There are *tremendous* compensations, and as time passes and the period of adjustment is over, & men are here, the situation will change completely. The *only* reason I speak of it is that I wanted you to know the conclusion to which I have come—that you and I *must* have a place to ourselves, not in the suburbs, but in a remote spot. It's a *spiritual* need.

Don't refer to this in your letter. I keep your letters. They lie about. I read parts aloud. Time enough when you come here, as you *will* July 28.

It seems it's been cooler in N.Y. than here. Last night a great storm broke the hot spell. Today it's lovely.

Love & love again, A.

Thomas Seltzer to Adele Seltzer

219 West 100th Street
New York

July 14, 1922

My dearest Darling:

Today came the first letter showing that you had received a letter from me. Things do arrive in the end after all.

Caesar will have told you of the dramatic occurrence or perhaps you have read about it before in The Times. I didn't want you to know about it a moment before it could be helped. I wanted you to enjoy the first days of your vacation and I was afraid you'd worry. Now don't worry. The case is being conducted properly, I think, and it looks hopeful. I have engaged an excellent lawyer for this purpose—Jonah Goldstein and he seems to know his business in this matter. I have many interesting things to tell you, but I won't tell them now. The papers are all with us and we are putting up a big fight. I have received a letter from a prominent lawyer, Miles M. Dawson, which, I am sorry, I haven't a copy of with me to send you. I'll try to get a copy tomorrow. He'll be a witness. So will Heywood Broun and Norman Hapgood and lots of other good people. Dr. Stragnell gave an interview to The Evening Post yesterday—splendid. He will be a witness and try to bring with him Dr. Kaempf. We are up against a gang of toughs, but Goldstein seems to know how to fight them.

Of course the burden upon me was terrific. At first I thought I'd break under it—all alone and with so much other work. However I had to let the other work rest for the time being except as much as the office force could attend to. Now I feel better. Beatrice called me up today on her way to camp and asked if she could help. Isn't she a dear girl?

I am awaiting H [Henrietta Szold]'s letter. Also a postal from Mrs. Schiff and the Wallenstein wedding announcement.

Lots of love, Thomas

Thomas Seltzer to Adele Seltzer

219 West 100th Street
New York

July 15, 1922

My dearest darling:

I started late tonight on the dictionary. It took me an age, and was rather trying on my eyes as I am tired. So I won't write all I expected. Just a word, a how-do-you-do and acknowledgment of your sweet letter about my being "a gorgeous erotic bird."

Am enclosing letter to Literary Review about Canby's article on D. H. L. If you have time and inclination you might answer pointing out that "Sons & Lovers" is *not* Lawrence's best. Don't use your own name. You might also hand out a compliment to Canby. We like appreciation, why shouldn't he? At least he makes an attempt to understand, and deserves praise for this.

Lots, lots and lots of love,

Yours, Thomas

219 West 100th
New York

July 24, 1922

My dearest:

No letter from you today. I missed it very much. Either you skipped a day or the mail, the wonderful mail, performed one of its customary tricks. I wonder whether the railway strike has anything to do with the irregularities.

Things are shaping themselves very favorably. The Supreme Court last Friday a week ago handed down a decision in favor of Halsey, a clerk of McDevitt-Wilson in the case of Mlle de Maupin. The opinion of the ten judges against two was published yesterday in The World. It more than pleads the case for us. But as precedents are so much, perhaps everything, in lawsuits, this is splendid.

The Sunday World will have a whole page on censorship in connection with our case. It is getting the opinion of American writers. Cosgrove is doing it, and it will be in our favor, I presume. I don't think it will appear before the trial, but it may prove valuable anyway.

I have not yet heard from Boss. I telegraphed him today. I hope he does not go back on us. I want Maya to come out on time.

Batouala is evidently going to be a big book. One of the colored agents in St. Louis, an important member of the Negro Associated Press and of the Negro newspaper, the St. Louis Argus, is taking up the work in a small part of the Middle West to the Pacific Coast and says he'll sell 60,000 copies. He seems to be a hustler. He has written a splendid review of the work. The Negroes have a great talent among them, more than I thought. Even if he sells only half for his share it's enough.

This is the worst day we have had yet. Last night I could not sleep, and the girls tell me they couldn't either. A steady rain has set in since about 5 o'clock and it seems the hot spell is broken. Let us hope so.

I await your letter tomorrow eagerly. I hope I have succeeded in reassuring you in my letters. Lots & lots of love,

Thomas

235

219 West 100th Street
New York

31 July 1922

My dearest:

Well, this was an arduous day. But also very interesting. Everything came off smoothly. Our witnesses were great, dignified, impressive and they talked well. Dawson is a big man and the judge showed the greatest respect for him. Van Doren *is* a dear and his testimony was fine. Dr. Sterne, Dr. Stragnell, Gilbert Seldes and others. I took the stand at the last and I felt apparently not the least nervousness.

Of course the judge is supposed to read the books and so he has to take about two weeks. A decision cannot be reached at once in such a case. Jonah Goldstein is a brick. He says the case is won. I do hope it's so.

I can't write you more now. I am exhausted. I did not sleep well last night and got up early at 7. I want to go out for a while. Soon I shall see you anyway; perhaps the day this letter reaches you if the mail plays one of its funny tricks. How I want to see you and have you in my arms, dear.

Lots, lots of love, Thomas

Adele Seltzer to Dorothy Hoskins

Thomas Seltzer, Inc.
Publishers
5 West Fiftieth Street, New York

August 29, 1922

Mrs. Dorothy Hoskins
306 Burr Street
"Oaklawn",
Houston, Texas.

Dear Dorothy:

You are a gem. Thomas and I so appreciate the pains you went to give us a verdict of the manuscript submitted. Thomas has not yet gone into the matter in detail so I don't know just what action we shall take.

From Canada I sent you a picture postal acknowledging your nice long letter, and telling you that I hoped to be able to answer it when I got to New York. *BUT*—when I got to New York. I don't swim very well in water and I feel like the same kind of a wretched swimmer in this element of surging details that is the publishing business. Every now and then I go down, down, down. What it is that pulls me up to the top, I don't know. At the present time Mr. Seltzer's secretary is on her vacation and I am trying to help a bit. I had a letter dictated to you last week, but the Public Stenographer engaged left in the middle of her work without finishing the typing.

Lawrence! You *will* have your essay, won't you? Well doesn't the very review you sent from the Westminster Gazette make you see what it is in Lawrence that so enslaves me? Doesn't the Westminster Gazette pay a tribute to his witchery? But he is lots more to me than that. Lawrence is the throbbing vital life of today with the genius of a sort of a combination of Shakespeare and Dostoevsky.

And that charge of sex obsession. To defend that charge would be as though I had to defend a charge against my own personality. If Lawrence is sensual and obsessed with sex then I am sensual and obsessed with sex. Now if I don't feel that he is obsessed by sex and you do feel it, it just resolves itself into a matter of feeling and what can I do to prove that he isn't obsessed by sex? If I don't feel it I don't know why other people feel it. Therefore, I don't know how to meet the charge.

I realize that in the Rainbow he goes into detail regarding the love life of several generations and my only feeling about that is that he didn't do it as well as he did with the sex torment of Aaron in Aaron's Rod. He was very very young when he wrote the Rainbow. He was fumbling around, groping around, but I don't mind that. It was not the fumbling of an inferior person. I loved it as I love the awkward gait of a puppy that I know absolutely is going to develop into a graceful fleet hound. Oh! Lawrence is so beautiful, so wonderful. How can I declare him to you? It would be like trying to declare the beauty of a tempest, of a mountain torrent, of a glacier.

You and I simply must meet. I know that I could make you love Lawrence as I do. I know that I could drive that idea of sex obsession out of your mind not by argument, but just by making you love Lawrence as I do.

We are going to send you his forthcoming book Fantasia of the Unconscious, and perhaps along with that volume I will write you again concerning my sympathy with his philosophy as expressed in that book.

Our office has orders to send all books to you at your home address. That is where Batouala should have gone. I hope it reached you safely.

Again lots and lots of thanks for the trouble you took about the automobile manuscript. Really it was so good of you. You are one of those persons that one can count on absolutely as one can count on a mountain not to move. Lots of love.

Cordially, Adele

AS / EN

Aren't my dictated letters horrid? This was dictated to a girl in for the day.

238

Thomas Seltzer to Robert Mountsier

Thomas Seltzer, Inc.
Publishers
5 West Fiftieth Street, New York

Mr. Robert Mountsier
Elizabeth,
Penna.

September 2, 1922

Dear Mr. Mountsier:

I am in receipt of your letter of September 1st.

Miss Kameny is away on her vacation, and I cannot get a statement of the balance due to Lawrence until her return. I will send you Four Hundred Dollars in about a week or ten days. This sum, as far as I recall, approximately covers the amount.

I expect to be able to publish *Fantasia of the Unconscious* on the 15th of this month, and *England My England* the first week in October.

As to copyright, I think it best to continue as heretofore, that is, take copyright out in our name and assign to Lawrence. I will try to get the accepted forms for this early next week and send them on to you in accordance with the contracts.

Have I your authority to start the printing of "A Gentleman from California" by Bunin on the basis of our verbal agreement for this book? That is—$100 advance; 10% royalty on the first 5,000, 15% above; $50 of the advance to be paid upon the signing of the agreement and $50 on publication.

Sincerely yours, Thomas Seltzer

239

Thomas Seltzer, Inc.
Publishers
5 West Fiftieth Street, New York

Mr. Robert Mountsier
417 W. 118 Street
New York City

September 5, 1922

Dear Mr. Mountsier:

In case Lawrence needs some money immediately, I am sending you enclosed a check for $200. I will send you another $200 check shortly.

Sincerely yours, Thomas Seltzer

Thomas Seltzer, Inc.
Publishers
5 West Fiftieth Street, New York

Mr. Robert Mountsier
c/o Walker
Elizabeth, Pa.

September 16th, 1922

Dear Mr. Mountsier:

As promised I am sending you enclosed another check for $200 on account of royalties for D. H. Lawrence.

I wonder if you have been getting the New York papers. It was double column display news in most of the evening papers, in the Sun on the first page, carried in all editions. The following day again prominent in the morning papers, with editorials which still continue. The Publishers' Weekly just out, has about four pages with the Judge's opinion complete.

240

Everybody is happy about it. It was really a popular cause in the true sense.

Sincerely yours, Thomas Seltzer

Adele Seltzer to Dorothy Hoskins

Thomas Seltzer, Inc.
Publishers
5 West Fiftieth Street, New York

Dear Dorothy:

Several days ago I returned the prayer for our dear maltreated beasts, and I couldn't get a chance to tell you until today that Stokes in N.Y. & the Clurgs in Chicago publish such cards. Success to you!

I'm so glad you feel about Batouala as you do. And of course I put back my ears and wag my tail when you pat me on the head for the translation. You should see some of the mean things the N.Y. critics say. One insinuated that I left out parts because they were too difficult for me. Parts *were* left out, but not by me. I translated every word & Thomas excised for the sake of the dear American public, which cannot stomach its literature too strong.

Have you been reading what Thomas has been thro lately—that the N.Y. Soc. for the Suppression of Vice raided his office, confiscated all copies (800 in all) [of] *A Young Girls Diary, Women in Love, Casanova's Homecoming,* & haled him to court on the charge of selling obscene literature. The weeks before the verdict was rendered were *hell*. But now it's all over. The Judge as you'll see from our ad. enclosed entirely exonerated Thomas & since then orders have been rushing in for the three "obscene" books. Can you understand that we've been busy?

Affectionately, Adele S. S.

Sept. 19

Thomas Seltzer, Inc.
Publishers
5 West Fiftieth Street, New York

Mr. Robert Mountsier
c/o Walker
Elizabeth, Pa.

October 5th, 1922

Dear Mr. Mountsier:

If you were in New York and dropped in the office occasionally and saw how rushed we are you would not blame me for not answering your letter promptly. I have been obliged to neglect the most important correspondence and you are among the first to whom I am writing.

The Bankers' Convention here will, I am afraid, not help your book. They are taking such a different attitude. And then McKennas's speech. I don't suppose any plan will be adopted. They talk of cancellation or partial cancellation of the debt. But it will probably never be done formally. What will happen, probably, is what nearly always happens in the case of a bad debt. It just has to be given up because it can't be collected. However, I am no competent judge in matters of finance. What I know is that in the past six or eight weeks, we have hardly sold a single copy of *Our Eleven Billions*, and yet most favorable reviews still continue to be written.

We have sent some review copies to England and will send some more. In addition to having a load of work on me, I am handicapped further by Miss Turman's absence. She has been away on account of illness for nearly two months. She had a bad cough and the doctor advised a complete rest.

There is great danger of losing *Sons and Lovers* entirely. This is an outrage. As nothing can be done with Kennerley the only thing left is to try to prevent Boni & Liveright from acting as an accomplice in this outrage. How to do it is the question. Perhaps it would be best for you to come here.

Have I used the word "ultimatum" wrongly? In that case, then, it was not an ultimatum and there is no reason why we should not come to an agreement. You are quite right in

wanting the transfers of copyrights promptly, and you shall
have them promptly henceforth. This will give all the
protection needed. But to make a complete change now is not,
in my opinion, a good thing. *Women in Love* I have
copyrighted in Lawrence's name, and so, for the new edition, I
am again copyrighting it in Lawrence's name, to avoid a
change. I do hope you will agree. I assure you it is all right.

We haven't a copy left of *Women in Love*. The new edition
will be ready in about three weeks.

Sincerely yours, Thomas Seltzer

Thomas Seltzer to Robert Mountsier

Thomas Seltzer, Inc.
Publishers
5 West Fiftieth Street, New York

Mr. Robert Mountsier
Elizabeth, Pa.

October 14, 1922

Dear Mr. Mountsier:

I have your letters of October 11th and 13th.

I am sending you enclosed a check for $500.00 on account of
royalties due to D. H. Lawrence up to June 30th of this year.
The total is about $700.00. A detailed statement will be sent to
you next Monday.

No deductions were made from the advance on *Psychoanalysis and the Unconscious,* according to Miss Kameny. The
deductions were from the royalties on that book only, which is
of course in order. However, I'll look into this matter and if any
error was made it will be corrected.

You yourself suggested that we consult Lawrence on the
royalty of *Sea and Sardinia.* So we had better not act on this
until Lawrence's wishes are known.

Fantasia of the Unconscious and *England My England* are
being bound now, and a change in the copyright is no longer
possible, even if I were willing to concede your point, which I
am not.

Women in Love also will be published next week.

With regard to your totally unwarranted complaint about payments, I have nothing to say.

I think that Kennerley has sold the rights of a cheap reprint only, but I am not sure. An appeal to justice would not work in those quarters, I am afraid, but they might be shamed into justice by publicity. The Authors' League might help, but I gather from a talk with Schuler that for this your presence as agent is necessary. I think the new edition is scheduled in about a month.

Some of the manuscripts Magnus submitted to me direct, others I received from the Paget Literary Agency, 62 West 47th Street.

Lawrence writes me that you are sending me the typescript of *Kangaroo*. I am awaiting it with interest.

Sincerely yours, Thomas Seltzer

Thomas Seltzer to Robert Mountsier

Thomas Seltzer, Inc.
Publishers
5 West Fiftieth Street, New York

Mr. Robert Mountsier
Elizabeth, Penna.

November 3, 1922

Dear Mr. Mountsier:

Women in Love was published October 18.
Fantasia of the Unconscious October 25.

A copy of *Fantasia* should have been sent to you with the other three books. My instructions were to send you all the three books together with *Maya the Bee.* But through some error in the shipping room it was not included. I am having it sent to you today.

The first edition of *Women in Love* was a little over 3,000 copies. I had to order a second printing three days before the date of publication. The first edition is entirely sold out and we are starting on the second one, which is out today. I shall write you soon again.

Sincerely yours, Thomas Seltzer

P.S. *England My England* was published October 24.

Thomas Seltzer to Robert Mountsier

Thomas Seltzer, Inc.
Publishers
5 West Fiftieth Street, New York

Mr. Robert Mountsier
417 W. 118th Street
New York City

November 22, 1922

Dear Mr. Mountsier:

Miss Bien of the Elks Magazine called up today and wanted information about you: whether you did writing for newspapers and magazines and whether you had written any other books.

The editor of the magazine read your book and was greatly impressed with it, and it seems he is considering ordering articles from you for his publication. I think it will be a good thing for you to get in touch with Miss Bien as soon as possible. The address is 50 E. 42 Street; the telephone Vanderbilt 8756.

How are you? Have you been operated on yet?

I am bearing the matter of reassignment of copyright in mind and will attend to it shortly. As usual, I am overburdened with work.

I hope you are well.

Sincerely yours, Thomas Seltzer

Thomas Seltzer to Robert Mountsier

Thomas Seltzer, Inc.
Publishers
5 West Fiftieth Street, New York

Mr. Robert Mountsier
417 West 118th Street
New York City

November 25th, 1922

Dear Mr. Mountsier:

If we are to publish any books by Lawrence in the Spring I ought to have copy at once. Most of our Spring books were handed in to the printer weeks ago. The only way to avoid typographical errors is by giving ourselves plenty of time.

I am glad you are getting on so well. Do you think you can see me next week.

Yours sincerely, Thomas Seltzer

"Women in Love" going well.

Thomas Seltzer to Robert Mountsier

Thomas Seltzer, Inc.
Publishers
5 West Fiftieth Street, New York

Mr. Robert Mountsier
417 West 118th Street
New York City

November 28, 1922

Dear Mr. Mountsier:

This being towards the end of the month Miss Kameny is very busy. So I am sending you on account a check for $300.00. I will let you have a corrected statement and also a statement for every title on December 5. If you must have it before let me know.

246

If Lawrence needs more money I may be able to let you have some next week.

Yours sincerely, Thomas Seltzer

Adele Seltzer to Thomas Seltzer

Schaar & Company
Manufacturers & Dealers
Laboratory Supplies
Scientific Instruments and Chemicals
556-558 West Jackson Boulevard
Chicago, U.S.A.

Dear Toby,

Here I am, with three hours in Chicago to spend with the Schaars. All the boys and Sarah & Clarence's wife are going to have lunch with me just before my train leaves.

You *did* have to spend two nights on the train, didn't you? And I seriously hope you obeyed my instructions on leaving Los Angeles & told the conductor you wanted to stop over at San Francisco. How many "Fred Harvey" meals did you have? I had two & breakfast on the train. I wonder what Lawrence would say to the American institution of Fred Harvey.

I read steadily, but even so got through only a half of *Mastro-don Gesualdo*. It's a superb thing, lusty & kicking with life, but after the middle of the book one get's a little weary of the perpetual Sicilian kicking.

I *hated* to be riding back without you. I'd even have preferred "Lawrence is great, *isn't* he?" "Lawrence is a remarkable character, *isn't* he?" "Lawrence is a wonderful man, *isn't* he?" all the way. However, I did get some reading done & made one worth while acquaintance.

I hope your trip has had its compensations. I'll do my best at the office.

Loads of love.

Adele

Friday, Jan. 5 / 23

247

219 West 100th Street
New York

Jan. 7 / 23

Dear Mr. Lawrence:

I have now read *Mastro-don Gesualdo*.

It is superb, so rich, so lusty, kicking with life. It is one of those few massive works of the whole of literature that tower monumental, apart, a world in themselves. Bitter, too, as you say, but in rare parts so beautiful. Nowhere that I know of has maiden awakening been done as exquisitely as with Isabella in the country, after her father and household have fled there before the plague.

As for your translation, I take it with the thrilled wonder and delight with which I take everything you do. (Singing of the old Christmas carol included). It seems to me perfection. The world is certainly fortunate that you of all people have done this work: and Verga unfortunate that he did not live to know you.

Yours sincerely, Adele Szold Seltzer

Thomas Seltzer to D. H. Lawrence

The Palace
Management of
Halsey E. Manwaring
San Francisco

Sunday Morning
Jan. 7, 1923

Dear Lawrence:

I just arrived in San Francisco and am staying in your hotel. What a pretentious place it is and how expensive. But as I expect to stay here only two days it won't break me.

Los Angeles—the book world of Los Angeles—gave me a hearty welcome. It is a flourishing city, growing very rapidly, and oh so proud of it. The book business was good during the

248

holiday season. You seem thoroughly established there. They tell me there is a good demand for *Fantasia* and *England my England,* and of course *Women in Love. Aaron's Rod* also seems to be selling still.

Otherwise Los Angeles doesn't interest me in the least. It has no distinction. They are building, building, building, like every American city that's booming. But their sole pride is in numbers—how fast the population is increasing; every 15 minutes, they tell you, a new building arises in Los Angeles, drab things, one much like the other, no real creations, not even a suggestion of creativeness. I do not want to encourage you in your attitude to America. I think in time you will come to see qualities, yes, "qualities" in America and Americans which you have not yet discovered. But much of what you say about us is so true that often I too can see nothing else, and then I have to pull myself together to try to see what else there is.

Have you been reading the newspapers? World politics, especially European politics are as bad as can be. You have heard of the break-up of the new conference of Allied Premiers in Paris and of the probability of France seizing the Ruhr? The only encouraging thing is that the year has begun so bad that nothing worse seems possible and perhaps the future will be an improvement.

For the present the interest of Warner Bros. in the motion picture rights of *Women in Love* is dormant.

Yours, Thomas Seltzer

Thomas Seltzer to Robert Mountsier

The Palace
Management of
Halsey E. Manwaring
San Francisco

Jan. 7, 1923

Dear Mr. Mountsier:

I wonder how the New Mexico climate and altitude is agreeing with you. If you have had a bath in the hot spring (I

249

see it *is* the famous Ojo Caliente) then I am sure you are partly reconciled to the cold.

I am sending you enclosed a check for $100.00. Thank you very much for the loan. San Francisco is a relief after Los Angeles.

Sincerely yours, Thomas Seltzer

Adele Seltzer to Robert Mountsier

219 West 100th Street
New York

Dear Mr. Mountsier:

Here I am in a cosy steam-heated flat, Do you envy me? Yes? I'd gladly change and be where you are.

Thank you so much for the loan of $100.00. I hope it hasn't been awkward for you to do without it so long.

Sincerely yours, Adele Seltzer

Jan. 7 / 23

Adele Seltzer to Dorothy Hoskins

219 West 100th Street
New York

Sunday
Jan. 7 / 23

Dear Dorothy:

Has it surprised or hurt you that xmas went by, and the New Year, without a line from me, not a word of thanks for your darling gift?

Guess the reasons. Do try to guess. Stop here and guess hard before you go on. Try. Don't read any further before you try.
- - - - - - - - - - - - - - - - - - - -
Have you heard that D. H. Lawrence is in the United States? On a ranch at Taos, New Mexico. *He's* the reason. Three days

250

before Christmas Thomas & I dropped all our chores and went west to spend a week with him and his wife on the ranch. I only got back yesterday.

Well, it was a stupendous experience, everything & more than I dreamt it would be beforehand. Lawrence is a Titan, a wizard, one of those human marvels like Shakespeare or Goethe. He loses nothing by being seen at close range. As for his wife, she's a Norse goddess. A great friendship sprang up between her and me, while Lawrence, I think, took more to my Thomas. I'm not jealous. I always do get on better with women.

I went out prepared with a riding habit (breeches & coat) lent me by a friend; and I galloped across the prairies with— Lawrence! Was I thrilled? You're laughing at me. Yes, you are. Silly sentimentalist, you're calling me. Go on, laugh at me. I'll join in. I'll laugh at myself. I *do* laugh at myself. But I can't help it, I was thrilled.

The whole thing thrilled me—the *mise en scène*, the vast prairies cupped in the serrated mountain ranges, the blue, blue sky, the dear little bull terrier who left his mistress to attach himself to Lawrence, obviously as "thrilled" by the great master as I am; the Norse goddess, and two Norse gods or Siegfrieds, two young Danish artists for whom Lawrence had rented a log cabin near his own on the ranch. Oh, it was wonderful.

Lawrence is a captivating personality, always flashing sparks. When he's in the mood to sing and make fun, he is utterly charming, with an elfish grace. My wholly masculine man, Thomas, has succumbed to him as completely as I. You should hear him imitate various American accents. It makes you roll with laughter. Don't think I'm giving you a picture or even a sketch of the man. As always, I'm too rushed. I came back alone, Thomas having continued further west, on business, and I must assume some of his duties while he's away in addition to the hundred or so that I already have.

Well, you're a dear, much, much too good a dear to send me gifts. I can't find proper thanks. Really, I'm wordless. I can only answer with love, because I know it's love made you send me something. Here's a kiss.

If I hadn't just *had* to come back by January 8th, I'd have descended from Taos to Houston. What's one day more of travelling when you spend days on days in the train. I liked it. I read and loafed & had a pleasant sense of leisure and aloofness from material cares.

The Indian pueblos and the art life centering at Santa Fé were a great revelation to me. We Easterners know nothing of it. Santa Fé had a distinctly old-world effect upon us. Is there any Indian life left as far south as Houston? Do you come in contact with it?

Needless to say, I'm glad you like my little bee. And you're quite right about the exclamations "My god!" & "oh God!" Hardly was the book printed when we noticed it ourselves and wondered how such a slip could have escaped us. The exclamations are corrected to "Goodness gracious!" or "Mercy me!" in the second edition.

Do let me hear from you soon again.

Yours, Adele

You're wrong! Absolutely wrong. The pecans were *not* consumed by anybody but Thomas & Adele and guests they once had to dinner. Thomas was particularly happy with them. He munched & munched & looked aggrieved when the last one went down his gullet.

A. S.

Adele Seltzer to Dorothy Hoskins

219 West 100th Street
New York

Jan. 15 / 23

Dear Dorothy:

You're so funny about Lawrence, terribly funny. I had to giggle over your letter all by myself, because Thomas is still in the West. You *must* be jealous of my liking him so. "Tell me *why* you like Lawrence so much. Tell me why. Why, why?" Your cry. "Why, why?" Dear Dorothy, I swear to you, I cannot tell you why anymore than I can tell you why I love the glow of a sunset, the opal of dawn, the murmur of running waters. In the field of human emotions, in the eternal passional struggle, that is what Lawrence is to me. Like the elements, he can be fierce and wild, tigerish, bearish (but *not* brutish). Ah, there I've got it. His tigerishness & bearishness seem brutishness to some people. His Q. B. knows he is not brutish. No, he is never brutish. And he is always chaste, in the sense in which that rank voluptuary Dame Nature is chaste. People don't like him, I suppose (those who *don't* like him, I mean. Because the numbers are passing into the thousands who do) because he expresses a harshness as raw as an unripe persimmon. This is not the supreme trait for which I love him, but it *is* a trait that pierces me with admiration. One feels a harshness these days, a mad swing away from the candied sweetness that forever murmured "love, brotherly love, sisterly love, neighborly love," when love was only a hypocritical cloak for hatred, rivalries & disloyalties. I know I was fooled by that "love." I, too, used to say: "the trouble is, we don't love each another enough." Now I say: "the trouble is, we haven't got the strength & courage of our hatreds." I don't love. I *hate* mean critics. I'd take a gun and shoot a certain Ernest Boyd who writes for the Freeman, The Nation, The N.Y. Evening Post, & now The Publishers' Weekly. I would. I'd do it gladly. No. I wouldn't take a gun. That's cowardly. But I'd go up to him & say: "Mr. Boyd, prepare. I'm going to slap you in the face. You deserve it, for the mean, sneaking cad you are." Well, that's the sort of feeling Lawrence expresses, only in a different realm of emotion.

Lawrence is *not* affected. The last thing in the world to say of him, and the last thing in the world that I can endure. He and the Q. B. were really roughing it. It was no show ranch, by no means. In fact, almost a little disappointing that way, as there were no cow-boys or Indians or half-breeds, only the ranch owner, a modest young fellow, and his wife, a pretty thing from the East. She helped feed & tend his hundred head of cattle, and he helped her with the housework. The Lawrences had to do all their own work—haul water from a hole in the frozen stream from a distance equal to three city-blocks, chop wood, keep fires going in the kitchen, dining-room & sitting-room, and cook. Lawrence himself cooks the main dishes. Whatever cooking his wife knows he taught her, as she comes of the German nobility—a baroness—and had never learned. She is quite simple about it, to the manner born, and when we were there, we helped with all the work. I'm very, very fond of housework, and I made Mrs. Lawrence rest a lot & chat with Thomas while I washed up. One whole morning I chopped wood. As for the bath question, one *can* keep clean with a all-over wash, can't one? And Lawrence is very generous. He had taken the five-room log cabin on the ranch for himself & Mrs. L., and another 3-room cabin for two young struggling Danish artists. There was scarcely any furniture or crockery or even kitchenware in the 5-room cabin. But from the little there was the Lawrences spared enough to make the 3-room log cabin habitable. The ranch owner lived in a regular frame farm house—ugly. The cabins at least were a good shape. The interior of the Danes' dwelling, with dark beams across the low ceilings, almost gave the sense of a peasants' hut in the old world.

It was exactly the old-worldliness of Taos and Santa Fé that delighted me so. I say this in answer to what you write—that the country would be nothing without its brilliance of sun and moon and atmosphere. I can imagine this would be true of elsewhere in the U.S. But here, in Taos, in Ranchez, in Santa Fé, in the Taos pueblo (an ancient, ancient castle-like, many-storied community dwelling pressed mysteriously against the flank of a mountain), one got a strange feeling of connection with things other than crass United Statesism. I had expected more Spanishness, too. No. It was old, but with an oldness preceding Europe. On the whole trip I saw only *one* Indian, plenty of Mexicans & Spaniards, but only one Indian. I merely got the *feel* of the Indians from the sight of the pueblos and from the works of Indian artistry at Santa Fé. It was very, very cold. And the Indians were staying indoors. No. On the ranch, it was just chatting indoors with the Lawrences or chopping wood or riding. We saw & spoke to nobody but the Danes, who came evenings to sit & smoke. It was a wonderful, wonderful week, Dorothy. Nothing like it, in my life. Lawrence is a Titan, and I go about with an ever-present sense of wonder that we, Thomas & I, little, little Jews, should be the publishers of the great English giant of this age, publishers of him, not because with Jewish shrewdness we outwitted some other publisher & got Lawrence first, but because Lawrence's "Women in Love" went begging for a publisher, and we were the only people who understood its greatness & had faith in him as a writer.

You ask for snapshots. Don't you know me yet? I'm not one of those clever, "handy," practical people who have a thousand & one accomplishments. I've never even held a kodak in my hand. But I'm glad *you've* got the kodak habit. You give me such a good idea of yourself, and your pets, & your home.

Your new home! How splendid! Of *course*, you're going to adore furnishing it. I've got some antiques—a superb desk, a gem of a tiny secretaire to match the desk, some lovely Colonial chairs etc. While my sister is in Palestine I have glorious old Oriental rugs & some other fine old pieces. My tiny home, consisting of the essential bed room, dining-room, living-room, bathroom & kitchen, with one tiny, tiny room that I use as a store-room & pantry, is said to be exceedingly cosy and home like. It is not "artistic." That is, I don't go in for color schemes, or specially artistic arrangements. Not because I wouldn't want to, but I haven't got the time. I was merely careful to buy, when I had to buy, "good pieces." My apartment gives the sense of a real home. One can even imagine children in it. The living-room consists of what in N.Y. are considered two rooms—a larger room with a smaller one off it and a broad doorway between without a door. N. Yorkers curtain the smaller room off & make a bed-room of it. We leave it open entirely, not even portières, and use it for a library. Thomas has about 3000 books in it. The walls lined with the books. The library gives our home distinction; the other rooms give it amiability & hospitality. There is nothing in it in bad taste; but there are no rare ornaments. Never could afford them.

Dear me! I nearly forgot one of the nicest things on the Ranch. Bibs, or Pips, or Bibelot, whichever one happened to call him. A Boston bull. The darlingest little fellow. How I adored his undershot jaw, two ever-gleaming little pearls of teeth, his whole monstrous little face and tight agile little body. I adored him. Could have huggged & hugged & hugged him all day long with my dog-hungery arms. You're fortunate, Dorothy. Will I *ever* be able to have a dog of my own again? Pips originally belonged to a woman in Taos. He was only a pup, and he attached himself to Lawrence. So the woman gave him to Lawrence. It's wonderful to see how attached the two are—dog to man, man to dog. Lawrence sitting on a low stool to the side of the hearth fire with Pips on his knees—well! go ahead, laugh at me. Anyhow you won't laugh at me for calling Pips a darling.

Yours, Adele

255

219 West 100th Street
New York

Jan. 28 / 23

Dear Dorothy:

I had a fragment of time, and I looked at you and Gus and the cat thro a magnifying glass. How handsome you are! My! And tall! It would take me a week at least getting over feeling a pygmy beside you. I'm only five feet two in my boots. Thomas is 1½ inches shorter.

Gus is adorable! Adorable puppy! Gracious, wouldn't I squeeze him! Squeeze him to death! He wouldn't mind. He'd love me for squeezing him to death. The dear! The way he stands on the upper step cocking his eye at the dog on the lower step. Yes, he has got more verve than the other dog. But we won't insult the other dog, who is probably a dear in his way. The enclosed is a snapshot of a new English author of Thomas's, Horace Wyndham. The dog in his arm is worth regarding thro a magnifying glass. The little rogue! He looks the perfect little scamp. I itch to squeeze him, too.

Aloisita is sitting beside Alois on my best parlor table, so glad to be reunited with her brother that I can't think of separating the two again. There she shall stay, and Alois, too. I shall look for something else for the giftee, and always smile affectionately —with affection for you and Alois and Maya—when my eye falls on my best parlor table. You're a dear for having gone to all that trouble. Thanks!

After I wrote you my last letter I went straight to bed and just as I was dozing off a line in your next to last letter, the one damning Lawrence, came to my mind and I had to laugh all over again at you. Of course, you've changed now in the Lawrence matter, but I *must* speak to you about that line, the full force of which missed me until I was just dozing off. You said: "I like your Thomas MUCH better than Lawrence. He is a man who works without affectations." You've got Thomas down all right. He certainly *is* free of affectations, if ever a human being was. He just can't play tricks. He can't sham even for fun. No use trying to draw him into fun that involves any feigning. Impossible for him. The joke in what you write is an implication I see in it. I may be wrong in this; perhaps there wasn't the implication that came leaping to my mind as I dozed off. Your line seemed to say to me: "Be true to your Thomas. Don't let the glamour about the great English writer make you see your Thomas in a lesser light." I suppose I needn't protest that it doesn't. Thomas, or my feelings for Thomas have never been involved in my attitude toward Lawrence. But no. That statement isn't true. They have. The other way, however. My feeling for Thomas has been very much affected by both Lawrence's writings & my stay for that one week with Lawrence and his wife. My feeling for Thomas has taken on a sane strength it never had before. That, however, is terribly difficult to explain, just as I find it terribly difficult to explain my tremendous, overwhelming admiration of Lawrence. One's whole psychological make-up is involved, every psychological and emotional process in one's whole life, no matter how subtle, how minute. You see, Lawrence is more than a writer of novels. He is a philosopher, and also an interpreter of his day. You must read him as a whole—Sons & Lovers—Rainbow—Women in Love—Psycho-Analysis & the Unconscious—Aaron's Rod—Sea & Sardinia—Fantasia of the Unconscious. *Women in Love* had already made Lawrence dear to me. I scarcely needed his other later works (By the way, *The Lost Girl* is only an excursion). I could go on with his philosophy alone. What I need his later works for is only for the glorious expression of that philosophy. *Sea & Sardinia*, you're right, was a revelation not an affectation. It was Lawrence splenetic, Lawrence venting his spleen at a war-desolated world. Perhaps it seems like a petty form for venting one's spleen. No, no! But there again, the explanation is too long & involved. Altogether I hate explaining Lawrence. I want him to be felt. Don't you remember, the cricket said to Maya "Why need everything be explained?" Isn't it, Dorothy, *feeling* right about things that counts? Not so much understanding right. A person must *feel* right—about all the outrages of the war, the peace (!!) treaty, the Ruhr business. Such a person doesn't need to read tomes explaining coal concessions etc. His right feeling makes him understand. So, I say, read Lawrence all over again, beginning with *Sons & Lovers*, right through in the order I told you. If you want *Psychoanalysis* & *Fantasia* I'll send them. I'll also lend you *The Rainbow* again. *Sons & Lovers* you'll have to buy. Shall I buy it for you?

Really, you must be indulgent with me for not writing an essay on Lawrence for you. It's a matter I feel so profoundly. Besides, one could go on explaining forever & still say something open to misunderstanding. For instance, you didn't get the fun with which I said that about us little Jews publishing the English Titan. If you'd ever talked with me face to face you've have seen me wink when I said it. I'm not humble about being a Jew. Heavens no! I haven't got an inferiority complex, racial, national or individual. The Jews, I feel, are the aristocrats of the intellect, as the English are the aristocrats of breeding and character. It tickled my sense of the drama of things to think of us publishing the works of the great English genius, just as it tickled my sense of drama to see Trotsky, the little Jewish Soviet war lord, dictating terms to the German junkers. I was looking at the situation from the outside, as an anti-Semite world might see it. You know, there really is a terribly strong feeling among the older publishers against the three rising Jewish firms—Knopf, Seltzer, Boni & Liveright.

Don't you think you'll ever come to N.Y.? No, you won't. You'll be prudent and save the pennies for the new house in the woods. Travelling *is* horribly expensive. It is. But Thomas & I are not thrifty. Thomas runs his business economically and I'm economical in small ways—save cord & bits of soap, make dresses do for years & years, and altogether spend the minimum on clothes. People give me so many garments. When I went West a friend gave me a riding suit she had discarded. *I* felt swell in it. Mrs. Lawrence saw me in it before she knew who I was & told me when she saw me she said to her husband: "That's the most distinguished figure I've seen for months." (I've got a neat figure in spite of the 5 feet two). I'm economical in small ways, but frightfully loose-handed in others—pay my colored Carrie $85.00 a month, use taxis freely, hand money out freely heaven knows where—in tips on the trip.

However, if *ever* we meet, I'll explain Lawrence. Shall we ever meet?

Good luck to your new home. Tell me how it progresses. I'll save up & send you something pretty for it when it's ready.

Yours, Adele

258

Thomas Seltzer to Knud Merrild

February 17, 1923

Dear Mr. Merrild,

I have your three jackets, two of which I like very much—
"Studies in Classic American Literature" and "The Captain's
Doll." "Kangaroo" I am afraid will not do. The jacket problem,
you know, is a very ticklish one. It is not merely a question of
art, but of advertisement. The book cover has to stand out
among hundreds of other books. This is especially true of a
novel. I do not believe yours will. However, I am retaining it
and paying you at the rate of $40 apiece. I may decide to use it
after all.

Enclosed is a check for $120.—

Sincerely yours, Thomas Seltzer

Adele Seltzer to Dorothy Hoskins

Birkindele (so-named after Birkin in Women in Love)

Oct. 1 / 23

Dear Dorothy:

Here I am the same as always even if I don't write for aeons.
My friends *must* have faith in me. Times come when I can't help
going completely under. That time, in a way, is still upon me.
For I have come to the top only for a day to write you and a few
other friends.

Where did I leave off? Did I ever tell you that Thomas took a
cottage in a remote section of the New Jersey hill country for
Lawrence & his wife? And that when they came to N.Y. they
asked us to live with them. We did—for a month. Then they left
again. Of that month I won't write you, because you're not in
sympathy with Lawrence, and you'll think Thomas & me
lunatics. We are if to worship sublime greatness is lunacy.

As we had had to take the cottage for the entire season, till
Oct. 15, Thomas & I continued to occupy it, but as the days
grew shorter & the weather colder, and the office busier,
Thomas commuted from the city with less and less frequency,

until now he pays me only week-end visits, and five days in the week I am absolutely alone, fending for myself, cooking, cleaning, splitting wood, translating (seven or 8 hrs. a day), and—playing with the cats.

One cat is full-grown, belonging to the owner of the cottage, the other—oh, the other! My kitten, my Schnitzler (so named by Lawrence because I was engaged on a trnsltn of a Schnitzler book at the time). Perfect type of the brown-grey tiger cat, black stripings, chestnut nose, brownish ears, black, black up the back of the lower hind legs, a black necklace on a downy, brownish breast. My perfection of a Schnitzler. And I must part from her. On Oct. 15.

You see she's a wild little country tiger of a cat, used to chasing wild creatures, and shinning high trees, and dozing in the sunny loft of the barn. How can I tear her from such delights to coop her up in a city flat? No, she shall stay here in the country with Mrs. H., who will be good to her. But will Mrs. H. love her in my special way? Will she take her out on long, long rampaging walks through woods and fields? Will she have her sleep under the covers in bed with her tucked right in the hollow of her neck? Will she say: "Schnitz, oh Schnitz, you charmer, you enchantress, you ravisher of my soul." And will Schnitz stare at her wide-eyed wondering what all the raving's about? Stare at her with wide eyes of pure old gold. Oh, what golden, real golden eyes. My Schnitz! And I must part from her on Oct. 15th!

During the week while I translate and fend for myself & play with the cats, I cannot, cannot bring myself to write letters. As a matter of fact, translating is a great strain on the mind & nerves; and additional writing would nearly be killing. I am writing you (and a few other people today) because I have deliberately taken the time off. Today no translating is being done.

Week-ends I have no time for anything but Thomas & guests. Weekends I become part of civilization. Weekends I drop the recluse and become the talkative member of society that makes all my guests wonder why of all people in the world I should enjoy being a hermit.

Can you imagine me a hermit? The cottage is 1/8 mile from nearest house and main road. It is down its own little private lane used only twice a day by the school children of the scattered farmhouses who use it as a short cut to school. It is set on the side of a hill in a cluster of old oak and maple trees with a view over to the other high hills (or really mountains) of the Orange range. The fields here are charmingly divided off by natural wild hedges of cherry trees, sassafras, birch, various flowering plants in season (like tall yellow daisies & golden rod), and endless coils of virginia creeper (now turned scarlet!). Some fields are like a cloistered quadrangle. You feel alone in them with God. Lawrence says the country is very, very, much like English Berkshire, and an English girl (teaching spoken English at Smith), who visited us, agreed with him. She was entranced by the country. Can you imagine how heartbroken I am to have to leave it and—Schnitz! Oh, that Schnitz!

And how do you like your own new house? This cottage we are in is old & has a good deal of charm. I'd love to possess it & its 7½ acres of field & woodland.

You were good to believe in me & send me your address. Now *write* me!

Yours, Adele S. Seltzer

Adele Seltzer to Dorothy Hoskins

219 West 100th St.
N.Y. Jan. 8 / 24

Tut, tut! What a jealous hussy! Going for the other one, forsooth, because she parts her hair in the middle and affects *ie.* Shame, shame. And she *doesn't* part her hair in the middle. She wears it drawn straight back into a "psyche" knob and fluffs it over the ears. She's *not* demure. She's a gay little sinner. But, unlike American misses, she can afford not to be demure. She doesn't pay by being rowdy. An American girl is either a prig or rowdy.

Well, Dorothy, you gave Thomas & me a good, good laugh & chuckle. He enjoyed your letter as an after-dinner treat, and gave me specific instructions about answering. I have forgotten his instructions but this is an opportune point at which to tell you something—quite bluntly—something about Thomas. You hear so little *from* him or *about* him that I cannot convey what I have to say by innuendo. I must state it baldly and bluntly.—Thomas is an admirer of yours. This last letter from you quite settled that he is. Yes, he's an admirer of yours. Feel flattered. Do. People rarely win Thomas's complete admiration. He's not lavish of his emotions, and he's very, very quick and subtle at smelling the faintest taint of commonness. For him to say of someone, "She's a real person," is equal to someone else's saying, "She's a goddess." He finds very few people "real." For that matter so do I. Beside Thomas & Lawrence I don't know a single real man. I have *one* N.Y. friend, only one, a woman, whom I call real.

Perhaps she'd surprise you. She's un-English, for one thing. She belongs to no country or race, but to all countries & races. She's an artist from top to toe—an artist in her paintings, an artist in the way she dresses her long, slim body, an artist in living, and an artist in the way she has fashioned her own being—chiselled away at herself until all the crudities have been refined out of existence. She's exotic, sometimes voluptous to behold, yet there's a sturdy robustness about her. She can plunge her exquisite hands into dish water and clean up messes after her sick kittens. (She always has "pedigree" Persian kittens that get fearfully sick & have to be sent to the Bide-a-wee Home). She and I meet occasionally for lunch and have long, long, deep, deep talks about men & marriage & love & life.

You say you want to know more about my life & my relatives. Here goes, then. Relatives first. The sister who was so ill went back in September to her house in Madison, Wisconsin, with her lung condition marvellously improved as a result of x-ray treatments, which had shrunk the malignant growth. The N.Y. physicians declare that her tissue shows a cancerous tendency throughout her system. The Madison physicians pooh-pooh this & say that as long as her lung trouble doesn't advance, she is safe. In the meanwhile she has been nursing her adopted child, who has been exceedingly ill, & her husband, who has also had his spells of not feeling well. And my Zionistic sister returned to Palestine at the end of November. *You* haven't heard about my relatives. Nor have my relatives heard about (or from) me. My Madison sister sent me superb hand-drawn & embroidered pillow slips made by herself, she had a birth day, & my Palestine & Baltimore sisters also had a birthday—and I haven't written a *line*!! Is *that* wanton neglect?

About myself, what keeps me so busy. Have I ever told you

that I am, besides a translator & Thomas's aide in the office, secretary to a millionairess? As a rule, I don't mention this because I detest it so. It is my Cross, my Calvary. I hang on to it because it pays well, especially this year. For about 12-15 hours of work a week, in 8 mos. of the year I earn enough to support myself. If I were living alone, I could get on splendidly with what I earn as her secretary. As Thomas's, the publisher's wife, it only covers rent & maid's wages and my pocket money. That's a good bit, though, & helps Thomas considerably, as it saves his drawing that amount from the business. Here's a sample program of a day on which I go to the millionairess.

8:30 A. M.—rise
10   A. M.—be at the M's desk in the breakfast room of her 5th Av. mans)ansion! Phew! Mansion! Charnel house of souls. That's what it is. The motto over its doorway should be: "All ye who enter here, leave your souls behind." Or more briefly: "Souls not wanted." Or "Entrance for souls and servants in the basement.")
1   P. M.—leave the M. & have lunch with Thomas down town.
2:30 P. M.—Thomas's office where I do all sorts of work. In every department.
6   P. M.—Leave the office—walk part of the way home with Thomas.
7   P. M. Dinner
8   P. M. Read Mss. till 1 A. M.

It's the reading of the Mss. that's the very devil. Of course, I don't by any manner of means read all the insane rubbish that finds its way into publishing houses. But eventually a large number are referred to me for a final verdict, and there are always masses of them piling up, piling up to rob me of my evenings. Really, Dorothy, I never have a moment's leisure. Something urgent on hand always. Very urgent. And so many authors & agents cross because they don't get prompter decisions. Even Lawrence writing me an annoyed letter from England. I haven't read a Ms. of his on which he asked my opinion in *September*. I haven't read *Kangaroo*, or *Studies in Classic Amer. Lit.* or the last story in the *Captain's Doll*, or *Birds, Beasts, & Flowers*. Would you believe it?

So I can't answer your question about Somers. But from

what Thomas tells me Somers *is* Lawrence, so I rather fancy he does talk like Somers.

Let me see—what else do you want to know?

Oh yes—Dorothie F. Pantling (who's a "miss" when she's demure. Because she acts demure when she's horrid. She becomes a demure miss. She's horrid when she dislikes people. She was *horrid* to one man I introduced her to. Her demureness convulsed me. I don't like the man myself).

Madge Jenison we know as a person, but in her capacity of Sunwise Turner. She's fine, very fine. Everything she tells of in her book took place *before* Thomas became a publisher. She had already given up her work there, and only helped in the shop occasionally.

No, I'm not translating anything at present, but soon will be, probably. The last book I did was *Heaven Folk* by the author of *Maya*.

Dorothie Pantling again. She's a Londoner by birth & upbringing. I doubt if she's more than merely visited Ireland. Her father is a dour Yorkshireman.—No, no. Worse. A Northumberlander. Her mother's an unacclimatized Irish lassie. Dorothie is forever pitying her mother.

But I *am* a scenty person. I use scent steadily—Coty, L'Arly, even more recherché parfumeurs, if I'm presented with their products. However, my dear pure English Dorothy, I do assure you, I *never* use scent to cover a smell. Perish the thought! Pah! A fine scent on a dirty body? Horrible. In the early days of Thomas & me knowing each other he was vastly amused & still more vastly astonished to hear me say, when I had met someone for the first time: "No, I don't like that person & never shall like him (or her). I know by his smell." As a matter of fact I don't like people whose natural body smell I don't like. Nor animals either. Some dogs have a sourish smell. I only like dogs if they have a peaty smell of sun-baked heaths. *You* know.

Please hurry up & tell me if *this* letter satisfies you. I don't want to withhold a thing from you that you wish. For one thing I love you, for another your very wish is flattering—your wish to know about me & everything pertaining to me, even relatives.

How—how is it that what you find now in Lawrence—that fine personal wholeness, like a sound hard apple hanging on a tree without reference to the other sound hard apples hanging on the same tree—sound & hard because it was sound & hard & not depending on another apple to make it sound & hard—*why* didn't you find this in the earlier Lawrence. That's just *the* thing in Lawrence. I'm *so* glad you found it yourself. Do write me soon.

Adele

The nut cakes came unbroken. The only drawback is that they quickly turn hard; & they don't taste so good when they're hard.

Adele Seltzer to Dorothy Hoskins

219 West 100th Street
New York

Easter Monday
1924

Dear Dorothy:

Give the little brown Adele hen an extra portion of laying mash by way of thanks for the two delicious coddled Adele eggs that I had for supper this evening. Or if there is a better way of conveying gratitude to an accommodating hen, convey it. Carrie had her two Carrie eggs for lunch and wanted to know what kind of a wonder you were. I tried my best to tell her.

Of course, I've made Thomas look foolish—that about kissing Dorothie. Lawrence (in *The Captain's Doll,* you remember) says nobody can make anyone seem so ridiculous as a woman can her husband. But, Dorothy, I'm afraid this time the fault is yours. I'm afraid you've got a wordly [sic] conception of Thomas & sex etc. etc. that absolutely does *not* apply. Thomas is a real man, very, very masculine, in fact, in his whole emotional & psychic make-up, and in his reticence and reserve; but he's absolutely free of sex consciousness. By that I mean he doesn't consciously carry the idea of sex about with him all the time. When he talks to a woman, it's as man to man, unless the woman deliberately introduces man-woman consciousness. That Dorothy [sic] doesn't do, certainly not with Thomas, and it's just as you say, she's like a charming Persian kitten. I don't mean to imply that if Dorothy were a boy, Thomas would pet her as he does. But a younger boy he would. I can see him, for instance, making the same fuss over Ronnie Pantling, the 15 year old brother of Dorothy, who wrote the enclosed letter. (Please return it). And, of course, I led you to believe that Thomas put his hands on her a lot. Which he didn't.

You see, I was assuming, foolishly, that you knew Thomas as well as I, that you knew how rare were his active manifestations of affection, and I only told you of his petting her to prove to you that she (whom you seem to distrust) must be charming indeed *if* she provoked in Thomas something so unusual in him. Thomas in man-woman matters (I'm *not* blind) is about the finest person in creation. There were many times in my life when I wished there were more of the flirt, the male seducer, in him. I felt he would understand me better then. I've got over that though.

One day at supper, after Dorothie was gone, and we were talking about her, Thomas said: "It's nice the way one likes Dorothie. It's a nice sweet simple affection she inspires." That's it—sweet & simple. No complications. No bothering about sex, or gratitude, or ingratitude. She's Dorothie, I'm Adele, Thomas is Thomas—give and take and enjoy each other. She falls in so nicely with us. No explanations. Here we are. There she is. Right-o!

Do you understand?

The Lawrences *are* different. Complicated, yes. But *not* the ingrates you think them. No, they fully stood the share of the cottage this summer, and really wanted, at least, to pay for their food the week they were here. I had to tear up the big check Lawrence left on my desk. And they simply shower gifts on us, *such* beautiful things, so colorful, so exotic, so different from anything I dare indulge in on my own account—a superb Genoan mosaic brooch set in a quaint gold English frame, a gorgeously painted great Mexican wooden bowl, a big brass Ceylon tray, a charming straw hat from Ceylon, two Mexican rugs, and last a painting—what a painting! Beautiful. Still-life. Nasturtiums and poppies in a grey bowl. Besides all that Lawrence gave *me* a full-length oil portrait of himself done by one of the Danish artists we met on the ranch and also a water-color done by himself in brilliant colors in imitation of the Italian primitives. And Frieda Lawrence knitted me a shawl and sent me stockings from England, and had her old mother in Baden-Baden crochet me a yard of quaint German lace because I'd gone into ecstasies over it when I saw it on an old torn night gown of Frieda's, and out of her torn nightgown had made myself a blouse for summer wear.

Yet the Lawrences are complicated. One's relation with them cannot be simple. Lawrence won't let it be. I can't say what one's relation with Frieda would be. He complicates things *for* her. I believe, without him she would be grandly simple. I don't know.

The fact is, I *do* know Lawrence. I know him through and through and through. I'm not a sophisticated sort (am I? do you think I am?) and my relations with people are usually on an agnostic plane. I accept them simply at face value, and trouble little about the springs of their conduct. Oh, but when they *do* certain things, things that seem to fly a warning, and I begin to probe, oh, then I delve mercilessly, and I *understand.* Lawrence is an open book. I could write an analysis of his character!! But I won't. Not yet. Perhaps never. Maybe, if you & I met, I'd tell you.

What fun it is writing to you!

Adele

I've *never* returned that lace waist. Wait until I do the spring cleaning.

P.S. Just read your letter again. *Must* rush to Lawrence's defense. He is *not* casual or rude. Never, never, never! Hates people to be casual or rude. (Is probably blind to the Brett's ways—or perhaps she is *not* what we think. He & Frieda seem to like her a good deal). He is most punctilious & scrupulous in the smallest matters. In fact, he gets after Harriet for being negligent. He is *too* polite, *too* courteous, *too* accessible to any fool who dares to approach him. In the ordinary, everyday relations of life he's your "perfect gentleman." Not an exaggerated, mannered politeness, either. Just fine, simple courtesy. No, the complications in him lie elsewhere.

And, I swear to you, he's been all he should be to Thomas & me, save in one instance only. But that's connected with something deep, deep & awfully hard to understand &

explain—something he can no more help than the wind can help blowing.

A.

[on separate smaller leaf]

Dorothie says he's such a handsome courtly creature. Isn't it wretched to think that this "priceless young gent," so obviously meant for Oxford & English culture, will have to be deprived of all that & turned into a wage-earning machine—an Americanized mechanism. If I were wealthy, I'd keep that boy at school till he graduated an A.B. at least. The dear lad. Isn't he amusing? Can you conceive of an American cub producing such an epistle?

A.

Adele Seltzer to Dorothy Hoskins

219 West 100th Street
New York

Monday
Oct. 27 / 24

Dear Dorothy:

Imagine what has given me the leisure to sit down & write you. A spell of illness. The grip. I had been fighting it off for a week. It got me finally last Thursday. I'm up now & going out tomorrow. Yes, that's the way I get leisure. And my lack of leisure is what I referred to in my postal. I have come to abhor this too-full life of mine as something monstrous. Life passes, and I don't live. I put off living. I seem like a seed carried in a hurricane and never getting the chance to take root. Thomas & I work & work & work. Bad times come just as we are built up and ready to go over the top, and pull us back. And we go on working and fretting and working and fretting. Of course, I should not like a life in which struggle is altogether eliminated, though perhaps I'd find enough struggle in, say, coaxing a rock garden of hardy perennials into existence. Is your life too *dolce far niente* for you? Do you envy us our life of a million contacts? Don't.

This reminds me of one of the books we've published *Who Will Remember?* Did you find it *very* exquisite? I did. Wasn't that beautifully indicated—the modern girl longing for dignified leisure, longing even to be bored, and the 18th cent. girl shedding a graceful tear when her days are so monotonous, so full of boredom that she can't squeeze even a line for her diary from her life's happenings? *Isn't* Julianna adorable? I love her. The very essence of exquisite maidenliness. Never "missish," as she herself says.

And don't you think some of the other books on our list are fine? *Some Do Not*, and *Boy in the Bush*. Even *The Burden & Simples* have their good points.

There was a lot, I know, in your last letter that I wanted to reply to. But your letter is in the office, and I shan't defer writing to you until I can have it at hand. Was it Lawrence you spoke about? No, I haven't read *Studies* yet. I *can't* find the time. Send me a mild poison that will keep me moderately ill for a month, and I'll read a whole library of books.

Lawrence! I'll talk to you about him. Or maybe I have. Have I ever written you how much I deplore his getting farther and farther away in his fiction from the universal things that touch the human soul most deeply. I coldly dislike his repudiation of love. I think I am not blind to my own traits, when I say that I do not want the selfless sort of thing called love preached by the preceding generation. I fully understand also that there can be passion without real warmth of feeling. But surely for one's mate, the man or woman you choose to walk by your side, you *must* have tenderness. I can also understand changing mates—easily. In fact, I think I can understand everything human. I think I can boast *nihil mihi alienum est*. I can steal and commit murder in my thoughts. I can hate & love at the same time. But Lawrence's repudiation of love is not human. It corresponds to nothing in human nature, to no deep need of love or hate. Humanity lives by its passions—by its greed, its lust, its covetousness, its love of beauty, its fervor for an ideal. Repudiation of love cannot be a passion. It can be only a mildly negative thing. Except in the case of Schopenhauer & Nietzsche, who did not "repudiate" love. They probably hated it, because they loved it too much. Lawrence wants something that has never been. He wants to

269

take a woman & exercise his cold man's passion upon her, and never utter a warm word of love. Well, we women won't have it so, will we, Dorothy? A man has got to love us before he can have us, doesn't he? No questions asked as to how long he will love us. We require no oaths, no protestations of undying faith. But at the time he must love us and be tender with us. Isn't it so? Certainly now is a bad epoch in which to plead his cause, now when women are economically independent & can make their own terms. No woman would have Lawrence on his terms, or rather Lawrence's men on their terms. In ancient times and in other lands when men were masters they could live without tenderness if so they chose. But I think men themselves have always loved that woman the best who evoked tenderness in them.

I went with Lawrence in his "passional struggle" as far as *Aaron's Rod*. I *do* see the fierce sex antagonism that exists today. That was what he expressed in those earlier books. But his later repudiation of love is no solution. I'm cross with him.

Do write me soon. Immediately, in fact. Does it surprise you to know that a letter from you is as keenly awaited an event as tho I lived on an R. F. D. route & got only one piece of mail matter a month.

I want to know all about you—if there's still a chance of your having to give up your home—all about you & your blue rug & the pets.

Love Adele

Adele Seltzer to Dorothy Hoskins

219 West 100th Street
New York

Jan. 10 / 25

Dear Dorothy:

Never again say there's anything wrong between us. Have faith in me and Thomas. How can you dream that your mirror images, those reflections of a beautiful body and beautiful soul, could ever produce damage with our relations? *Don't* you know yet, Dorothy, that you are as alive and real in my life, in every day of my life, as though you were my next-door neighbor?

The trouble isn't spiritual; it's material, grossly material, and the trouble isn't with *you* that you haven't enough to offer, but with *me* that I haven't time.

It's as though a drab destiny (I see my Destiny with a complexion like a tapeworm and garments like a mop cloth) pursued me all my life holding my nose to the grindstone. Just before xmas, *just* as I was clearing away odds and ends of work, preparing for a few hours of holiday leisure (*only* a few hours, that's all I ever ask, only a few hours to be human in, and see my friends & write to my friends)—just as I saw a streak of light, a large, really onerous task fell upon me unexpectedly. It's work that consumes every moment. It will be three weeks still before I'm rid of it. All my other work has to be concentrated upon furiously so that it is condensed into fewer hours to leave me some hours every day for the Task. Same old story. Translation of a book contracted for in England. Then when it comes, such a mess that I have to do it all at any rate.

Don't think Thomas & me absurd perfectionists. We're willing to accept something a little worse than the best; but this stuff is almost gibberish.

You, in a quiet Southern town, probably envy me all this activity. I admit my life is interesting, yet possibly not so interesting as you conceive. The intensity of my work cuts me off from people. Thomas & I don't "mix." Only yesterday we lunched with a man, because he's going to Europe, whom we had been meaning to "cultivate" ever since Thomas began to publish, and that was our first social engagement with him, our first—now that he's leaving, when it would have been better to be close to him while he was staying.

Try to picture me busy like this, won't you? Then when letters from me don't come, you'll say: "Adele is squeezed dry." Really, Dorothy, I *am*. I *can't* sit down & write a hearty letter at twelve o'clock at night after having racked my brain steadily for twelve hours during the day. Can I? No, all I can do is romp with Peeps.

You don't even know Peeps yet, though she and Thomas and I have been friends since August.

But before I tell you about Peeps—but maybe I have told you, have I? Write saying whether or not I have. If I haven't,

I'll tell you about her in my next letter.

Your new little kitten is a character. Delightful! The primitive little thing! How can you bear to civilize her.

Before your letter, there came a note from you about "rags" —handkerchiefs, I take it. The handkerchiefs didn't come, and I *love* to get handkerchiefs. I can't have too many handkerchiefs. Our family is teased for its passion for handkerchiefs— especially fine ones, not too small, of linen.

I've got to get to work now, else I'd tell you an interesting story, a life-story that culminated at our cottage in Connecticut where we spent the xmas weekend—I happy as happy could be, everybody else freezing.

Write me soon again. Do. And if I can't do any better, I'll write a postcard.

> Love (which you *must* believe in) from
> Yours A.

It occurred to me to add that I adore writing to you. Not writing is a real grief. It's sadder than any of the other "nots" in my life, like not going to the theatre, or art exhibits, or loafing on Sat'y & Sunday etc.

Adele Seltzer to Dorothy Hoskins

Thomas Seltzer, Inc.
Publishers
5 West Fiftieth Street, New York

February 10th, 1926.

Dear Dorothy:

As Thomas has lost his bridal feeling for D. H. Lawrence, he is willing to part with the enclosed letter to me. A year ago he wouldn't have parted with an envelope addressed in Lawrence's handwriting.

As for Nathalia Crane, it may seem strange, but we haven't got a single thing in her handwriting. The child uses the typewriter exclusively, and lately when there was all that question of her authorship, we parted with what few poems there were with corrections in her handwriting. They served as documentary evidence. At the present moment the child is so busy going to school and writing a novel, that I hesitate to ask her to write any of her poems out in longhand. But someday I will, and then will gladly send you any bit I may have.

Of course, of course, the "rag" note dates from last year. It all comes back to me now. Not that I ever forgot the previous gift of handkerchiefs or cologne, but I forgot the note went with it. There was a clearing up in our office recently, and I suppose this personal note strayed into my correspondence basket and I thought it was a new letter.

I am still in the throes of that awful translation and a lot of other detail work. All dried up inside. No juice to spurt into a nice letter to you. Maybe soon. But lots of love just the same. That doesn't dry up.

Yours, A.

Mrs. Dorothy Hoskins
Route F. Box 237
San Antonio, Texas

Adele Seltzer to Dorothy Hoskins

Thomas Seltzer, Inc.
Publishers
5 West Fiftieth Street, New York

March 12th, 1926.

Dear Dorothy:

That last letter of yours all about Lawrence came just when I needed it most. I was in bed with the grippe. I'm all over it now. It wasn't a very bad attack.

You are funny about Lawrence. Now that I am cooling off, you are getting all "het" up. Didn't I tell you you would find your own way to Lawrence, and wasn't I right not to fling passages at you, but let you discover the beauties for yourself? I find the greatest beauties (of the sort that you select, but only enhanced) in the first part of *The Rainbow*, in the description of the Italian mountains in *The Lost Girl*, and acme of all, in the Alpine scene at the end of *Women in Love*. Lawrence's "sex" did not bother me until he wrote *Aaron's Rod*. I allowed him *Aaron's Rod*. But I disliked *England, My England, The*

Captain's Doll, and all his later works. I did not read *Kangaroo.* When I say I dislike Lawrence, I never mean that he isn't great. Whatever he does is stupendous. What I dislike is the point of view, not the treatment. The trouble with Lawrence is, that there's not another human being in the world who can feel about things as he does. He has a morbidity that sets him apart from the rest of humankind. I know that all geniuses are supposed to have morbidities, but usually their morbidities are simply an accentuation of the universal, not a departure from it. In other words, if they love, they simply love more violently; if they hate, they hate more violently. But Lawrence neither loves nor hates. He has feelings for which there is no name. He is not either in himself or in his writings erotic. On the contrary, he is austere. It is simply that he is warped on the sex side. What a shame, what a shame! Because I feel that as a genius, he is as great as the greatest.

It is disgusting of me to be so long writing you when the last paragraph in your letter tells of you in pain. I cannot, I simply cannot associate you with pain. Do write me a line telling me you are quite well, and if you don't write that you are quite well, I insist upon radium treatment. It is perfectly absurd, an energetic, vital creature like you, spending so much time flat on your back. I won't have it. The doctors can cure you. And you must let them. Come here to New York to have yourself made well. We can manage to look after you.

[manuscript ends]

Thomas Seltzer to Dorothy Hoskins

219 W 100th St.

July 12, 1926

Dear Dorothy:

I never thanked you for those fine handkerchiefs you sent me. After having my nose manhandled by the doctor for weeks with all sorts of instruments your gentle treatment of it touches me to the very depths. Many, many thanks.

You can still get a kick out of modern books. This means that all is well with you. I have experienced a revulsion against them in the last year or so. There are no real great men or women writing today. Lawrence is the one great man and the one great writer, but he suffers from the trifling character of the age which has no room for greatness. He suffers because until he can go his own way and does go his own way, the very sensitiveness which is part of his greatness makes him susceptible to the slightest movement that is stirring around him, intellectual, social, spiritual. It is this that makes him rebel so violently. He is of this age because he senses it so finely and he hates it because it is so inadequate to the feeding of his great inner being and of his art. His first three books are his greatest. Sons & Lovers draws its chief sustenance from the solid, substantial, mysterious past. The Rainbow is the exuberance of youth with the background of a society that has begun to disintegrate but is still vigorous and strong; Women in Love—the disintegration has proceeded apace, yet it is not beyond hope and as long as there is life Lawrence can fight. The War has wiped away all hope and Lawrence is using his wonderful gifts on material that is rotten. So we get his later books.

But I didn't start out to write you about Lawrence.—Oh, yes, I have turned to ancient Greek literature. Perhaps the soothing quality of it lies in its being so far, far back that we don't care very much, are not involved. Perhaps it's due to its own innate calmness. I hope though—and this is what I started out to say, that it will be many many years before you will go to the Greeks for balm. Remain young and stay right with this world. After all, it's the only world we have. And don't get acquainted with too many authors. Don't get disillusioned.

Yours, Thomas

Thomas Seltzer to Knud Merrild

November 5, 1934.

Dear Merrild—

We were both glad to receive your letter. The times you refer to have already passed into history and it is a queer feeling to see our friends and ourselves in a historical background. Each time you write, this sense of a large part of me belonging to the past strikes me with renewed vigor and I don't know whether I ought to be glad or sad that a portion of myself is, so to speak, a fossil. In advance, I suppose, one would try to avoid spending a memorable week at the end of 1922 and the beginning of 1923 on Del Monte Ranch with Lawrence and Frieda and two picturesque Danish artists, if one but knew that in a few years one would be relegated thereby to a period distinctly removed from the present. But at the time when we gathered in Lawrence's log house to celebrate New Year's Eve, none of us thought of anything but the enjoyment of the moment in pleasant and far from Philistine company, and each contributed his share to make the modest little party as cheerful as possible. What I was struck by especially was the small but sweet voice of Lawrence. Do you remember his singing some English Christmas carols? I was particularly touched by his rendering of "Good King Quentin." I have heard it sung many a time and was never impressed. Everyone seems to consider it a trifle and so it is. But the way Lawrence sang it, it had a haunting beauty that gripped you. I have often since tried to recapture that beauty and mentally I can do so but not if I try to sing it myself. I have asked others, with good trained voices, to sing it for me in the hope that they would reproduce for me the feel and the tang which it had in Lawrence's perfectly simple and unstrained recital, but always I was completely disappointed.

I mention this because to me it is typical of Lawrence the man as I perceive him. He is known to the world as a great poet and novelist, and as a curiosity, a piquant character, a sort of Don Juan who never practised his theoretical Don Juanism. But except for the fact that he was indeed a great novelist and poet, this conception of him as a man is, I know it for certain, all wrong. It is a fearful distortion. Lawrence was as great a man as he was a writer. In every aspect of life he was natural without pose and at bottom, sane. Follow him in the kitchen when he cooks, when he washes and irons his own underwear, when he does chores for Frieda, observe him when he walks with you in the country, when he is in the company of people whom he likes and to a certain extent respects—how natural he is in every movement and yet how distinguished, how satisfying because he is inspiring and interesting because of his extraordinary ability to create a flow, a current between himself and the other person. He had

276

Last photograph of Thomas Seltzer.
(Alexandra Levin)

extraordinary poise, too. I wonder if you know what I mean? So many people dwell only on his fierce outbreaks. But to me his outbreaks, even if they belonged to the man, were not of the essence of him. The times and his environment are more to blame than himself.

You ask me to recall incidents of our visit. But how can I without writing a book? And I do not want to write one other book on Lawrence. Sometimes I have much to say about him. Sometimes I think I have nothing at all to say. If you were here and we could talk together, it would be much more satisfactory. You could perhaps get things out of me that might be useful to you. But I am afraid it's too great a task to write, though I should very much like to help you. . . .

With best wishes from Adele and myself.—Yours,

Thomas Seltzer

THOMAS SELTZER PUBLICATIONS OF D. H. LAWRENCE:
A Chronological Listing

Touch and Go, 5 June 1920
Women in Love, 9 November 1920
The Lost Girl, 28 January 1921
The Widowing of Mrs. Holroyd, February 1921
Psychoanalysis and the Unconscious, 10 May 1921
Tortoises, 9 December 1921
Sea and Sardinia, 12 December 1921
Aaron's Rod, 14 April 1922
Fantasia of the Unconscious, 23 October 1922
England, My England, 24 October 1922
The Gentleman from San Francisco and Other Stories, 10
    January 1923
The Captain's Doll: Three Novelettes, 11 April 1923
Studies in Classic American Literature, 27 August 1923
Kangaroo, 17 September 1923
Birds, Beasts, and Flowers, 9 October 1923
Mastro-Don Gesualdo, 13 October 1923
Sons and Lovers, November 1923
The Boy in the Bush, 30 September 1924
The Rainbow, November 1924
Little Novels of Sicily, 9 March 1925

LOCATIONS OF MANUSCRIPTS AND PHOTOGRAPHS

All of the letters from D. H. Lawrence and Frieda Lawrence to Thomas and Adele Seltzer are located in the Humanities Research Center, The University of Texas at Austin, except as noted below.

> Letter of 3 June 1921: The Alfred M. Hellman Collection, Columbia University Libraries
> Letter of 7 November 1920: Cornell University Library
> Letter of 13 November 1926: Mr. W. Forster
> Letter of 20 February 1923: Mr. Gerald M. Lacy
> Letter of 8 April 1923: Mr. George Lazarus
> Letters of 3 February 1923, 9 October 1923, 13 May 1925, 28 December 1925: McFarlin Library, University of Tulsa
> Letter of 9 October 1923: Mr. William Pieper
> Letter of 12 August 1921: Special Collection Department, Northwestern University Library
> Letter of 10 February 1923: Princeton University Library
> Letter of 27 April 1923: The Beinecke Rare Book and Manuscript Library, Yale University

All of the letters from Thomas and Adele Seltzer, except the two letters to Knud Merrild, first published in Merrild's *With D. H. Lawrence in New Mexico*, are located at the Humanities Research Center, University of Texas at Austin.

The location of each photograph has been noted in the captions. *HRC*: Photography Collection, Humanities Research Center, University of Texas at Austin. *Lazarus*: George M. Lazarus. *Levin*: Alexandra Lee Levin. The frontispiece portrait of D. H. Lawrence is a previously unpublished photograph by Edward Weston, courtesy of Andreas Brown, Gotham Book Mart, New York City. The photographs of D. H. Lawrence's first editions are by Ray Hartman.

ACKNOWLEDGEMENTS

I would like to acknowledge my obvious debt and to express my sincere appreciation to the following individuals and institutions for the use of their D. H. Lawrence materials; without the thoughtful cooperation of Lawrence collectors, librarians and libraries, a project of this nature would be impossible. For their generous allowance to use manuscripts, photographs, and other materials, my gratitude is due to Mr. W. Forster; Mr. George Lazarus; Mrs. Alexandra Lee Levin; Mr. John Martin; The Beinecke Rare Book and Manuscript Library, Yale University; The Alfred M. Hellman Collection, Columbia University Libraries; Cornell University Library; Special Collections, Northwestern University Library; Princeton University Library; McFarlin Library, University of Tulsa; and the Humanities Research Center, The University of Texas at Austin. As most of the material for this volume came from the Humanities Research Center, I would like to indicate a special note of obligation to its director, Dr. Warren Roberts.

I would also like to express my thankfulness to a number of individuals who have assisted me in the research and preparation of this manuscript. An exemplary essay, "The Thomas Seltzer Imprint" by G. Thomas Tanselle, has proved to be the indispensable research source for the notes on the publishing association between D. H. Lawrence and Thomas Seltzer. In addition, Professor Tanselle has graciously given of his time to respond to all my queries for additional information. Mrs. Lin Vasey, Research Assistant, and Professor David Farmer, Assistant to the Director, both at the Humanities Research Center, have conscientiously answered my numerous letters and last-minute phone calls concerning what might at times have appeared to them to be rather trivial details. Professor Farmer is preparing a new text of *Women in Love,* and it is my particular hope that he may find some bits and pieces here relating to Seltzer's publication of that work which will assist him in the preparation of his volume. Ross Parmenter, formerly of *The New York Times* and now of Oaxaca, Mexico, and for many years one of the most earnest and diligent researchers in the Lawrence field, was generous with his time and knowledge; he supplied me with clippings from *The New York Times* files on Thomas Seltzer and identified several of the photographs. Mrs. Alexandra Lee Levin, a freelance writer and literary heir of the Seltzers, has allowed me to use her extensive collection of Adele Seltzer materials, and has written with Lawrence L. Levin the "Biographical Narrative" of the Seltzers included here. Mrs. Louis Cohn, Mr. Larry Lacy; and Professors Charles Endress, Michael Jenkins, Otto Tetzlaff, and Neil Devereaux of Angelo State University have helped me considerably. Finally, this project, like all Lawrence studies, is possible only with the cooperation of Laurence Pollinger, Literary Executor of the D. H. Lawrence Estate.

In closing, I would like to again state my gratitude to the Leverhulme Trust for what is now the second of three books which I began to prepare while a Leverhulme Fellow at the University of Manchester. Angelo State University has liberally granted me two Faculty Research Grants to assist with the financial costs of the preparation of the volume. Seamus Cooney of Western Michigan University, and editor of the Black Sparrow Press, has again served, as he did with my editing of *The Escaped Cock,* as the kind of vigilant reader such volumes of D. H. Lawrence require and deserve. And a very special appreciation to my assistant, Miss Nancy Bynum, for her devotion over several months in the preparation of the final manuscript.

GML
San Angelo
4 March 1976

282

BIBLIOGRAPHY

Bennett, Arnold. *Letters of Arnold Bennett, Volume I: Letters to J. B. Pinker.* Edited by James Hepburn. London: Oxford University Press, 1966.

"Book Censorship Beaten in Court." *The New York Times*, 13 September 1922, p. 23.

Bradbury, Malcolm. *The Social Context of Modern English Literature.* Oxford: Basil Blackwell, 1971.

Brett, Dorothy. *Lawrence and Brett: a Friendship.* London: Martin Secker, 1933.

Bynner, Witter. *Journey with Genius: Recollections and Reflections Concerning the D. H. Lawrences.* London: Peter Nevill, 1953.

Carswell, Catherine. *The Savage Pilgrimage: a Narrative of D. H. Lawrence.* London: Martin Secker, 1932.

Carter, John. "The Rainbow Prosecution." *Times Literary Supplement*, 27 February 1969, p. 216. Also see letters to the *TLS*: 17 April, 24 April, and 4 September 1969.

Clark, L. D. *Dark Night of the Body: D. H. Lawrence's "The Plumed Serpent."* Austin: University of Texas Press, 1964.

Cooney, Seamus. "The First Edition of Lawrence's Foreword to 'Women in Love'." *The Library Chronicle of the University of Texas at Austin*, Spring 1974, pp. 71-81.

Damon, S. Foster. *Amy Lowell: a Chronicle.* New York: Houghton Mifflin, 1935.

Ellmann, Richard. *James Joyce.* New York: Oxford University Press, 1965.

Foster, Joseph. *D. H. Lawrence in Taos.* Albuquerque: University of New Mexico Press, 1972.

Gross, Gerald, ed. *Publishers on Publishing.* New York: Grosset & Dunlap, 1961.

Harvey, Sir Paul, ed. *The Oxford Companion to English Literature.* Oxford: The Clarendon Press, 1967.

"Important Censorship Case." *The Publishers' Weekly*, 5 August 1922, pp. 463-464.

Joyce, James. *Ulysses.* New York: Random House, 1946.

Lawrence, D. H. *Apocalypse.* Introduction by Richard Aldington. London: Heinemann, 1972.

—————. *The Collected Letters of D. H. Lawrence.* Edited by Harry T. Moore. 2 vols. New York: Viking, 1962.

_____. *The Complete Poems of D. H. Lawrence.* Edited by Vivian de Sola Pinto and Warren Roberts. 2 Vols. London: Heinemann, 1964.

_____. "D. H. Lawrence: Twelve Letters." Edited by Paul Delany. *The D. H. Lawrence Review 2* (1969): 195-210.

_____. *Letters from D. H. Lawrence to Martin Secker: 1911-1930.* Iver, Bucks: Martin Secker, 1970.

_____. *The Letters of D. H. Lawrence.* Edited by Aldous Huxley. London: Heinemann, 1956.

_____. *Phoenix: The Posthumous Papers of D. H. Lawrence.* Edited with an Introduction by Edward D. McDonald. London: Heinemann, 1961.

_____. *Phoenix II: Uncollected, Unpublished and Other Prose Works by D. H. Lawrence.* Collected and Edited by Warren Roberts and Harry T. Moore. London: Heinemann, 1968.

_____. *The Quest for Rananim: D. H. Lawrence's Letters to S. S. Koteliansky, 1914 to 1930.* Edited with an Introduction by George J. Zytaruk. Montreal: McGill-Queen's University Press, 1970.

Luhan, Mabel. *Lorenzo in Taos.* New York: Alfred A. Knopf, 1932.

MacKenzie, Compton. *My Life and Times: Octave Five.* London: Chatto & Windus, 1966.

Merrild, Knud. *With D. H. Lawrence in New Mexico.* London: Routledge & Kegan Paul, 1964.

Moore, Harry T. *The Priest of Love: A Life of D. H. Lawrence.* Revised edition. New York: Farrar, Straus, and Giroux, 1974.

Nehls, Edward, ed. *D. H. Lawrence: A Composite Biography.* 3 vols. Madison: University of Wisconsin Press, 1958.

Roberts, Warren. *A Bibliography of D. H. Lawrence.* London: Rupert Hart-Davis, 1963.

Saunders, J. W. *The Profession of English Letters.* London: Routledge and Kegan Paul, 1964.

Secker, Martin. *Letters from a Publisher, 1911-1929, to D. H. Lawrence & Others.* London: Enitharmon Press, 1970.

Tanselle, G. Thomas. "The Thomas Seltzer Imprint." *Papers of the Bibliographical Society of America* 58 (1964): 380-448.

Tedlock, Ernest. *The Frieda Lawrence Collection of D. H. Lawrence Manuscripts.* Albuquerque: University of New Mexico Press, 1948.

" 'Women in Love' Again." *The Publishers' Weekly,* 24 February 1923, p. 580.

ABOUT D. H. LAWRENCE

"In the face of formidable initial disadvantages and life-long delicacy, poverty that lasted for three-quarters of his life and hostility that survives his death, he did nothing that he did not really want to do, and all that he most wanted to do he did. He went all over the world, he owned a ranch, he lived in the most beautiful corners of Europe, and met whom he wanted to meet and told them that they were wrong and that he was right. He painted and made things and sang and rode. He wrote something like three dozen books, of which even the worst pages dance with life that could be mistaken for no other man's, while the best are admitted, even by those who hate him, to be unsurpassed. Without vices, with most human virtues, the husband of one wife, scrupulously honest, this estimable citizen yet managed to keep free of the shackles of civilization and the cant of literary cliques. He would have laughed lightly and cursed venomously in passing at the solemn owls—each one secretly chained by the leg. . . . To do his work and lead his life in spite of them took some doing, but he did it, and long after they are forgotten, sensitive and innocent people—if any are left—will turn Lawrence's pages and know from them what sort of a rare man Lawrence was."

—Catherine Carswell

Printed June 1976 in Santa Barbara & Ann Arbor
for the Black Sparrow Press by Mackintosh & Young
and Edwards Bros. Inc. Design by Barbara Martin.
This edition is published in paper wrappers; there
are 1000 hardcover trade copies; & 126 numbered
copies handbound in boards by Earle Gray, each
containing a direct print of a previously unpublished
photograph of D. H. Lawrence.

7/26
5.00